Essentials of
Orchid Growing

Essentials of
Orchid Growing

Gordon C. Morrison
Photographs by Mark A. Webb

Kangaroo Press

First published in 1991 by Kangaroo Press Pty Ltd
3 Whitehall Road (P.O. Box 75) Kenthurst NSW 2156
Typeset by G.T. Setters Pty Limited
Printed in Singapore through Global Com Pte Ltd

ISBN 0 86417 399 7

Contents

Preface

We refer to ourselves as orchid groweres but this is not strictly true. We do not grow orchids, they grow themselves. All we can do is to facilitate their well being (or otherwise) by catering for their needs. But what are their needs? Among other things this book sets out to explore the nature of these.

The theme here is not 'how to grow orchids' but rather 'how do orchids grow'.

Plant science is a complex subject covering many disciplines. My aim here is to simplify this complexity and give the grower only a resumé of the relevant factors required for a broad understanding of the subject.

In the text I have used many words without defining these, but an extensive glossary is attached which will not only serve this book but act as a mini-dictionary and reference for all orchid occasions in the future.

Throughout this book I have placed emphasis on the use of correct terminology, something that is lacking among a lot of growers. Old habits die hard so I suppose this strategy is aimed mainly at newcomers who hopefully will use the correct terms and not follow the bad habits so prevalent today.

Reading alone cannot replace hands-on experience, so for Chapters 1 and 3 dissection of plant material is needed. Use a ×10 hand lens to look at and count pollinia and examine viscid discs and the stigmatic surface. Cut a root and look at it; develop an intimacy with all parts of the plant.

G.C.M.

Acknowledgments
The author is indebted to Mr P. Collin for the loan of the photograph shown in Fig. 1.4.

Mark Webb says special thanks to the numerous orchid growers who have allowed him to photograph their plants over the years with particular thanks to the members of The Orchid S.P.E.C.I.E.S (NSW) Inc.

Gordon C. Morrison is the author of *Growing Orchids in Australia and New Zealand* (1982) and *The Orchid Grower's Manual* (1988). He has worked with horticultural plants for over 30 years and with orchids for 18 years, and has studied orchids growing in their natural habitats both in Australia and overseas. His current interest is the classification of orchids and their phenology in both the wild and in cultivation.

He is a Bachelor of Science in Plant Biology, a Fellow of The Linnean Society of London and a Fellow of the Australian Institute of Horticulture.

Mark A. Webb B.Sc. has been growing and photographing orchids for a number of years. His prizewinning photography has appeared in journals and magazines both locally and overseas. With his wife Allison he runs Orchid Publications, a business specialising in computer design and nature photography. He is an Associate Judge of the Australasian Native Orchid Society and regularly lectures on orchids and photography. He currently resides in the Blue Mountains, west of Sydney with Allison and son Andrew.

Descriptions of Plants Illustrated by Colour Plates

Descriptions and photographs by Mark A. Webb

The descriptions given augment the information available from the photographs.

Those plants marked with an asterisk (*) are ideal for those starting to grow orchids. The newcomer is frequently confused by names and whether any particular orchid is easy or difficult to grow or requires special conditions. However, this whole book is devoted to the essentials of orchid culture and the descriptive text no way negates the need to apply the principles expounded in the chapters relevant to plant growth.

Protection from frost is a universal requirement and most plants can do with some shading in the afternoon to reduce their leaf temperature. Any reference to 'heat' being required means a minimum temperature of 13°C unless otherwise stated. A general rule for any tropical orchid is a minimum temperature of 10°C although some which grow high up in mountains can withstand lower temperatures with retarded growth.

If the temperature requirement cannot be met try reducing the amount of water normally supplied. Give just enough water to retain turgor. The plant will not grow but it will live through the difficult period. If low temperatures cause leaf fall, the plant will either expire or require one or two seasons under optimum conditions to recover. Newcomers should grow only those plants whose requirements they can meet, as it is very disheartening to lose plants early in your orchid career.

In general orchids can be divided into the following minimum temperature tolerances.

      4°C   10°C   13°C   15°C   17°C

The exposure time of plants to temperatures below these can often be lessened by placing the plants in sheltered locations, away from wind and against brick walls, or in some cases by bringing them indoors at night.

G.C.M.

Ada aurantiaca Lindley

This attractive easy-to-grow species from the Andes mountains in Columbia, South America, is well suited to pot cultivation due to its upright habit and fine root system. It is cold resistant and will grow in most parts of Australia with minimal protection. A spotted variety *punctata* is also known.

Aërides odoratum Lour.

An extremely variable species distributed over a wide area from the Philippines, China, Vietnam, Burma, the Himalayas, Nepal, Thailand, the Malaysian Peninsula and on through Indonesia into New Guinea. *A. odoratum* is the commonest species of the genus in cultivation. Plants can become quite large, up to 1.5 m in height, with profuse branching. In cultivation it is best grown either in a timber slat basket in fairly open media, or attached to a live host tree. In temperate regions this species may need the protection of a glasshouse, depending on the origin of the plant. Flower colour may vary from pure white to white with pale mauve or purple markings. Flowers are highly scented.

Ansellia africana Lindl.

A terrestrial species from tropical and southern Africa, this tall plant with strappy leaves is quite attractive. The flowers are variable in colour from greenish to bright yellow with chocolate-brown spots or bars and a yellowish or pale brown labellum. The branching inflorescence is up to 1 m high and carries many flowers. In cultivation this species requires high light levels and the protection of a glasshouse.

Ascocentrum curvifolium (Lindley) Schltr.

A species native to Burma, Thailand and India. The flowers range in colour from orange through vermillion to a rich reddish-brown and are borne on densely packed racemes to 15 cm in length. The display on a well-flowered plant is quite spectacular. This species is well suited to cultivation in slat baskets where the roots are free to hang in the air. A glasshouse is necessary to grow it in temperate regions.

Barkeria skinneri Lindl.

From Mexico and Guatemala, *B. skinneri* grows to 30 cm high. Twenty to thirty lilac, rose or magenta flowers are produced on stems to 60 cm during winter. It is one of the easiest species to grow of this sometimes rather difficult genus. It is essential that the roots are well ventilated, and the species is best grown mounted on treefern or hardwood. The plant requires plenty of water when actively growing—but must not remain wet—and plenty of light without high temperatures.

Baskervillea paranaensis (Krzl.) Schltr.

A terrestrial species from central Brazil, *B. paranaensis* has small flowers which are borne in large numbers on stems to 60 cm. The leaves are large, fleshy, dark green in colour and add variety to the foliage of any orchid collection. The plants die back each year after flowering and produce one or two new leads from each growth. As this species is a vigorous grower with thick fleshy roots it requires a large pot containing a nutrient-rich medium. Protection from extreme cold is necessary as it flowers during the winter months in cultivation.

Bothriochilus bellus (Rchb.f.) Lem.

A spectacular species from Central America, *B. bellus* is one of four species in this unusual genus. The egg-shaped pseudobulbs support several upright, ribbed leaves. Up to six 5 cm fragrant flowers are borne on a 16 cm sheathed inflorescence. In cultivation this species prefers to be underpotted in an open medium that retains some moisture at all times and grown in bright, indirect light.

Bulbophyllum barbigerum Lindl.

An intriguing, spring-flowering species from tropical west Africa, *B. barbigerum* has round, flattened pseudobulbs bearing a single leaf. This species has up to fourteen 2.5 cm foul-smelling flowers per inflorescence. The most striking feature is its very mobile labellum which is covered in long, blood red hairs that dance and flutter at the slightest air movement. In cultivation this species does well on a treefern slab in moist, warm conditions.

Bulbophyllum globuliforme Nicholls

A temperate epiphytic species endemic to southeastern Queensland and northeastern New South Wales, *B. globuliforme* is one of the world's smallest orchids with pseudobulbs to 2 mm. Like *B. weinthallii* R. Rogers, it prefers the rough bark of the branches and upper trunk of *Araucaria cunninghamii* (Hoop Pine). It is an easy species to cultivate under bushhouse conditions and grows well on mounts of weathered hardwood or natural cork. The solitary 3 mm flowers are produced in spring and last for a number of weeks.

Bulbophyllum macrobulbum J.J. Smith

The world's largest *Bulbophyllum* species with pseudobulbs to 18 cm in diameter and solitary leaves to 2 m in length, this species is found growing on cliff faces and large trees in dense tropical rainforest of the coastal lowlands and islands of Papua New Guinea. Flowers are borne in large clumps of up to 40 from the base of the pseudobulbs, individual deep purple-red flowers being up to 10 cm in length. This species is blowfly pollinated and therefore has a somewhat putrescent smell (like an animal that's been dead for some time).

Bulbophyllum weinthalii R. Rogers

This species has the largest flowers of the temperate *Bulbophyllum* species of Australia. It is found growing on *Araucaria cunninghamii* (Hoop Pine) at altitudes of 600–1200 m from northeastern New South Wales to southeastern Queensland. The 8–20 mm pseudobulbs of this species are packed tightly together and encased in woolly bracts. Solitary 20 mm diameter white, cream or pale green flowers with red to purple markings are produced in autumn. In cultivation *B. weinthalii* is best grown under cool to cold, moist conditions on a slab mount of weathered hardwood or treefern fibre. This species is long lived and free-flowering.

Ceratostylis retisquamea H.G. Reichb.

Native to the Philippines Islands of Mindanao and Luzon, this species was formerly known as *Ceratostylis rubra.* The glossy brick-red flowers are widely opening and 2.5 cm across. They are solitary or in pairs but are produced in large quantities by mature plants, sometimes several times throughout the year. The plants are clustered and the stems covered with brown papery bracts which contrast with the bright green leaves. In cultivation this species requires heated glasshouse conditions.

Cochlioda noetzliana (Rchb.f.) Rolfe

A high altitude epiphytic species from the Andean mountains of Peru, *C. noetzliana* is characteristic of the genus with its large (5 cm), scarlet flowers borne on dense, arching racemes. This cold growing species flowers in the late summer to autumn and has been extensively used in hybridising with other closely related genera such as *Odontoglossum, Oncidium* and *Miltonia.*

*Coelogyne amoena

A lovely cool growing species which is very rewarding in cultivation. It flowers freely producing racemes of two or three white flowers in spring. In cultivation it can withstand some hard treatment but thrives in reasonably high light levels, but not full sun, with regular watering during hot weather.

Coelogyne primulina G. Baretto

A recently described miniature species from Hong Kong with flowers which are translucent pale yellow, 2.5–3 cm across and are borne in pairs but open singly on an upright, apical raceme. The small pseudobulbs are well spaced (2–5 cm apart) along a creeping wiry rhizome. The plant grows well overflowing from a shallow pot or on a mount of natural cork where the rhizomes can spread.

Cymbidium canaliculatum R. Br.

A hardy species of the dry eucalypt forests of northern and inland Australia, this species has leathery, deeply channelled, grey-green leaves to 50 cm. A pendulous inflorescence to 40 cm with 60 or more fragrant flowers is quite common. Flower colour varies from the almost black-red of the so-called variety 'Sparkesii' to the rarer pure apple-green form. Other colour forms are also common with varying amounts of blotching and marking in browns, tans and greens. In cultivation *C. canaliculatum* must be given good air movement and be kept dry during winter. Daily watering during the growing season is beneficial. *C. canaliculatum* has a very extensive root system running for many metres inside its host tree and therefore does not like being disturbed once potted; so a long lasting medium is necessary for the successful cultivation of this rewarding species.

Cymbidium devonianum Paxton

A cool growing miniature species from Nepal, India and northern Thailand from altitudes of 1450–2200 m. The heavily textured flowers are variable in colour ranging from olive-green with purple spotting to buff-yellow streaked with dark purple. Fifteen to 35 tightly spaced flowers are borne on a pendulous raceme which can be at least 30 cm in length. The pseudobulbs are almost nonexistent being only swellings at the base of the rather broad leaves.

*Cymbidium floribundum Lindl.

This is a miniature species from southern China and Taiwan which was previously known as *Cymbidium pumilum.* The flowers of this species are usually reddish-brown with yellow margins. The lip is white with red markings. There is a green colour variant which is cultivated as variety *album.* As this species is from mountain regions where it grows lithophytically it can be grown with a minimum of protection in temperate regions. Due to its dwarf habit this hardy species will make an ideal indoor plant if plenty of light is available and it is not overwatered.

Cymbidium madidum Lindl.
An epiphyte of the tropical and subtropical rainforest, swamps and open forests from northern Queensland to northeastern New South Wales, this species rapidly develops into large specimen plants and is the easiest of the Australian *Cymbidium* species to cultivate. Flower colour can be yellow to brown, with the north Queensland variety *leroyi* being bright green. This species often germinates in other epiphytic plants such as ferns and will grow quite happily mounted in this manner. Plants grown in pots need to be hung to best display the pendulous racemes and to allow air movement around the leaves.

Dendrobium aberrans Schltr.
A small epiphyte from the moss forests of eastern New Guinea (300–1900 m), this species has 2–3 apical leaves on a 3–20 cm pseudobulb. The long-lasting, small (25 mm) flowers are iridescent white, later fading to creamy-yellow with the column often pink in colour. The most striking feature of this species is the three-lobed, fleshy labellum. A very rewarding species in cultivation, with seedlings being easy to grow and quick to flower.

Dendrobium antennatum Lindl.
One of the most widely distributed and best known of the section *Spathulata* dendrobiums, *D. antennatum* is found from Queensland, northeastern Australia through New Guinea and the Solomon Islands. It has 15–75 cm pseudobulbous stems with an inflorescence to 35 cm, bearing up to 15 green and white flowers. Cultivation of this species in temperate regions requires high light levels and glasshouse conditions.

Dendrobium bracteosum Reichb.f.
This species is referred to in some parts of New Guinea as the Coconut Orchid because of its habit of establishing on coconut palms in old plantations. It is found on the coastal fringe growing high up on the branches of tall trees and on the trunks of coconut palms. Flower colour can be variable, from pure white with a yellow-tipped labellum through all shades of pink, from pale to dark rose with an orange labellum. It gets its name from the persistent bracts which surround individual flowers. Flowers are borne from nodes on leafless pseudobulbs which can be up to 45 cm in length. Plants not in flower have a somewhat scruffy appearance. In cultivation *D. bracteosum* requires bright light and perfect drainage with moderate air

movement to thrive. It is best grown in a small pot or on a mount.

Dendrobium capitisyork M. Clements *et.* D. Jones
A species endemic to the northeastern portion of Queensland, *D. capitisyork* is found growing as an epiphyte in rainforest at low to moderate altitudes. This species is quite cold tolerant and will grow and flower under bushhouse conditions as far south as Sydney, New South Wales. *D. capitisyork* was previously known as *D. tetragonum* var. *giganteum* Gilbert and unlike other species in the *D. tetragonum* complex will flower at any time during the year, with the peak flowering between autumn and spring. Yellow to gold, red-marked flowers to 12 cm in height are borne in groups of 2 to 5 flowers on a short raceme.

Dendrobium cariniferum Reichb.f.
A small species occurring from India to Thailand, *D. cariniferum* has pseudobulbs to 10 cm. The flowers are borne in pairs on a terminal inflorescence and have a bright orange and cream labellum with the other segments cream. They are up to 4.5 cm across and very highly scented. In temperate regions this species requires the protection of a glasshouse.

Dendrobium cuthbertsonnii F. Muell.
A miniature species 2–8 cm tall found growing as an epiphyte on shrubs and tree ferns or as a lithophyte in moss on rocks, road cuttings and exposed cliff faces, *D. cuthbertsonnii* is one of the most attractive dendrobiums found in the highlands of New Guinea. It is often incorrectly known by the more popular synonym *D. sophronites*. The flowers vary in colour from orange to mauve-pink with white and yellow less common. Bicolour forms are also known. The most common colour form is bright red with a yellow-marked labellum. This species can be difficult in cultivation if its requirements of high humidity and air movement are not met. Fortunately nursery-raised seedlings of this very rewarding species are becoming more readily available.

Dendrobium kingianum Bidw. ex Lindl.
A temperate lithophytic species distributed from central New South Wales to central Queensland, *D. kingianum* is probably the most common of the Australian dendrobiums. In cultivation it is a most rewarding species to grow and flower, doing well in open media in pots which are not too deep. Daily watering during the summer months is beneficial, although plants should be

allowed to dry out between waterings. The flowers of *D. kingianum* are up to 30 mm across and are usually carried on an upright or arching raceme of 2 to 17 flowers. The flowers come in a range of colours from pure white, through pink to the darkest magenta 'reds'. Some plants have a contrasting labellum. Line bred cultivars are sought after by enthusiasts and are generally horticulturally superior to wild plants.

Dendrobium laevifolium Stapf.
A species similar to *D. cuthbertsonnii*, *D. laevifolium* is found growing in cloud forest in moss and lichens on small shrubs. Flower colour varies from a pale cream-lilac to the more common bright pink. In cultivation *D. laevifolium* has proven to be a vigorous grower from seed, requiring similar cultural conditions to *D. cuthbertsonnii*.

Dendrobium lawesii F. Muell.
Named after Dr Lawes, one of the pioneer missionaries to Papua in the 1800s, it is one of the best known species of *Dendrobium* section *Calyptrochilus,* characterised by pendulous flowers with labellum that is cowl-shaped, toothed, bent or folded at the apex. This epiphytic species from the highlands of New Guinea (1000–1500 m) grows on trees in deep shade, within a few metres of the ground. Flower colour is variable with red and purple being the two most common colours, but with yellow, apricot, white and bicolour forms also existing.

Dendrobium margaritaceum
Another miniature *Dendrobium* species, *D. margaritaceum* comes from Thailand. The pseudobulbs, which are covered with dark hairs, can grow to 8 cm tall and bear solitary flowers from the upper nodes which are up to 4 cm across. The flowers are a brilliant white with a labellum marked with bright orange and are heavily scented. As with the other species in the nigro-hirsute group an open mix is required in cultivation and regular watering is only necessary when plants are in active growth producing new roots; excessive water at other times will cause the roots to rot. As the growths of these species are fleshy, protection from cold is necessary.

Dendrobium stratiotes Reichb.f.
A species closely related to *D. antennatum*, *D. stratiotes* is found from the Moluccas through Sulawesi and New Guinea. It is a most striking species with flowers to 10 cm, and has been used extensively in hybridising. It is a species worthy of wider cultivation. An albino form is known from the island of Morotai in the Moluccas.

Dendrobium strepsiceros J.J. Smith
Another species closely related to *D. antennatum*, *D. strepsiceros* differs from the above in that its flowers are predominately yellow-green with a faintly striped labellum. It is found in western New Guinea and the Moluccas.

*Dendrobium striolatum H.G. Reichb.
A temperate, lithophytic species occurring from central New South Wales to Tasmania, *D. striolatum* forms large mats on cliff faces and rock outcrops. It is easily distinguished by its short, curved, terete leaves which take on a reddish hue when grown in bright conditions. Flower colour can vary from a rich golden yellow through to a pale cream, usually with brown to red stripes on the backs of the segments. *D. striolatum* is easy to establish in cultivation, either on suitable mounts such as treefern fibre, weathered hardwood or in a hanging basket or pot of very open medium.

Encyclia alata (Bateman) Schltr.
An unusual Mexican species that sprouts its inflorescence from a short, stem with stiff oval leaves in late winter. The inflorescence continues to grow throughout the rest of the year, with the first flower opening in spring. Flowers are solitary, rarely in pairs. After opening, the ribbon-like petals slowly elongate until they reach their final length of 5 cm. Another unusual feature of this orchid is its shiny, heart-shaped labellum which has the appearance of being wet.

Encyclia bractescens
A spring flowering species found from Mexico to Honduras and the Bahamas that has conical pseudobulbs to 3 cm tall and grasslike leaves to 12 cm. Five to 12 flowers are borne on an upright willowy inflorescence. The 6 cm flowers are coppery coloured with a white labellum veined with pale pink.

Epidendrum pseudepidendrum Reichb.f.
A terete-stemmed species from Costa Rica and Panama, notable for its unusual combination of contrasting flower colours. Plants of this species will grow to about one metre in height with narrow leaves to 15 cm in length. Three to 5 flowers are borne on an open inflorescence, with flowers ranging from 3 to 5 cm in size.

Haraella retrocalla (Hay) Kudo
A monotypic genus from Taiwan, *H. retrocalla* is a favoured species with enthusiasts. It is found growing epiphytically in the warm, humid lower

mountain regions (300–1000 m). Two to three flowers 2 cm in height are borne on a raceme to 4 cm. This species does well grown on a mount of natural cork under humid conditions. In temperate regions the protection of a heated glasshouse is required.

Masdevallia amabilis Rchb.f.

A cool growing species from northern Peru found in cloud forests where it is subjected to heavy dews and fogs. In cultivation this species must be kept moist and cool but the medium should not be allowed to become stagnant. Good air movement is also required. The distinctive and unusual flowers are borne singly on stems to 30 cm.

Masdevallia strobelii

This Equadorian species grows to 4 cm in height. The flowers are orange and yellow and are borne singly on stems to 4 cm tall. The sepaline tube is furry inside. In cultivation this species requires moist conditioins.

Mediocalcar bifolium J.J. Smith

An epiphytic species from the highland montane forests of New Guinea, M. bifolium has pseudobulbs spaced 1–1.5 cm apart. This gives the species a somewhat spread out appearance. It is a rambling, branching species which quickly forms specimen plants. Cultivation is the same as for M. decoratum Schuiterman, the two species being reasonably closely related. Flowers are bright red with white tips and are jug-shaped in appearance. The 1.1 cm long flowers are borne from the base of pseudobulbs on a pedicel which can be up to 1.8 cm in length.

Mediocalcar decoratum Schuiteman

A recently described species from the highland montane forests of New Guinea at altitudes of 900–2500 m, M. decoratum is a free-branching, mat-forming epiphytic species. The pseudobulbs are tiny and have between 3 and 6 leaves. It is usually found growing in shaded areas, and plants grown in higher light levels develop a purple tinge to their pseudobulbs. The flowers are balloon-shaped and generally orange with yellow tips, although other colour forms have been reported. In cultivation this species has been grown in shallow pots, saucers and on treefern mounts. It responds well to daily watering during the growing season. The 7 mm flowers are produced from the base of older pseudobulbs on a short pedicel in late autumn and early winter.

Oberonia carnosa Lavarack

The smallest of the Australian Oberonia species, O. carnosa is found growing in bright light on sparse scrub or thickets, in humid locations. In cultivation this species is best grown on a mount of weathered hardwood, treefern or natural cork. One millimetre orange to gold flowers are produced on arching or pendulous racemes to 6 cm in length. In temperate regions this species needs the protection of a heated glasshouse.

Paphiopedilum armeniacum S.C. Chen & Liu

Probably the most vibrantly coloured of the Paphiopedilum species from southern China. Unfortunately, since its description in 1982 by Chen & Liu this beautiful species has been all but wiped out in its natural habitat by over-collection. P. armeniacum is found growing on limestone hills and has proven relatively easy to grow in cultivation. This species produces new growths from stolons which, in its natural habitat, travel through the litter. In cultivation accommodation needs to be made for these or they may appear from drainage holes, making it difficult to maintain new growths.

Paphiopedilum bellatulum (H.G. Reichb.) Stein

This species was introduced into cultivation from Burma, and was first described, by Reichenbach in 1888. It is typical of those species in section Brachypetalum of subgenus Brachypetalum in that it has dark-green mottled leaves. A large, white, maroon-spotted flower is borne on a short stem just above the foliage. It grows in cracks and crevices on limestone outcrops in the region bounded by southwest China, western Burma and Thailand. In cultivation it can be a difficult species to grow unless given perfect drainage and good light. Pieces or chips of limestone in the media seem to be beneficial.

Paphiopedilum bougainvilleanum Fowlie

A spring-flowering member of section Barbata, P. bougainvilleanum is found only on the island of Bougainville, east of Papua New Guinea, growing around and on granite outcrops at 1200 m. This species can be difficult in cultivation if its requirements of bright light, excellent drainage and plenty of moisture while making new growth are not met. Single growths may produce multiple new leads after flowering, so it can soon develop into a specimen plant.

Paphiopedilum glanduliferum var. glanduliferum (Blume) Stein

One of the earliest described tropical Asian Paphiopedilum species (Blume 1848), P. glanduliferum is lithophytic and sometimes epiphytic. It inhabits the limestone cliffs of islands in eastern Indonesia and New Guinea (sea-level to 200 m). In cultivation this species likes bright light and good air movement. Its root system differs from that of the other paphiopedilums in that it is wiry and smooth. Flowering may be irregular, occurring at any time during the year, as each growth flowers when it is mature.

Paphiopedilum spicerianum (Reichb.f. ex Masters & T. Moore) Pfitzer
This charming autumn-flowering species was first flowered in Europe by Mr H. Spicer after whom it is named. It comes from the limestone hills of northern India between 1000 and 2000 m where it grows in shallow humus-filled niches. It is an easy species in culture, requiring cool moist conditions.

Paphiopedilum sukhakulii Schoser & Senghas
A species from northeast Thailand which is now nearly extinct in the wild due to over-collecting. The flower to 12 cm across can be very impressive with its widely spreading, green-spotted petals and reddish labellum. The leaves are tessellated green and yellow making this species an interesting foliage plant when not in flower. It is very popular in cultivation but does require some protection from the cold.

Phaius bernaysii Rowland ex H.G. Reichb.
A much sought-after evergreen terrestrial species, *P. bernaysii* is endemic to the low-lying sand islands of Morton Bay in southeast Queensland, where it is found growing in conditions which are best described as swampy. Cultivation for this species is the same as for *P. tankervilleae* (Banks ex L'Hert) Blume.

Phaius francoisii (Schltr.) Summerh.
A very attractive member of the genus from Madagascar, *P. francoisii* has pseudobulbs to 1.7 cm in diameter with leaves typical of the genus, but only to 45 cm in height. Inflorescences are to 45 cm with up to 12 flowers 4 cm in diameter. This evergreen terrestrial species inhabits dense, wet, semi-deciduous forest, where in the dry season temperatures can reach 40°C. Cultivation for this species is the same as for *P. tankervilleae* (Banks ex L'Hert) Blume.

Phaius tankervilleae (Banks ex L'Hert) Blume.
A widespread evergreen terrestrial species distributed from China throughout southeast Asia and New Guinea to the northeast coast of New South Wales, Australia, *P. tankervilleae* is an easy and rewarding species to grow in cultivation. A well-drained medium rich in organic material is required, and during the active growing season copious amounts of water with small amounts of nitrogen-rich fertiliser are beneficial. One successful method of cultivation is to stand pots on gravel in a water-filled container that has drainage holes at the height of the gravel. This allows the plant to take as much water as it requires without the medium becoming sodden. The broad soft leaves are easily damaged by frost, so winter protection is required.

Phalaenopsis pulchra (H.G. Reichb.) H. Sweet
A striking species from the Philippines, *P. pulchra* was once considered to be a colour form of *P. lueddemanniana* H.G. Reichb. It is easily distinguished from this species by its narrower floral segments and overall uniform colouration, which may vary from pink through to deep magenta. Like other *Phalaenopsis* species, *P. pulchra* needs the protection of a heated glasshouse in temperate regions during winter. It is best grown either on a slab mount such as treefern or hardwood, or alternatively in a timber slat basket filled with very open medium of bark, charcoal and fern fibre.

Phalaenopsis schilleriana H.G. Reichb.
A species native to the Philippine Islands of Luzon and Mindanao, it is found in the mountains at altitudes of 800–2000 m. The flowers can be up to 6 cm in diameter but are variable in size. They are a lovely pink with a golden lip marked with red and are displayed on long, arching racemes which can be up to a metre in length. The plants have dark green leaves which are mottled with silver-grey and are often magenta underneath. In cultivation this species requires the protection of a heated glasshouse in temperate regions.

Phalaenopsis violacea Teijsm & Binn.
An attractive species from peninsular Malaysia, Borneo and Sumatra, *P. violacea* is found growing at low altitude in shady areas on tree trunks overhanging watercourses. Two colour forms are known. The large Bornean form has sepals and petals that are white to light green in colour, with lateral sepals that are mostly violet. The smaller Malaysian form has flowers which are pink-violet to strong crimson over most of the floral segments.

Promenaea xanthina (Lindl.) Lindl.
A very appealing species from Brazil with flowers which are highly fragrant, it was previously known as *P. citrina*. The flowers are

up to 5 cm in diameter and are citron-yellow in colour with a red-spotted labellum. In cultivation this species requires some protection and grows well in medium light levels with high humidity.

Restrepia hemsleyana Schltr.
This miniature species from Venezuela and Colombia forms dense clumps. The red flowers are to 5 cm long and are borne on slender stems. In cultivation this species requires protection from cold. Plants should not be overpotted and will soon grow into large clumps if provided with high humidity and plenty of light, but not direct sunlight. They must be kept from drying out.

Rhynchostylis gigantea (Lindl.) Ridl.
A vandaceous species from Burma, Thailand and Laos, R. gigantea can grow to 1.2 m in height, forming large clumps of multiple growths. Inflorescences to 40 cm are pendulous and densely packed with flowers which range from white with varying degrees of red-violet to magenta spotting and solid magenta. The labellum is usually heavily coloured. The flowers have a heavy, waxy texture and are very strongly scented.

Robiquetia bertholdii (Reichb.f.) Schltr.
A beautiful green-tipped, pink-flowered Robiquetia species from Vanuatu, the Solomon Islands and Fiji. In cultivation this species grows best mounted in a moist environment. Like many other vandaceous species, R. bertholdii will produce side growths and quickly develop into a large plant. Flower colour varies from white through pale pink to dark pink. The dark pink form illustrated is from Vanuatu.

*Sarcochilus falcatus R. Br.
Found growing on the trunks and branches of trees in the temperate rainforests of eastern Australia, S. falcatus is the most common and most widely distributed of the Australian Sarcochilus species. Plants are easily recognised by their falcate (sickle-shaped), yellowish-green leaves. Three to 12 white flowers are borne on a pendulous raceme. Flowers are between 2 cm and 5 cm in diameter and are often vanilla-scented. The labellum is white with varying amounts of yellow and/or purple marking. Plants may develop into large clumps over time, producing a spectacular display when in flower. This species is very easy to cultivate in cooler regions of Australia, growing best on natural mounts such as weathered hardwood, natural cork or live host trees with smooth-bark, such as citrus.

*Sarcochilus fitzgeraldii F. Muell.
A temperate, lithophytic species of the ravines and gullies of northeastern New South Wales and southeastern Queensland, S. fitzgeraldii was once very abundant, but unfortunately has suffered from over-collecting. Like other lithophytic Australian Sarcochilus species it will form large clumps over a number of years. In cultivation it grows particularly well in the colder southern regions of Australia and New Zealand, and is best grown in a fairly open mix in shallow terracotta saucers. Flower colour is basically white with varying amounts of pink to red central marking.

Sophronitella violacea (Lindl.) Schltr.
A cool growing monotypic genus from Brazil, S. violacea was first described by Lindley in 1847. Pseudobulbs on well grown specimens are ovoid in appearance to 3 cm in length. The species does particularly well grown on a mount of natural cork or weathered timber. Flowers are a uniform violet-cerise and up to 2.5 cm in diameter.

Sophronitis cernua (Lindl.) W.J. Hook
A small cool growing species from south-central Brazil, S. cernua was first described by Lindley in 1826. It is an autumn/winter flowering species with bright red-orange flowers up to 2.5 cm in diameter. In cultivation it grows best on a mount of treefern. It will grow well in a bushhouse if it is given cool and moist conditions.

Sophronitis coccinea (Lindl.) Reichb.f.
This species was discovered in 1837 at fairly high altitude near the city of Rio de Janeiro, Brazil and is probably the most popular of those in the genus. It has the largest flowers (5–7 cm) and they are bright red. In nature S. coccinea is found growing as an epiphyte or sometimes as a lithophyte in cool, moist conditions. In cultivation Sophronitis species in general do not like to be overpotted or disturbed once growing, so potting media and mounts have to be long lasting. Once repotted, plants may sulk for quite some time before starting to make new growth. In temperate regions they will grow under bushhouse conditions if given an airy, moist environment.

Spathoglottis affinis de Vr.
A terrestrial species from the mountains of northern peninsular Malaysia, Burma, Thailand and Java. The flowers are golden yellow with reddish purple stripes on the lateral sepals and often on the labellum. They are borne on stems to 30 cm tall which carry many flowers,

although only two or three are open at any one time. The pseudobulbs are small and flattened in appearance. This species is easy to grow in cultivation with protection from the cold, but it should be remembered that it is deciduous in the dry season when it requires only a minimum of water. High light levels are required when the new shoots appear.

Thunia venosa
Like other species in this genus, *Thunia venosa* is an interesting plant when not in flower with tall reedy stems. This species is deciduous over winter and produces new leads which quickly mature in spring. The pink tinged, white flowers are striking and are borne in drooping clusters from the tops of the stems. *Thunia* species are easy to grow in cultivation, requiring a rich mix with enough food to provide for rapid growth. The leafless canes are best unpotted and all remaining roots removed. When the new growths begin to appear the plant should be potted and staked until new roots are produced. A quick method for producing specimen plants is to layer the previous year's stems after they have produced their new growths.

Vanda hindsii Lindl.
This species has a distribution from New Guinea into northeast Queensland. Specimen plants will reach 1 m in height with straplike leaves to 45 cm. Up to 12 flowers are borne on a raceme that can be to 40 cm. The flowers are up to 35 mm in diameter, somewhat waxy in appearance and are generally brown with yellow margins. A pure yellow form is known from New Guinea.

Zygopetalum maxillare Lodd.
A much sought-after species from Brazil and Paraguay, *Z. maxillare* is difficult to keep in cultivation unless perfect drainage is achieved. In its natural habitat it grows exclusively on treefern trunks in gullies and on humid slopes. Showy flowers to 6 cm in length are borne on an upright raceme supporting 5 to 8 flowers.

References

Barretto G. (1990) A new species of *Coelogyne* Lindl. *The Orchid Review.* Feb; 37–41

Bechtel H., Cribb P.J. and Launert E. (1981/86) *The Manual of Cultivated Orchid Species.* Blandford Press.

Black P.M. (1980) *The Complete Book of Orchid Growing.* Ward Lock Ltd, London.

Clements M.A. (1989) Catalogue of Australian Orchidaceae. *Australian Orchid Research.* 1; 1–160.

Cohen S.H. (1990) *Epidendrum*—The neglected Genus. Part VI *Barkeria. The Orchid Review.* March; 77.

Cribb P.J. (1983) A revision of *Dendrobium* Sect. *Latouria* (Orchidaceae). *Kew Bulletin.* 38(2); 229–306.

Cribb P.J. (1986) The Antelope Dendrobiums. *Kew Bulletin.* 41(3); 615–92.

Cristenson E.A. (1988) Species Portrait. *Sophronitis pterocarpa* Lindl., with the correct citation for *Sophronitis cernua* (Lindl.) W.J. Hook. *The Orchid Review.* June; 179–81.

Das S. and Jain S.K. (1980) Orchidaceae: Genus *Coelogyne. Fasciles of Flora of India, Fascile 5.* Botanical Survey of India, PO Box Botanic Garden Howrah-711103.

Dockrill A.W. (1969) *Australian Indigenous Orchids.* The Society for Growing Australian Plants.

Hawkes A.D. (1981) *Encyclopaedia of Cultivated Orchids.* Faber & Faber Ltd, London.

Hillerman F.E. and Holst A.W. (1986) *An Introduction to the Cultivated Angraecoid Orchids of Madagascar.* Timber Press, USA.

Hunt, P.F. (1979–84) *The International Book of Orchids.* Cavendish House, London.

Isaac-Williams M.L. (1988) *An Introduction to the Orchids of Asia.* Angus and Robertson Publishers, Sydney.

Jones D.L. (1988) *Native Orchids of Australia.* Reed Books Pty Ltd, Sydney.

Jones D.L. (1990) *Exotic Orchids in Australia.* Reed Books Pty Ltd, Sydney.

Lavarack P.S. and Gray B. (1985) *Tropical Orchids of Australia.* Thomas Nelson, Melbourne.

Lewis B. and Cribb P.J. (1987) *Orchids of Vanuatu.* The Royal Botanic Gardens Kew in association with Colingridge, Great Britain.

Millar A. (1978) *Orchids of Papua New Guinea—An Introduction.* Australian National University Press, Canberra.

Northern R.T. (1980) *Miniature Orchids.* Van Nostrand Reinhold Company, New York.

Du Puy D. and Cribb P. (1988) *The Genus Cymbidium.* Timber Press, USA.

Reeve T.M. and Woods P.J.B. (1989) A revision of *Dendrobium* section *Oxyglossum* (Orchidaceae). *Notes from the Royal Botanic Garden Edinburgh.* Volume XLVI. No. 2, 161–305.

Schlechter R. (1982) *The Orchids of German New Guinea.* Translated by R.J. Rogers, H.J. Katz and J.T. Simmonds, edited by D.F. Blaxell. Australian Orchid Foundation, Melbourne.

Sheehan T. and Sheehan M. (1979) *Orchid Genera Illustrated.* Van Nostrand Reinhold Company, New York.

Schuiteman A. (1989) Two new species of *Mediocalcar* (Orchidaceae) from New Guinea. *Blumea* 34, 167–72.

Teo C.K.H. (1985) *Native Orchids of Peninsula Malaysia.* Times Books International, Singapore.

Tibbs M. (1990) Orchid Portrait *Sophronitella violacea. The Orchid Review.* March; 94–95.

1. *Ada aurantiaca*

2. *Aërides odoratum*

3. *Ansellia africana*

4. *Ascocentrum curvifolium*

5. *Barkeria skinneri*

7. *Bothriochilus bellus*

6. *Baskervillea paranaensis*

8. *Bulbophyllum barbigerum*

9. *Bulbophyllum globuliforme*

10. *Bulbophyllum macrobulbum*

11. *Bulbophyllum weinthalii*

12. *Ceratostylis retisquamea*

13. *Cochioda noetzliana*

14. *Coelogyne amoena*

15. *Coelogyne primulina*

16. *Cymbidium canaliculatum*

17. *Cymbidium devonianum*

18. *Cymbidium floribundum*

19. *Cymbidium madidum*

20. *Dendrobium aberrans*

21. *Dendrobium antennatum*

22. *Dendrobium bracteosum*

23. *Dendrobium capitisyork*

24. *Dendrobium cariniferum*

28. *Dendrobium lawesii*

26. *Dendrobium kingianum*

25. *Dendrobium cuthbertsonnii*

27. *Dendrobium laevifolium*

29. *Dendrobium margaritaceum*

32. *Dendrobium striolatum*

30. *Dendrobium stratiotes*

31. *Dendrobium strepsiceros*

34. Encyclia bractescens

33. Encyclia alata

35. Epidendrum pseudepidendrum

36. Haraella retrocalla

26

39. *Mediocalcar bifolium*

40. *Mediocalcar decoratum*

37. *Masdevallia amabilis*

38. *Masdevallia strobelii*

41. *Oberonia carnosa*

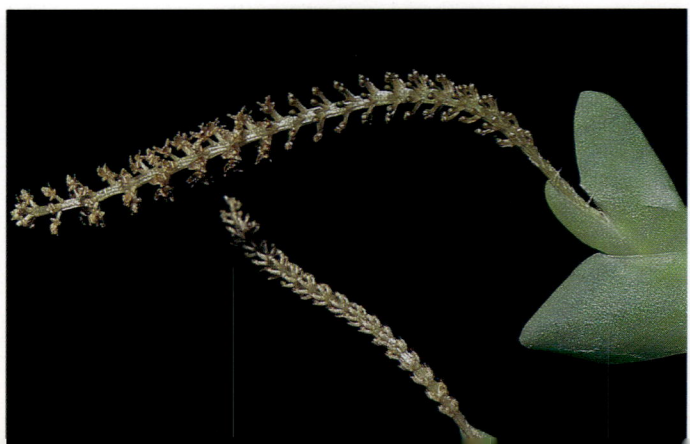

42. *Paphiopedilum armeniacum*

44. *Paphiopedilum bougainvilleanum*

45. *Paphiopedilum glanduliferum* var. *glanduliferum*

46. *Paphiopedilum spicerianum*

43. *Paphiopedilum bellatulum*

48. *Phaius bernaysii*

47. **Paphiopedilum sukhakulii**

49. *Phaius francoisii*

50. *Phaius tankervilleae*

51. *Phalaenopsis pulchra*

52. *Phalaenopsis schilleriana*

54. *Promenaea xanthina*

55. *Restrepia hemsleyana*

53. *Phalaenopsis violacea*

56. *Rhynchostylis gigantea*

57. *Robiquetia bertholdii*

58. *Sarcochilus falcatus*

59. *Sarcochilus fitzgeraldii*

60. *Sophronitella violacea*

61. *Sophronitis cernua*

63. *Spathoglottis affinis*

62. *Sophronitis coccinea*

64. Thunia venosa

66. Zygopetalum maxillare

65. Vanda hindsii

1 The Flower and Fruit

The first problem encountered by newcomers to orchidology is recognising an orchid as such. This is not quite as simple as it sounds for there are over 700 different genera of orchids and more species than in any other plant family. Added to this is the wide diversity of appearance of orchid flowers. To assist the newcomer to identify a flower as a possible orchid a simple key is given below, but before proceeding with this one must be familiar with the basic anatomy of the orchid flower as shown in Fig. 1.1. This shows the monandrous orchid flower which has one anther; most orchids in collections are monandrous with one exception which will be dealt with later. The difficulty comes when translating these anatomical components to the more bizarre forms of orchid flowers such as *Masdevallia, Coryanthes* and *Catasetum* to mention just a few.

An orchid plant is a monocotyledon (Chapter 4) and has its major floral parts in multiples of three, that is three sepals and three petals. In some plants the sepals are more prominant than the petals, such as *Bulbophyllum,* where the sepals are large and the petals are so small that a close examination is needed to find them. In *Coelogyne* many newcomers mis-identify the narrow petals as sepals. The column is a conjunction of both the androecium (male) and gynaecium (female) parts, for with few exceptions the orchid flower is hermaphroditic.

To simplify the key, explanations and exceptions are given in the notes which follow.

Key for monandrous orchids

1. The ovary is inferior	go to 3
2. The ovary is superior	not an orchid
3. The flower segments are six	go to 5
4. The flower segments are 4, 5 or many	not an orchid
5. The flowers are zygomorphic	go to 7
6. The flowers are regular	not an orchid
7. A gynostemium is present	most likely an orchid
8. Anthers and stigma are separate	not an orchid

Notes

1. As shown in Fig. 1.1 the ovary is inferior when located immediately below the sepals, that is towards the rachis. The immature ovary is not swollen and is sometimes difficult

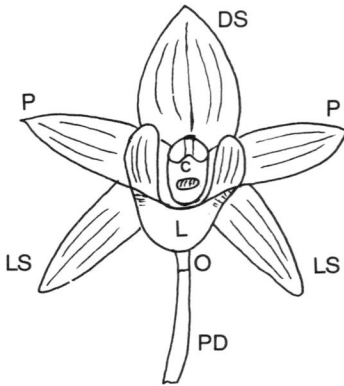

Fig. 1.1   A typical monandrous orchid flower. Dorsal sepal = DS; lateral sepals = LS; petals = P; the third petal is in the form of a lip or labellum = L. The column = C arises from the ovary = O, partly obscured by the lip. The column contains the anther (pollinia) under the top anther cap and the stigmatic surface (cross hatched) lower down. The flower is attached to the rachis by a stalk, the pedicel = PD

to distinguish from the pedicel; the ovary is ridged or grooved while the pedicel is mostly smooth.

2. Superior ovaries are situated above the sepals and petals and do not occur in orchids.

3. The flower segments consist of 3 sepals and 3 petals, one of the latter is usually different from the other two and is often striped, ridged or hairy and is called the labellum or lip. The flower may be as shown in Fig. 1.1 or turned through 180 degrees giving an inverted appearance.

4. These floral segments are found in dicotyledons.

5. Zygomorphic flowers can be cut in only one plane to produce two equal parts. Some orchids have twisted parts, such as the column of *Mormodes,* which is one exception to this rule. However, the rule aplies to most monandrous orchids.

6. Regular flowers can be cut in more than one plane to produce equal portions (actinomorphic).

7. A gynostemium or gynandrium or column is that part of the flower containing the pollen and stigma when these are combined into the one structure. Several other plant families have this feature but they are dicotyledons (Chapter 4). These are eliminated earlier in the key.

Floral patterns

The orchid flower is thought to have originated from a primitive lily type plant or perhaps an ancestor from which both lilies and orchids arose through evolution. Both Liliales and Orchidales (orchid-ah-leez) are included in Liliidae (Chapter 4) and both are recognised as originating in the Cretaceous Period (Chapter 13). The most primitive orchid found today is *Neuwiedia* from Indonesia and Malaysia, which is triandrous, having three stamens. Other primitive orchids are the *Apostasia* and *Cypripedium* (and its related genera) which have two anthers or pollen sacs.

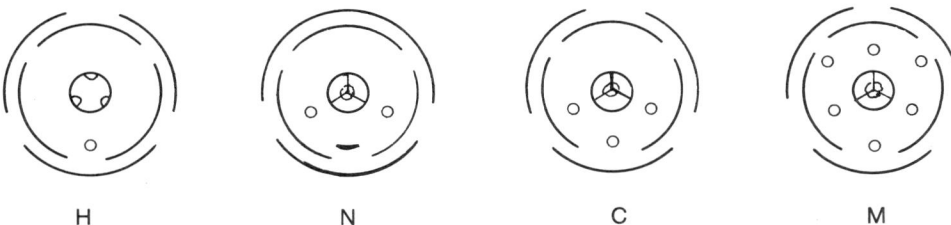

H   N   C   M

Fig. 1.2 Floral diagrams of *Hypoxis* = H; *Neuwiedia* = N; *Cypripedium* = C and a monandrous orchid = M. *Hypoxis* is a primitive monocotyledon with an inferior ovary and is shown for comparison with the orchids. The axile placentation in the ovary is a primitive characteristic. Monandrous orchids have a more advanced parietal placentation of the seeds. The general arrangement of the perianth and stamens is in four whorls. The two inner whorls contain all six stamens in *Hypoxis*. The primitive orchid *Neuwiedia* has only three stamens, two in the inner whorl and one in the second whorl. In *Cypripedium* and other genera in the Cypripedioideae, the stamen in the second whorl has been reduced to a staminode; two stamens remain in the inner whorl. In the monandrous orchids there is only one stamen in the second whorl, all others have been lost

Fig. 1.2 shows the floral patterns of *Neuwiedia* and *Cypripedium,* plus a typical monandrous orchid. Also shown for comparison is the pattern of *Hypoxis* (Amaryllidaceae), a primitive monocotyledon with an inferior ovary from Central and Tropical Africa.

Floral segments

To most orchid growers it is the sepals and petals, including the labellum, which are of major interest. Each flower consists of these floral segments plus the anthers (androecium), the stigma, styles and ovary (gynaecium), and the pedicel or stalk by which the flower is attached to the flower stem (rachis). Some flowers have a long nectar tube to provide pollinating insects with an energy source. Others have a scent which is either pleasant or abhorrent to humans; some have no scent at all. The total number of flowers on a stem arising from the vegetative part of the plant (peduncle) is called the inflorescence. This and other parts of the flower will be dealt with in turn.

The sepals and petals are collectively called the perianth. The sepals protect the bud while it is developing but nothing protects the sepals, hence holes in these from insect attack spoil the open flowers. This is not so important if the sepals are small and green and do not form part of the coloured display, but in orchids the sepals are of importance to exhibitors. In nature the importance of the sepals is probably diminished as the petals can attract the pollinator to the sexual parts of the flower, which after all is their sole function.

In some flowers the two lateral sepals are permanently joined along their edges for their entire length (connate) or part thereof. These are called synsepal and are prominent in *Cypripedium* and similar genera. The dorsal sepal is frequently of a size, shape and colouring which is used as part of the identification of a species. This is again especially so for *Cypripedium* and allied genera.

The two petals are usually identical, but the petal opposite the anther (monandrous orchids) is modified to form the labellum or lip which is a major feature of all orchids in collections. Not only are its size and shape important, but a fleshy lump called a callus (plural calli) on the lip varies from genus to genus and from species to species within a genus. This callus is prominent in *Phalaenopsis* and its shape is species diagnostic. There is quite a large variation of colour in orchid flowers within a single species so colour is not considered important from a diagnostic viewpoint.

The labellum is often loosely pivoted, very loosely in some genera, to the base of the column and moves freely up and down. In other genera it is securely fixed to the column base and any attempt to move the lip moves the whole flower. This is a useful diagnostic feature, particularly for those genera which have very similar flowers.

Fruit

The fruit of an orchid is a capsule. It is often referred to incorrectly as a pod but a pod is the fruit of Fabaceae, not Orchidaceae.

Fig. 1.3   Orchid fruits. Capsules have formed along the rachis. Some capsules have opened discharging the seed, some of which has been caught in a spider's web between two capsules

The fruit is formed from the fertilised ovary and has three carpels in all orchids, that is it is tricarpelate. In most species of orchid there is only a single locule or cavity with parietal placentation, that is the seed embryos are located around the inner periphery of the ovary. In the primitive orchids the ovary is trilocular with axile placentation as in the genus *Hypoxis* as shown in Fig. 1.2. The fruit is dehiscent when ripe and splits open to release dry seed. In primitive orchids the seeds are in a pulp.

The seeds are very small when not fertilised and the ovary is not much thicker than the pedicel. The plant does not waste energy on the production of large seeds and a large ovary until it is necessary to do so and this energy can be diverted to flower production. Orchids are prolific seed producers: 28 000 in *Cypripedium* is a small number, the fruit of *Cycnoches* species may contain three million. All of these are not necessarily fertilised or viable and it is common opinion that those seeds nearest the column have the best chance of being fertilised by the male gametes contained in the pollen tubes which grow into the ovary from the stigmatic surface on the column.

The seeds vary considerably in size; a typical value is 400 micrometres long and 100 micrometres in diameter. The actual growing part, called the proto-embryo, is much smaller and is encased in an open-work, mesh-like structure which forms the visible seed. (Fig. 1.4) The weight of a typical seed is about 3 micrograms and it is readily blown about to lodge in bark crevices, humus clumps and lichens and mosses growing on tree branches (Chapter 14). Unlike most larger seeds orchid seeds do not possess endosperm as a food reserve for

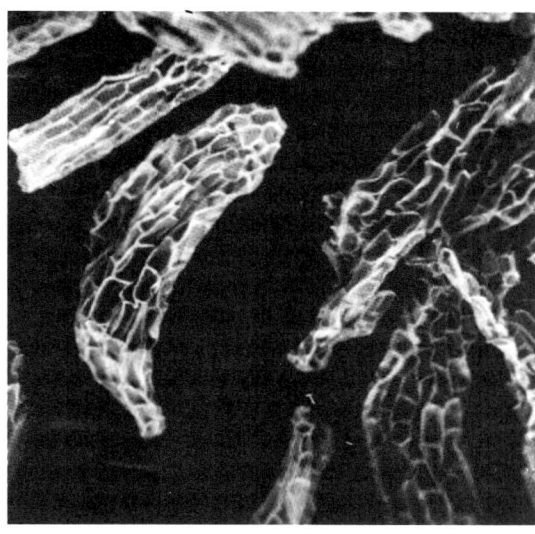

Fig. 1.4 A typical orchid seed magnified 140 times. The open-mesh framework holding the proto-embryo is clearly evident

use during germination. They do have a small oil droplet which provides enough energy for respiration to sustain life, but to germinate they require an outside source of energy (Chapter 14).

For further information on the inflorescence and the flower refer to Chapter 3.

2 The Naming of Orchids

After learning to recognise an orchid plant as such (Chapter 1) the newcomer to orchidology has to master orchid names. The common names much used in horticulture such as bottlebrush, she-oak and lords and ladies just will not do. The international scope of orchid growing and the large number of species and hybrids demands something better than this and failure to recognise and learn botanical names will soon leave the newcomer on the outer fringe of orchid growers.

However, this chapter is not only for newcomers to orchidology. Notwithstanding the articles published in orchid journals, many who have grown orchids over decades still do not understand or use orchid naming principles. One has only to look at catalogues, plant labels and advertisements in journals to see that many growers and nurserymen do not write orchid names correctly, even if some licence is allowed for advertising gimmicks to attract attention. So this Chapter should be of interest to all persons concerned with orchids or indeed any other plant.

This discussion has, therefore, been kept to a simple and quickly digested level. The more complex aspects of orchid nomenclature are dealt with in Chapter 4 for those who wish to know more. Discussion covers the format of botanical names of species and then of hybrids, who names what and why names change. Finally some help is given with the pronunciation of orchid names.

What is a species

This question is frequently asked by orchid growers and has some bearing on the naming process. The word 'species' has no special connotation. In Latin it simply means 'kind' and the kinds of organisms are called species. This is a rather circular type of definition and various taxonomists have their own ideas on the differences which justify classifying plants within, or not within, a given species.

One might answer by saying it is other than a hybrid, but this negative approach is unsatisfactory and also requires definition of a hybrid.

Three definitions are given below which, when taken together, given some idea of the concept.

1. Groups of actually or potentially interbreeding natural populations which are reproductively isolated from other such groups.

2. A naturally occurring collection of plants which can interbreed in nature and bear a resemblance to each other.

3. A group of plants showing intergradation among its individuals and having in common one or more characteristics which definitely separate it from any other group, i.e. it is distinct from other kinds.

The terms 'natural populations' and 'naturally occurring collection' raise the question whether cross pollination by man of two plants of the same species results in the progeny also being species? One would tend to say 'yes, they are', but if the two plants have some special attributes such as intense flower colour or extra thick petals as a result of some genetic variability in only these two plants, can the progeny displaying these attributes truly be considered a species? They are not a natural population. This problem has not been resolved universally so orchid growers tend to regard the progeny as a species, sometimes acknowledging the special attributes by the addition of a cultivar name (see below).

The difficulty here is that man usually only cross pollinates two plants when some attribute appeals to him and one can see that ultimately, with continued breeding, plants unlike the naturally occurring populations may be produced and named as species. This possibility occurs because some growers aim only for show bench success and the general opinion is that 'big is beautiful' or some other favoured characteristic. Breeding for the show bench is popular but the result may be a distortion of the species.

Until this matter is resolved I believe that these plants will be regarded as species with scant regard for the definition. But it is hoped that orchid societies will become conscious of this aspect.

Botanical names of species

The following is intended for orchid growers and not taxonomists. It describes the correct way to write orchid names for catalogues and plant labels (both frequently written incorrectly). All botanical names, whether for orchids or not, are formed from at least two words, the generic name and the specific epithet, both together constituting the name of the plant. The generic name is indicative of the genus to which the plant is assigned, e.g. *Cymbidium, Vanda, Cattleya*. It is always a singular noun (hence a name); whenever 's' is added, e.g. cymbidiums, it becomes a common name. This form is much used in speech about orchids but there is little reason to use it in print, in titles of books or in any serious work on orchids. Note in particular that the generic name is written with a capital letter and printed in italics, or underlined if italics are not available. When the plural is used (a common name) it is neither capitalised nor italicised, as shown above.

The second word is an adjective describing the generic name hence this word is an epithet and not a name. It is called the specific epithet as it identifies a species within the genus. As it is not a noun any reference to 'specific name', which one sees quite often, is incorrect. The two words together, generic name plus specific epithet, form the botanical name of the plant. It is also quite incorrect to use the specific epithet on its own, e.g. *Cattleya granulosa* and *Dendrobium speciosum* are correct but *'granulosa'* or *'speciosum'* is incorrect and horrible even in speech. Note that the specific epithet is also in italics and commences with a small letter irrespective of whether or not it is commemorative, e.g. *Vanda hookeriana* (named after Hooker).

The botanical name may have one or two other epithets added to it. One commonly seen is variety (var.). This epithet is written in italics, such as *Phalaenopsis fimbriata* var. *sumatrana*. Varietal names may only be applied to species and by the taxonomist naming the species or the variety. Do not confuse varietal epithets with cultivar names. See later in this Chapter.

A fourth epithet may also be added to describe the 'form' (f). This is not used very often but it appears occasionally to indicate a colour or the place of origin when the plant differs slightly from the normal species or variety. Chapter 4 describes the proper use of variety and form. Both epithets are written in italics, or underlined, and also commence with a small letter.

In orchid nomenclature a cultivar name may also be added to a species which has been cultivated from a wild plant or has been raised from a single seedling when the plant has special merit which warrants the added cultivar name. This is written in Roman letters, is a fancy name, is always the last word in the name and is enclosed in single inverted commas, e.g. *Phalaenopsis lindeni* 'Malibu'.

The naming of species

The naming of a new orchid species is not something to be undertaken lightly and is usually done by an orchid taxonomist who has a good practical knowledge of the regional flora where the plant was found and who has an extensive library, a wet and dry herbarium and/or living collection of other orchids known in that and adjacent regions. Frequently other established herbaria need to be consulted and it is not always easy to have herbarium staff drop their own work and search their records at the request of others. In the early days of orchid collecting communication and publication was not as easy as today and many orchid descriptions were in obscure publications or put away in herbaria without much attention given to the collection. A good search may reveal that the orchid plant in question is not new and has already been named. Under international convention the first published name has priority except in special circumstances (see below).

Synonyms and the priority rule

The International Code of Botanical Nomenclature (ICBN) specifies that the earliest correctly published name must have priority and be the recognised name. The accepted publication date of *Species Plantarum* by Linnaeus, 1 May 1753, is recognised as the commencing point and the names in this work have priority over others. However, this priority relates only to a taxon and not necessarily to a combination of taxa, e.g. genus and species.

Communication between orchid taxonomists was poor during the hey-day of orchid collecting when men like R. Brown, Schlechter, Reichenbach, J.J. Smith and Lindley named any orchids they could find or were sent irrespective of one another. As a result any Flora we consult usually contains one or many alternative names or synonyms. These synonyms are invalid names under the priority rule and they should not be used at all. They only serve to indicate the history of the plant's name.

If you refer to a list of synonyms you may find some of these pre-date the accepted name. This is frequently because the plant was not allocated to the correct genus or a new genus has been erected. For example, the present *Phalaenopsis amabilis* was called *Epidendrum amabile* in 1753 by Linnaeus when all epiphytic orchids were classed in the genus *Epidendrum*. In 1825 Blume erected a new genus which he called *Phalaenopsis* for these plants. Sometimes the earlier name for the plant was not validly published which makes the name illegitimate. The several reasons for invalidity are beyond the scope of this Chapter.

Taxonomists have realised that priority rules and name changes of families and genera can be inconvenient if these have a large number of species, particularly if a name has been in lengthy service, perhaps because the original name was obscure and unknown for some time. Under the ICBN rules it is possible to conserve the name currently in use by publishing this as a *nomen conservandum* in the ICBN rule book. Examples of conserved names are *Bulbophyllum, Calanthe, Miltonia* and *Dendrobium*. There is not a procedure for conserving specific epithets.

This system is not to be confused with the so-called 'Horticultural Equivalents' given in the *Handbook of Orchid Nomenclature and Registration*. This list of 'equivalents' is largely based on long established commercial usage, the commercially used name being recommended. It is more for convenience than botanical accuracy and is in no way a set of rules to be followed by everyone. It is largely up to the individual whether to be guided by the listing or to adopt the botanically correct name if this differs from the listing.

Name changes

A plant's name is changed for several reasons but do we have to change the label every time we see a name change?

The answers are Yes and No. If the change is made in accordance with ICBN rules the answer is Yes. The priority rule has already been mentioned. Another rule covers 'valid publication'. The plant name and description (a diagnosis in Botanical Latin) must be validly published in a recognised journal of botanical substance and a type specimen lodged with a herbarium. If the name has just been marked on a herbarium sheet or a plant named from a painting or photograph, such name is illegitimate until validly published and a type specimen lodged.

If the change is made simply because a taxonomist chose to do so by exercising his judgement then the answer is No, you do not have to make the change unless you agree with the proposal. Far too many orchid growers make the change without assessing the reasons for the change, or they are not aware of their freedom of choice. Many become embarrassed when told of the 'error in their label' and rush into acceptance of the change to avoid further embarrassment.

You will not be alone; every taxonomist will be assessing the change and deciding whether to accept it or not. Eventually, with the passing of years, the change will be accepted or not by most people.

When Shim in 1984 proposed a new generic classification for the *Phalaenopsis* complex I did not see any enthusiastic rush to embrace this change. As far as I can see most growers still accept the classification of Sweet (1980). Another example is when Wood (1976) changed *Paphiopedilum victoria-mariae* to *P. victoria-regina* and reduced the species *P. chamberlainianum, P. glaucophyllum, P. liemianum* and *P. primulinum* to subspecies of *P. victoria-regina*. This change has not been universally accepted, let us hope for valid reasons.

Most of these 'judgement' changes are done by elevating a variety to species rank or conversely transferring a species to a variety of another species. Sometimes two species of plants are considered to be conspecific (i.e. the same species) and one plant is simply made a variety of the other species if there is some slight difference.

Hybrid names

What is a hybrid? It may be defined as an organism which is the offspring of a union between two different races, species or genera. So a union between pollen gametes and the egg gametes of two different species is a hybrid. A plant derived from two species is called a primary hybrid and these, if fertile, may then be used to create further hybrids and so on and so on. The possibilities seem endless and many thousands of hybrids have been created and registered with the International Registration Authority for orchids.

Only those hybrids which are registered have any standing among hybrid enthusiasts and commercial orchid growers. There are many thousands of hybrids produced which the owner did not bother to register, possibly because of the effort or because the plants were not worth doing so. Not all hybridisers or owners are enthusiastic about registering the result of their handiwork. Registration is left to commercial growers and dedicated hybridists.

The Registration Authority

The International Society of Horticultural Science based in the Hague has established several Commissions each dealing with some facet of horticulture. One such Commission is for Nomenclature and Registration. This Commission then appoints various International Registration Authorities for the hybrids of various plant genera. The IRA for orchids is the Royal Horticultural Society, Vincent Square, London SW1P 2PE.

The code governing the registration of hybrids is the 'international code of nomenclature of cultivated plants'. However the naming of hybrid orchids has special problems made more difficult by the extreme promiscuity of orchids generally, where not only different species but also many genera interbreed readily. To provide a reference to the problems of orchid hybrid nomenclature the International Orchid Commission has produced a handbook on the subject. A preliminary edition appeared in 1965, the third edition is dated 1985. The registration authority uses this handbook, so anyone contemplating registration of a hybrid should obtain a copy. It can be obtained from the Royal Horticultural Society in London or from the American Orchid Society in the USA.

What does the IRA register?

Most registration authorities register the cultivar name (note the code calls this a 'name', taking precedence over the handbook which calls it an 'epithet'). The IRA for orchids registers only the 'grex'. Orchid growers have used fancy names for many years to describe a cross-bred plant but in a manner which was contrary to the rules of nomenclature and to the practice of breeders of all other plants. The solution to the problem was resolved at a meeting between Dr W.T. Stearn and David Sander, where it was agreed that the multitude of plants produced by orchid hybridists should be called a 'grex', meaning a swarm or flock. The adoption of this system then allowed the addition of a cultivar name in the same manner as used by other horticulturists. Orchid growers had come back into the nomenclatural fold.

The method used to show the parentage of a hybrid is called a formula. An example of this is

Cattleya bowringiana × *Cattleya elongata*

and this is the formula used whenever these two species are hybridised. Upon registration the above formula is converted to a grex epithet, which for this example is Elbowri (a fancy name capitalised but not in quotation marks and not italicised). The plant is now called *Cattleya* Elbowri and this applies to all hybrids of the above formula anywhere in the world, irrespective of who makes the cross and irrespective of which plant is the pollen parent.

Without an up-to-date hybrid listing one would not know the parents of *Cattleya* Elbowri whereas the formula gives a clear indication of this and may be a method of label marking preferred by many growers. It is not incorrect to use the formula as some may think; it is a matter of individual preference.

It is an onerous and costly enough task to register the grex; it would create an impossible situation if the IRA registered cultivar names.

More on hybrid names

Two hybrid plants may be interbred, e.g. *Oncidium* Susan Perreira × *Oncidium* Persian Red. This hybrid has now been registered as the grex *Oncidium* Fire Opal. A grower with an outstanding clone of this plant, after it has flowered, may wish to add a cultivar name and call this one plant and only this plant, *Oncidium* Fire Opal 'Goldilocks'. All offshoots, subdivisions, back bulbs and the like of this one plant can be known by this name.

Perhaps a species may be bred with a grex, e.g. *Oncidium* Pert × *Oncidium henekenii*. This has been registered as *Oncidium* Wild Honey. It must be becoming more difficult to think up grex names as the years go by.

How should intergeneric hybrids be named? The answer was given by the naming of a cross breeding of two non-orchid genera *Lapageria* and *Philesia*. The hybrid was given the generic name of *Philageria*. So an intergeneric hybrid between *Laelia* and *Cattleya* became *Laeliocattleya*. A few examples are listed below:

Epiphronitis is *Epidendrum* × *Sophronitis*
Brassidium is *Brassia* × *Oncidium*
Ansidium is *Ansellia* × *Cymbidium*
Arachnoglottis is *Arachnis* × *Trichoglottis*

However, this simplification did not last for long. With four genera contributing to the hybrid a generic name like *Brassosophrolaeliacattleya* was just too much to say and write on a label. The difficulty was resolved in 1950 at the Stockholm Botanical Congress when words ending in -ara were used, e.g. *Potinara* for the hybrid mentioned above. This becomes a true generic name and the plant must be listed under this name.

A new generic name formed from three or more generic parents is derived often from the name of an eminent orchidologist and terminated in -ara, e.g. *Wilkinsara*.

It is incorrect to use a grex epithet which has not been registered. Any hybrid of stated parentage can have only one grex epithet and one task of the IRA is to prevent duplication of grex epithets and the allocation of another grex epithet to a parentage already registered. Once registered, the grex epithet for that particular genus becomes the property of the world. Any hybrids resulting from a cross between the stated parents, whenever and wherever made, are known by this grex epithet. This may sound peculiar to many plant hybridists but any other method would result in hopeless confusion.

Whereas the allocation and use of grex epithets is reasonably well controlled, the use of cultivar names for orchids is wide open and uncontrolled except in a gentlemanly way.

If you have an outstanding plant you may select and apply a cultivar name, but before doing so you would be morally obliged to seek advice and consult the literature as to whether this name had been used before for the genus in question. Furthermore you should arrange for some recognised orchid journal to publish the cultivar name along with a description of the plant and a photograph. This at least informs others that you have some claim to this name. Unless this is done others cannot be expected to acknowledge your prior claim. If this plant is subsequently divided up and disposed of, the recipients should continue to use this cultivar name and pass it on with future divisions of the plant. Note that seedlings from this plant are not entitled to this name but it may be quoted as one of the parents.

The treatment of the subject here is not exhaustive but it should be sufficient for growers to appreciate the basic rules of orchid naming. The requirements are clear and only confused by those who seemingly try not to follow the system or are ignorant of it.

Pronouncing orchid names

Botanical names are of Latin or Greek origin or the latinised form of other languages. The language of Botanical Latin originated in the 1700s so it is a comparatively modern language. Scholars of the day learnt Latin and often this was their only non-native language, so travellers to other countries were forced to converse in Latin, perhaps using terms unknown to the Romans of old. Letters between naturalists were often written in Latin so its use became universal in the scientific world of that time.

Some present day Latin scholars disagree with the pronunciation of some plant names or with some descriptions of plants written in Botanical Latin. However, as one prominent botanist, Professor E.J.H. Corner, pointed out, Botanical Latin is as different from classical Latin as present day English is from Chaucerian English.

In offering the following guide to pronunciation I have assumed a knowledge of English, hence I have used the English form. I venture to say that non-English speaking persons will have their own ideas of how the words should sound.

The first hurdle in pronunciation is learning to recognise diphthongs consisting of two vowels together but said as one. Table 2.1 lists diphthongs and the suggested method of pronouncing these. Again this is the English form and not the classical sound. If we are going to adopt some standard method of saying words, and there are two or more methods of doing so, then I feel we should toss out all methods but one, and keep to this, no variations being allowed, classical, Roman or otherwise. As stated before I have opted for the English form. Common usage is a great modifier of language.

Table 2.2 shows the vowels in various forms with indicators as to how they should be pronouned.

Table 2.3 sets down guidance for pronouncing some consonants, although these are rather straight forward except for c, g, and y plus the two letters ch occurring together.

Table 2.1

Pronunciation of diphthongs

diphthong	pronunciation
ae	as ee in meet
au	as au in taught
ei	as ei in height
oe	as ee in meet
eu	as ew in yew
ui	as oo in food

Notes

1. The two adjoining vowels 'oi' do not appear in the table as this is not a diphthong and should be said as o-i. This is so difficult to say that common usage in many countries has made it into a pseudo-diphthong said as oy as in boy. Using it in the former way would produce some blank looks from others.
2. A diaeresis (··) is sometimes placed over the second vowel to show that it is sounded separately, e.g. Aërides where otherwise the Ae would be a diphthong. Diaereses are frequently omitted in error and sometimes it is difficult to determine whether the dots should be present or not.
3. The terminal ending 'ensis', often used to end a specific epithet, means 'from the place'. If the place name ends in o then an apparent diphthong is formed where not intended, hence a diaeresis is not used in this case. The o is sounded separately, usually in its ō form, e.g. rioensis. There could be many other examples with other vowel combinations forming apparent diphthongs.

Table 2.2

Pronunciation guide to vowels using indicators

ā as in mate	ō as in quote
ă as in cat	ŏ as in not
a as in about	ū as in cute
ē as in beef	ŭ as in cut
ě as in pet	
ī as in dice	– is a long sound
ĭ as in pit	˅ is a short sound

Here are some rules.

1. Divide a strange name into syllables containing just one vowel (or diphthong) each. Look after the vowels and the consonants will largely look after themselves.

Examples
a) Neobenthamia when divided is Ne-o-ben-tham-i-a. Notice that two vowels occur together, e and o; i and a. Neither form diphthongs so all are pronounced, as nē-ō-bĕn-thăm-ĭ-a.
b) Calanthe when divided is Cal-an-thē.
   The c when hard (see Rule 3) is represented by the letter k (as in kitchen) so we have kăl-ăn-thē. This name illustrates that the final silent e is always sounded in botanical names. English speaking people are so accustomed to a final e, as in have, alternate, mole, furore etc. that they often tend to keep the botanical e silent.
c) Cattleya when divided is Catt-ley-a which becomes kăt-lēa.
d) Ionopsis when divided is i-o-nop-sis which becomes ī-ō-nŏp-sĭs. Here we have both a long o and a short o.
These examples suffice to demonstrate the operation of Rule 1.

2. Many generic names and some specific epithets commemorate some person, a botanist, horticulturist, plant collector or even a person who provided finance for a project. The latinised version of the name should, therefore, be pronounced as near as possible to the person's name. A good illustration of this is example a) of Rule 1. Neobenthamia commemorates Englishman George Bentham. Without knowing this one may be inclined to say nē-ō-bĕn-thām-ĭ-a, not a very grave error to be sure, but avoidable with care. This rule is usually simple to follow for English names but names of foreign origin may present some difficulty.

3. The consonants c and g change in sound according to the vowel following. A hard sound is used before a, o and u as in cat, cot and gut. A soft sound is used before e, i and y as in cent, cinder, gin, cynical and cypher. The epithet coccinea is a good example, coc-cin-e-a becomes kŏk-sĭn-ē-a. Cymosa becomes sī-mōs-a.

4. A bi or a di in front of a word means two, so say with a long i (ī) before saying the remainder of the word. For example bigibbum is bī-jĭb-bŭm as per Rule 3. This epithet is often said with a hard g but this is not the normal English version.

5. Which syllable is emphasised? This probably causes more both than any other factor. If the vowel in the second last (penultimate) syllable is long (ō) then this syllable is emphasised.
For example canaliculatum becomes can-al-i-cu-la-tum or phonetically kăn-ăl-ĭ-cū-lā-tum. As the la is long this syllable is emphasised.
If the vowel in the penultimate syllable is short then emphasis is on the third last (antepenultimate) syllable which may, at times, be the first syllable of the word.
For example, mutabilis becomes mū-tăb-ĭl-ĭs so the tab is emphasised. Minima becomes mĭn-ĭ-ma so the min is emphasised.
The above five rules will usually provide a correct and understandable English version of Botanical Latin especially if the word sounds reasonable.

Readers will frequently hear other ways of saying the names of orchids. Once a person has formed a habit of saying a name one way it is often difficult to change the habit without a good deal of conscious thought. This emphasises the need to adhere to a single method of pronunciation and this section of the chapter hopefully describes a reasonable method for English speaking persons.

Table 2.3

Pronunciaton of some consonants

c	as a k before a, o and u
	as an s before e, i and y
ch	mostly as k but at times may be ch as in church at beginning of word, e.g., Choysia
g	hard as in grab before a, o and u
	soft as in ginger before e, i and y
j	as in jolly
ph	as f
ȳ	as in cypher
y̆	as in cygnet
y	as ee in jolly

References

Shim P.S. (1984) A new generic classification in the Phalaenopsis-complex. *Malayan Orchid Review,* 18; 49-61.

Sweet Herman R. (1980) *The Genus Phalaenopsis.* The Orchid Digest Inc.

Wood M.W. (1976) *The Orchid Review.* (English) May 1976.

3 The Orchid Structure

This Chapter covers the external appearance of the orchid, that is its morphology, and then proceeds to describe some of the inner tissue, the anatomy. Some stress is laid on the use of the correct words to describe parts of the plant as currently many orchid growers use a variety of terms, often quite incorrectly, when referring to plant parts.

All professional people have a language pertinent to their own craft. For the continued sanity of motor and aircraft mechanics it is vital that the correct names be used, consistently, for the parts of their charges. Why then should not 'orchidologists' have a correct and commonly used language based on the relevant and fundamental concepts of the botanical language? I suspect that orchid growers' lack of interest in and failure to interpret botanical literature is largely due to their not speaking the language.

There is nothing difficult about the use of the correct term, for example 'raceme' is no more difficult to say than 'spike' and most orchids do have a raceme but none have spikes. Tissue culture results in clones, not seedlings, and only species have varieties, hybrids have cultivars. Unfortunately, despite the efforts of many orchid writers to change this, the old terms persist.

The glossary given at the end of this book, if it is used, should assist growers in interpreting descriptions and culture articles given in reputable journals, although these latter are not always blameless when it comes to incorrect terminology.

Morphology

Habit of growth

There are three major growth patterns of orchids. The one most commonly encountered is 'sympodial' meaning 'feet together'. Fig. 3.1A illustrates this type of growth where the new stems (sometimes called pseudobulbs) arise from a continuously growing rhizome or creeping stem. A rhizome is a root-bearing stem from 'rhiz' meaning root. The distance between the stems arising from the rhizome is called the internode, which may be short of long. Long internodes are seen in some *Bulbophyllum* and *Cattleya* while short internodes occur in many *Dendrobium*.

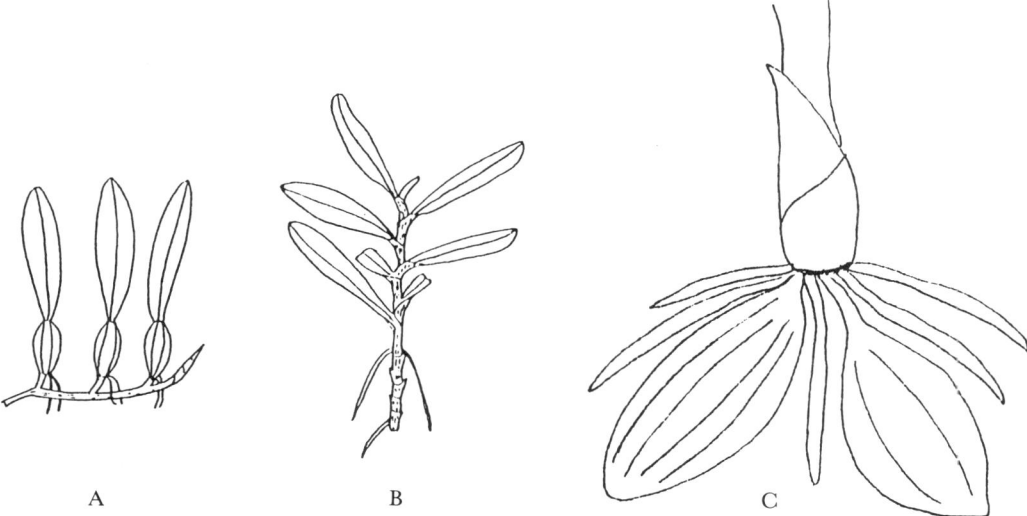

Fig. 3.1 Diagram A shows sympodial type growth. Diagram B shows monopodial growth. Diagram C shows the base of the stem and root growth of a typical geophytic orchid. The large swollen vesicles are swollen root stocks

Pseudobulbs have evolved as water and food storage stems and have a great diversity of shapes. The life of each pseudobulb is limited and as the plant ages so the old pseudobulbs, having given up their stored water and nutrients, shrivel and die. Some sympodial orchids do not develop thickened stems or pseudobulbs, e.g. the Pleurothallidinae; each leaf is attached at an abcission layer to a leaf stem or petiole arising from the rhizome.

The second type of growth is 'monopodial' or 'one foot' as typified by *Vanda* and *Ascocentrum*. The growing point is at the upper tip of the plant which continues to send out new leaves from this point. Adventitious roots arise in the stem and in time new young shoots are produced from near the base. (Fig. 3.1B)

The third type of growth is that seen in many geophytic orchids. (Fig. 3.1C) In this case the food and water storage organs appear to be swollen rootstocks as all growth occurs from the one point. These are not tubers as they are commonly called, however in some texts these fleshy organs are called tuberoid structures, that is tuber-like in appearance.

Stems and leaves

Stems which are swollen are often referred to as pseudobulbs or false bulbs. In fact they are not bulbs of any sort in the true meaning of the word but more closely resemble corms in that they are a food and water storage organ having dry scale leaves protecting axils. However, the term pseudobulb is likely to persist in general usage. Those stems which are not swollen are simply stems, nothing more nothing less; they also have nodes and internodes.

The arrangement of leaves on the stem is referred to as 'opposite', 'alternate' and 'whorled'. Opposite leaves are situated on opposite sides, 180° displaced, of the same node. Alternate leaves are placed one above the other on separate nodes, usually but not always, on opposite sides of the stem. Whorled leaves arise from a common node but placed around the stem at regular intervals and at the same level. The length of the internodes, the width and length of the leaf, the leaf shape and the nature of the leaf apex, whether it has one, two or three points, are all diagnostic characteristics appearing in plant descriptions.

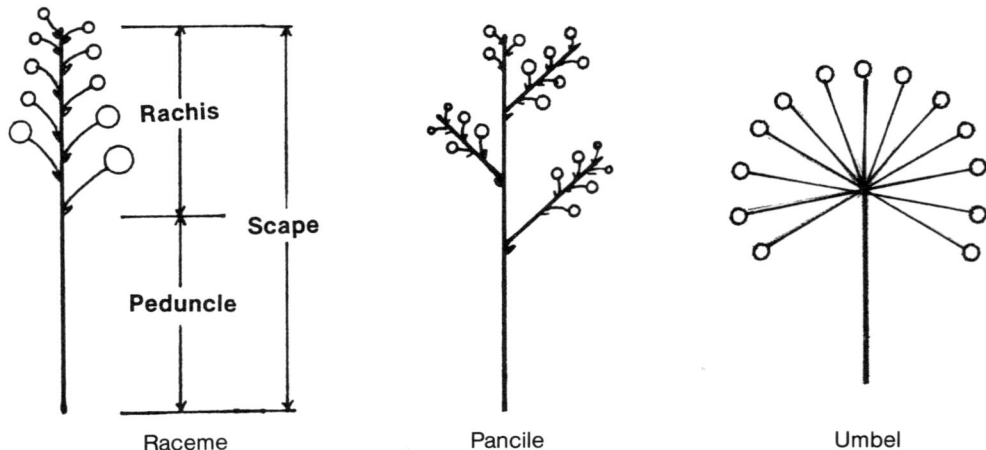

Fig. 3.2 Commonly encountered types of inflorescence

Inflorescence

Fig. 3.2 shows the commonly encountered types of inflorescence of orchids. The raceme is the most frequent as seen in *Cymbidium, Vanda* and many others. The panicle is an inflorescence having multiple racemes, the most obvious example being *Oncidium*. The single flower stalk is often called a scape but it could just as correctly be called a peduncle and is typical of some *Paphiopedilum*. The umbel is seen in the section *Cirrhopetalum* of *Bulbophyllum*. There is one other type, the capitulum or head seen only in *Rhizanthella gardneri*, R. Rogers, a saprophytic species of orchid spending its entire life underground.

The inflorescence may be terminal, basal or lateral and this characteristic is usually diagnostic at generic level. Examples for terminal are *Habenaria* and some *Dendrobium;* basal, *Bulbophyllum;* lateral, *Vanda*.

Another typical generic diagnostic feature is whether resupination has occurred, i.e. is the lip towards the top or free end of the rachis or is it downwards towards the base of the peduncle. In most cases resupination occurs by the twisting of the flower pedicel to give a 180° reversal in the flower orientation. In other cases the pedicel simply causes the flower to 'flop over' and it appears on the other side of the plant stem.

In most orchids the flowers on the raceme commence opening from the base upwards and this is called an 'indefinite inflorescence'. In a few species the flower may open from the top downwards, a 'definite inflorescence'.

Diagnostic features at specific level are length of peduncle and rachis, peduncle straight or arched, peduncle and/or rachis smooth or hairy, the length and even the persistence of bracts and sheaths.

The flower

This, along with the fruit, is the subject of Chapter 1.

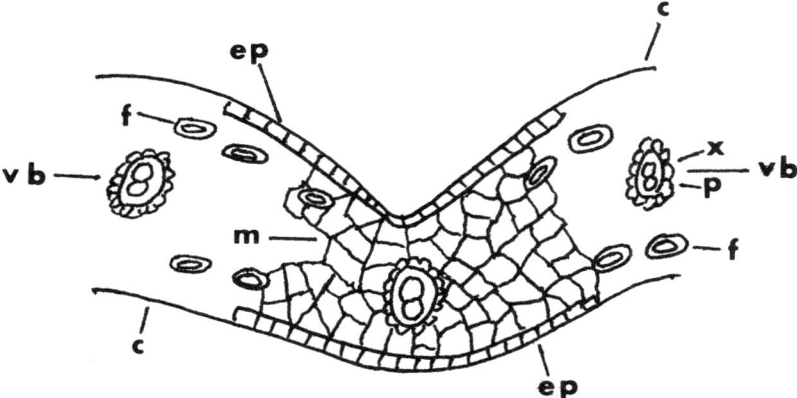

Fig. 3.3 Transverse section of a typical orchid leaf. c-cuticle; ep-epidermis; f-fibre cell; vb-vascular bundle; x-xylem; p-phloem; m-mesophyll cell

Anatomy

The leaf

A transverse section of an orchid leaf is shown diagrammatically in Fig. 3.3 and consists of a cuticle (non-living) on the upper and lower surfaces over the thick walled cells forming the upper and lower epidermal layers. The upper surface of the leaf, usually exposed to more sunlight than the lower surface, has a thicker cuticle, although with vertically oriented leaves the cuticle thickness is much the same on both sides. The cuticle or waxy covering is essentially a waterproof jacket over the leaves to protect the epidermal layer, to minimise water loss by evaporation from a heated surface and to reflect light from the leaf surface to avoid overheating.

Vascular bundles are scattered throughout the leaf. These contain the xylem vessels for the transport of water and nutrients from the roots and also the phloem cells to conduct sugars and other substances from the photosynthetic sites in the leaf to other parts of the plant. The vascular bundles are surrounded by thick walled fibre cells and similar fibre cells are scattered throughout the leaf, but particularly near the upper and lower epidermal layers to give strength to the leaf.

The tissue contained between the two epidermal layers is the mesophyll tissue and in the orchid leaf it consists mainly of parenchyma cells which contain chloroplasts.

The lower epidermal layer of an orchid leaf is punctured by stomata (Plate 3) through which CO_2 enters and water exits. These stomata open and close, as required by environmental conditions within and external to the plant (see Chapter 6). In all orchids so far examined stomata appear only on the lower (abaxial) epidermal layer whereas many plants have at least some stomata in the upper epidermal layer. In the orchid, the stomata are eliptical in shape with the long dimension running parallel to the length of the leaf as shown in Plate 3B. Notice the heavy deposit of rills of wax around the stoma in Plate 3A. These make it difficult to wet the leaf. The roughness of the leaf undersurface on *Vanda* is also apparent in Plate 3B.

Goh (1974/75) gives the stomatal density for various orchids; the number varies over a wide range from 18 000 per square centimetre for *Arundina graminifolia* and 14 000 for

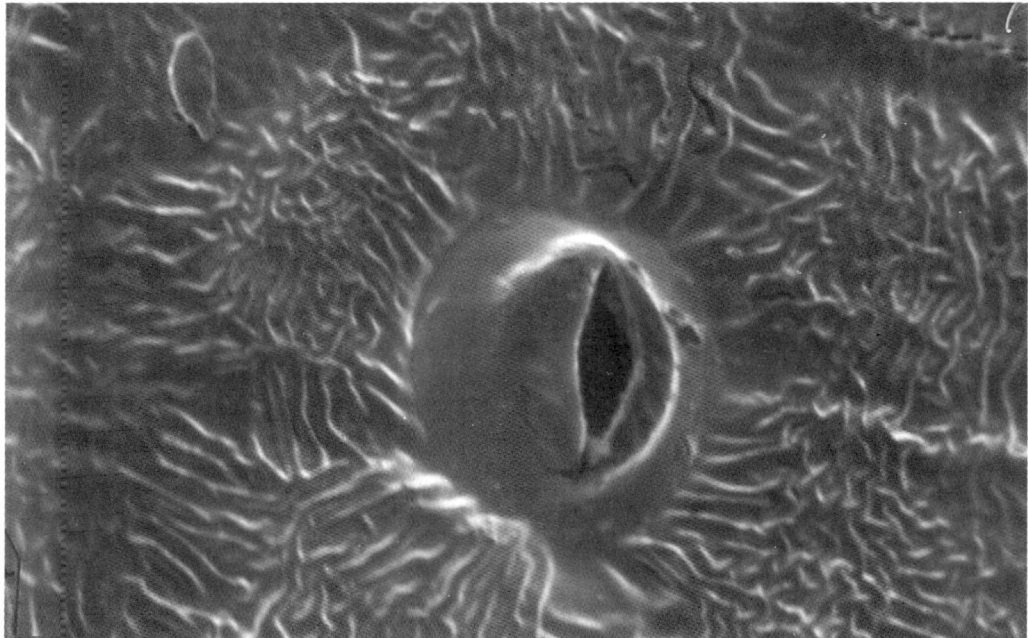

Plate 3A   A single stoma with rills of wax from the underside of a *Dendrobium* leaf magnified 2000 times as seen with a scanning electron microscope

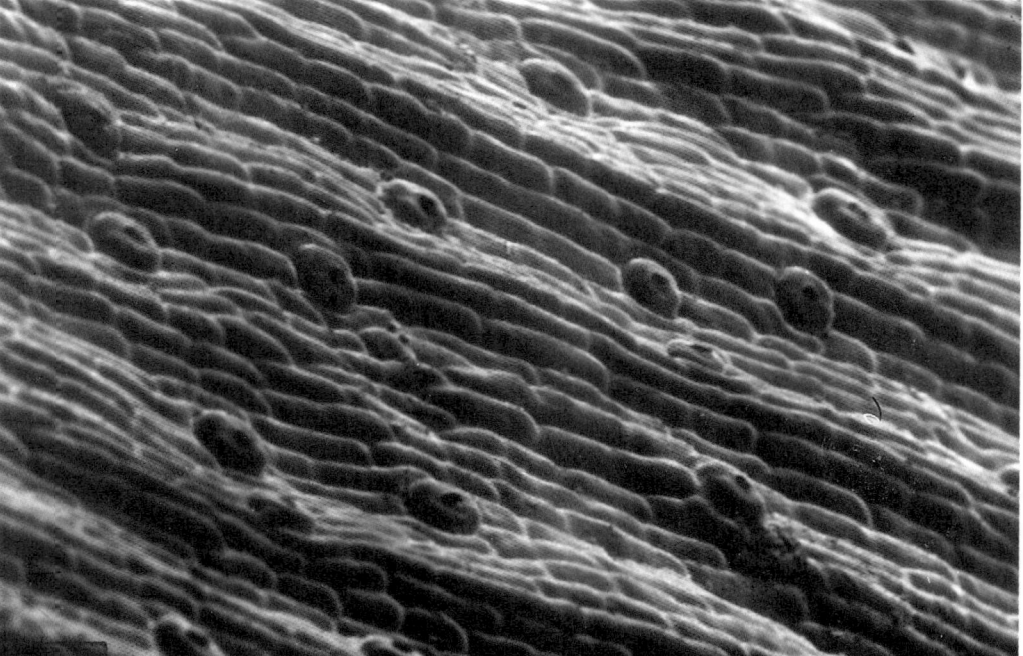

Plate 3B   The underside of a *Vanda* leaf at a magnification of 500 times. The stomata are oriented along the length of the leaf in regular rows

Spathoglottis plicata, both of which are geophytes, down to 800 per square centimetre for *Phalaenopsis violacea;* but a figure of around 3000 per square centimetre seems to apply to several species and hybrids.

As shown in Plate 3 each stoma consists of two sausage-shaped guard cells which open and close the aperture by the influx or efflux of potassium ions in response to internal control mechanisms. Behind each stomatal aperture there is an inner air chamber, the substomatal cavity, which contains a saturated atmosphere of water vapour and some carbon dioxide. See Fig. 3.4. The carbon dioxide has to pervade the spaces in the cell walls and between the cells and be absorbed through two membranes in order to supply carbon dioxide to the photosynthetic machinery.

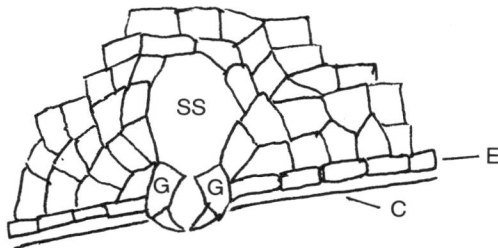

Fig. 3.4   Section through a stoma. SS-sub-stomatal cavity; G-guardcell; E-epidermis; C-cuticle

The stem

As mentioned under the heading of morphology stem formation varies widely in the orchid genera. The orchid is a monocotyledon, so has vascular tissue (its xylem and phloem) distributed in bundles throughout the stem. A dicotyledon has rings of vascular bundles close to its outer surface or bark, and in the ring a cambium layer of meristematic cells which each season form new vascular bundles and produce the well known 'tree rings', which expand the size of the trunk or stem each year as the plant grows. This cambium tissue is not present in monocotyledons so the stem diameter only increases with the expansion of the existing cells in the early stages of stem growth and after this it does not expand at all. Sushan (1959) working on the anatomy of a *Cattleya* hybrid counted some 200 vascular bundles in the stem, each bundle being surrounded by very thick walled fibres to give strength to the stem. Even the cells surrounding these fibre cells were very thick walled and lignified to give additional support.

The root

Unlike most plants the roots of epiphytic orchids are visible and most orchid growers are well aware that roots are indicative of the plant's health and condition. For this reason the anatomy of the root will be treated in some detail. That the root system of epiphytic orchids is of major importance is shown by those leafless and shootless plants which consist almost entirely of roots, which contain chloroplasts and act as both the absorptive and photosynthetic tissue of the plant. The shoot, if any, is very small and serves only as a junction point for the many radiating roots and the bearing of a flower.

The orchid does not have a primary or tap root, the roots being secondary and adventitious, arising from the stem. The major sections of a typical epiphytic root are shown

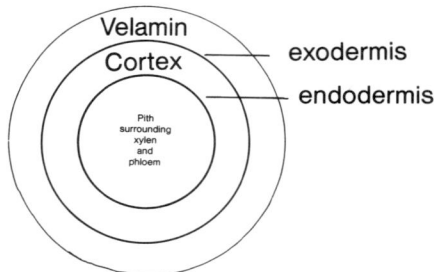

Fig. 3.5 Map digram showing location of root sections

in Fig. 3.5. The outer coating or velamen is where the action commences so this will be explained first; followed by that ring of thick walled cells, the exodermis, surrounding the cortex. Inside the cortex is another ring of thick walled cells called the endodermis which encloses the pith containing the vascular tissue.

The velamen of several orchid species has been studied. Recent papers on the subject are Benzing, Ott and Friedman (1982) and Benzing, Friedman, Peterson and Renfrow (1983), and the results of these studies will be quoted extensively here although not exclusively. Other studies of interest are Sushan (1959) and Sanford and Adanlawo (1973).

The thickness of the velamen varies from one to eighteen cells; in many cases there seems to be between 2 and 6 layers but *Bulbophyllum* is reported by Sanford *et al.* (1973) to have only one layer. Benzing *et al.* (1983) give the thickness of the velamen for several orchids studied. Leafy orchids such as *Epidendrum radicans* and *Encyclia tampensis* have a thick velamen of about 290 μm with five to eight layers. A shootless orchid, *Polyradicion lindenii,* has much the same velamen thickness with seven layers although this large size is not characteristic of shootless orchids; *Harrisella porrecta* has a thickness of only 27 μm with two cell layers.

The thickness of the velamen or its number of cells correlates very poorly with the ability of the root to avoid water loss. The surface to volume ratio of the roots is the most important single factor in minimising water loss from the root.

The roots of *Epidendrum radicans* and *Encyclia tampensis* with thick velamen containing several cell layers have S/V ratios of about 2 and these desiccated faster than *Polyradicion lindenii* or *Phalaenopsis amabilis,* both having only modestly thick velamen but S/V ratios of 1.4 and 1 respectively. For example *P. amabilis* took 318 $\pm$ 212 hours to lose 30% of moisture. As a further example *Vanda parishii* with a S/V ratio of 0.65 took 437 $\pm$ 116 hours to lose 30% of moisture. Epiphytic orchids are usually subject to wet and dry seasons in the tropics and periodically rain-free periods in temperate climates, even in some cases to drought, so minimising water loss from the roots is a vital factor towards survival.

The velamen, being the external part of the orchid root, is easily seen. It appears as a whitish covering around the roots commencing some one or two centimetres back from the greenish root tip and consists of cells which have lost their nucleus and cytoplasm, hence are dead cells, but are sculptured in various shapes all being open to the air via eliptical slits. Where more than one layer of velamen cells are present, the outer layer consists of smaller cells than those of the inner layers and is called 'epi-velamen' by Sanford *et al.* (1973).

The velamen-equipped orchid root is ideally designed for the rapid capture of water and dissolved nutrients washed down from the tree canopy (see Chapter 14). For some time argument raged whether velamen did play any significant role in nutrient absorption, but

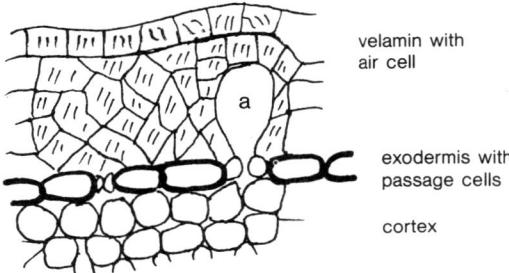

velamin with
air cell

exodermis with
passage cells

cortex

Fig. 3.6 Enlarged view showing velamen with slits and air cell, the exodermis and cortex

work with radioactive elements has demonstrated that nutrient solutions captured by the velamen do pass into the root. Once the captured solution passes into the root the velamen is again ready to capture more stemflow or throughfall (Chapter 14) and at each shower of rain it becomes recharged, like a sponge, and constitutes a reservoir of nutrients for the plant. Once the liquid has been removed from the velamen cells, air enters and is trapped, relatively immobile, in these cells and acts as a boundary layer of considerable thickness, protecting the inner root from the effects of air turbulence and so limiting water vapour loss from the root to that of molecular diffusion across the boundary layer (Chapter 6).

Zankowski, Fraser, Rost and Reynolds (1987) investigated the anatomy of aerial roots of *Epidendrum ibaguense* and noted that immature velamen can be seen within a distance of 0.5 mm from the root tip and within 2 mm from the root tip the velamen and cortical cells contain numerous vacuoles and chloroplasts resulting in the typical green colour of the root tip. As the velamen cells become older their cell walls thicken and become mature and empty at about 10 mm from the root tip giving the root its silvery white appearance when dry.

The next major region in the root is the cortex, composed of parenchyma cells internally but with two layers of thick walled cells at its outer and inner limits. The outer layer adjacent to the velamen is the exodermis, the inner layer is the endodermis.

Fig. 3.6 shows an enlarged view of the velamen, exodermis and part of the cortex. The exodermis contains two major types of cell. The first type consists of long vacuolated cells parallel to the root axis; these produce thick secondary walls and Zankowski *et al.* (1987) have proposed that at least part of the exodermal layer contains a Casparian Strip. This is part of the primary wall formation that contains suberin and lignin and is impervious to water, providing a barrier to apoplastic water or solution flow. Apoplastic flow is when the fluid passes through the 'free space' within the roots, that is the cell walls proper (without penetrating the interior of the cell) and the air gaps between the cells.

The opposite to apoplastic is symplastic where the fluid flow is through the cytoplasm of the cells, usually from cell to cell via thin strands interconnecting them. The symplast can be considered a continuous flow system.

The second type of cell in the exodermis is the 'passage cell'. It is thin walled and very active and forms the symplastic channel from the velamen to the cortex.

The cortex proper contains many multi-purpose cells having chloroplasts which show green when the air in the velamen is displaced by water. The cortex also contains some large cells called idioblasts which are used as storage cells; some people consider these to have some secretory function for removing and storing unwanted substances. Most orchids seem to store needle-like crystals of calcium oxalate in these idioblasts; perhaps the calcium can be recycled but little is known about this at present. The apoplast in the cortex is reasonably high due to the considerable air space between cells where the calcium pectate has not cemented the cells along their entire margins (Fig. 3.6).

The inner layer of the cortex is the endodermis. This develops within 0.5 mm of the root tip with small cells 13×13 μm but at maturity they can extend in length to 500 μm and 35 μm in width (Sushan 1959). Passage cells are again present, these being thin-walled non-lignified cells which occur in the endodermal 'ring' as several cells opposite the xylem vessels (the upward conducting pipe lines to the leaves) and which allow water to pass readily from the cortex to the xylem. The phloem tissue (distribution channels for sugar and other substances) is protected from leakage back into the cortex by the thick walled cells. A Casparian Strip is invariably present.

Inside the endodermis is the pith, a collection of parenchyma cells forming a matrix in which are embedded the elements of xylem and phloem forming the vascular tissue (Fig. 3.5). The pith cells contain chloroplasts, store starch and have numerous air spaces between the cells, which may become 200 μm long and 80 μm wide (Sushan 1959) at maturity.

The fact that roots possess chloroplasts and carry out photosynthesis with a high rate of carbon fixation (Ducker & Arditti 1968) indicates that air must be able to penetrate the root quite easily, yet roots do not possess stomata. There are aeration cells in the exodermis immediately adjacent to the velamen and it is possible that turgor pressure in the cortical cells adjacent to these aeration cells allows them to open and close the passage of air into the cortex where it is then free to circulate in the air spaces (Benzing *et al.* 1983).

References

Benzing D.H., Ott D.W., Friedman W.E. (1982) Roots of *Sobralia macrantha* (Orchidaceae): Structure and function of the velamen-exodermis complex. *Am. J. Bot.* 69(4); 608-614.

Benzing D.H., Friedman W.E., Peterson G., Renfrow A. (1983) Shootless, velamentous roots and the pre-eminence of Orchidaceae in the epiphytic biotrope. *Am. J. Bot.* 70(1); 121-133.

Ducker J., Arditti J. (1968) Photosynthetic CO_2 fixation by green *Cymbidium* (Orchidaceae) flowers. *Plant Physiol.* 43; 130-132.

Goh Chong Jin (1974/75) The anatomy of orchid leaves. *Malayan Orchid Review* 12(2); 14-23.

Sanford William W. & Adanlawo Ilesanmi (1973) Velamen and exodermis characteristics of West African epiphytic orchids in relation to taxonomic grouping and habitat tolerance. *Bot. J. Linn. Soc.* 66; 307-321.

Sushan Sam (1959) Development anatomy of the orchid *Cattleya* × Trimos. In *The Orchids, a Scientific Survey.* Ed. Carl L. Withner, Ronald Press.

Zankowski Paul M., Fraser David, Rost Thomas L., Reynolds Thomas L. (1987) Developmental anatomy of velamen and exodermis in aerial roots of *Epidendrum ibaguense*. *Lindleyana* 2(1); 1-7.

4 Classification and Nomenclature

Before an organism can be named it must be classified and this holds good for all plants including orchids. Classification is a process of producing order out of chaos; organisms are separated into large 'boxes' and thence into smaller 'boxes' until finally each type of organism is identifiable and can be given a name. Classification is not an exact science and depends to some extent on the opinions and determinations of the person doing the classifying.

The highest rank in classification is the Kingdom and it is generally recognised that there are five Kingdoms as shown in Table 4.1. As orchid growers we are concerned mainly with the Plantae and it is for this Kingdom that the International Code of Botanical Nomenclature (ICBN) sets down some rules for classification and naming.

Table 4.1

The Five Kingdoms

1. Monera	Includes bacteria and cyanochloronta, the latter often erroneously called blue-green algae.
2. Protista	Unicellular or colonial unicellular organisms possessing nuclear membrane and mitochondria.
3. Fungi	Absorptive nutrition; all fungi.
4. Animalia	No photosynthetic pigments, ingestive nutrition; all animals.
5. Plantae	Multicellular with frequently vacuolate cells and photosynthetic pigments in plastids. Primarily non-motile. Structural differentiation producing specialised organs.

Table 4.2

The hierarchical system

rank	ending	example
Kingdom	—	Plantae (or Phyta)
Division	-phyta	Spermatophyta
Subdivision	-phytina	Magnoliophytina
Class	-opsida	Liliopsida
Subclass	-idae	Liliidae
Order	-ales	Orchidales
Suborder	-ineae	
Family	-aceae	Orchidaceae
Subfamily	-oideae	Orchidoideae
Tribe	-eae	Orchideae
Subtribe	-inae	Orchidinae
Genus		
Subgenus		
Section		
Series		
Species		
Subspecies (subsp. or ssp.)		
Variety (var.)		
Subvariety (subvar.)		
Form (f)		

Notes

1. The name/s of the Subgenus, Section and Series are to follow in round brackets immediately after the generic name.
2. Those ranks in bold type are those recognised by the ICBN as being major.
3. The ranks are strictly hierarchical. A Form of a Variety is permitted as is a Section of a Subgenus, but a Variety of a Form and a Subgenus of a Section are not permitted.
4. The above ranks, or words indicating such rank, must not be used for other purposes. The *Dendrobium* Family is quite incorrect. Use words like group, complex or alliance which only have the meaning given to them by the author, to indicate some association of plants.

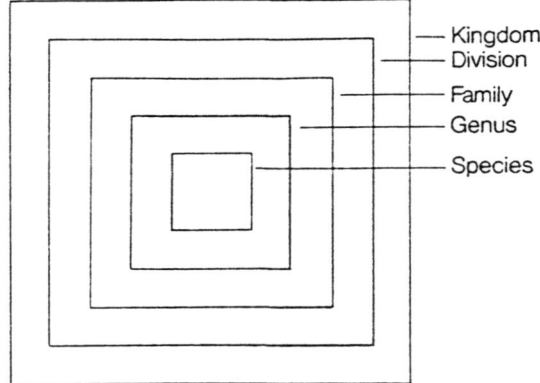

Fig. 4.1   The box within a box scheme showing only five ranks of the twelve major ranks

The classification system is hierarchical in that ranks are allocated to the groupings, each superior rank encompassing all inferior ranks. A species is allocated into an ascending arrangement of successively wider categories until a single all-embracing category is reached which includes all plants (Plant Kingdom). This is often called a box-within-a-box system where any one box includes all the boxes enclosed by it. (Fig. 4.1)

The ICBN recognises twelve main ranks in the hierarchy, although only five are shown in Fig. 4.1. These are shown in bold type in the left hand column of Table 4.2. To these may be added prefixes for super and sub, such as Superorder and/or Suborder so that many more ranks are available if required. In a very large family, such as the orchid family, it is necessary to add additional recognised ranks such as Subfamily and Subtribe. These will be treated in due course. Each of these ranks is known as a taxon (pl. taxa), hence the name taxonomy to denote the classification of plants (or other organisms).

In order to see the relationship of orchids to other plants it is necessary to review the higher ranks, i.e. above that of Family, which in line with the approved endings shown in columns 2 and 3 of Table 4.2 becomes **Orchidaceae** (pronounced as orchid-ace-ee-ee). The box-within-a-box system would place **Orchidaceae** into the **Orchidales** (pronounced orchid-ar-leez).

Stebbins (1974) places the **Geosiridaceae,** the **Burmanniaceae,** the **Corsiaceae** and the **Orchidaceae** all into **Orchidales.** He quotes the **Orchidaceae** as having 30 000 species but the total of the other three families comes to only 140 species showing that the **Orchidaceae** clearly predominates. Dressler (1981) (pp. 5 and 6) sees little reason to incorporate these other families into the **Orchidales,** there being insufficient resemblance to do so, and prefers the **Orchidales** to contain the **Orchidaceae** only. However, the *Flora of Australia,* Vol. 1 places **Burmanniaceae, Corsiaceae** and **Orchidaceae** all into the **Orchidales,** so various authorities have various ideas on classification.

Readers will note that nowhere have I used terms like 'the family Ochidaceae' or 'the Order Orchidales' as this is incorrect and repetitive. The ending on the words (see Table 4.2) indicates the rank. However, it is acceptable to say 'the genus Leptotes' as genera have no restrictions imposed on word endings.

It is opportune to state here that these ranks (taxa) should only be used in their approved sense. It is nonsense to say the '*Dendrobium* family' when speaking about the genus

Dendrobium. It is equally nonsensical to say the Family of Australian Orchids as though other countries also had their families of orchids. If the correct term is unknown or inconvenient to use then taxonomically neutral words such as 'group', 'complex' or 'alliance' may be used as this then has only the meaning the author allocates to it at the time.

Having placed the **Orchidaceae** into the **Orchidales,** agreeing with Dressler's analysis, we need only, as orchid growers, consider this Order as having one Family. As there have been recent modifications to the higher taxa it is necessary to examine these from the Kingdom downwards before we return to the **Orchidaceae** and concentrate wholly on the break up of this into smaller taxa.

The major split of Plantae is into Divisions; some botanists use Phylum (pl. Phyla) as used by zoologists, but the ICBN rules dictate that Division is correct. Various authors advocate a varying number of Divisions. Bold *et al.* (1980) have created 19 Divisions which tells one only that all plants in a Division are in Plantae (hence are plants) but fails to show any relationship between the plants in one Division and another Division. Other authors prefer three or four Divisions. In this text, for simplicity's sake and because readers are interested in orchids and need only a slight appreciation of their relationship with other plants, I shall keep to four Divisions as follows:

Thallophyta, mainly the algae, undifferentiated tissue.
Bryophyta, mainly the mosses and liverworts.
Pteridophyta, the ferns.
Spermatophyta, the seed-bearing plants, highly differentiated in tissue.

From this listing it is clear that our Division of interest is Spermatophyta, the seed bearing plants. Some plants bear seeds encased in an ovary (angiosperms) others have uncased or naked seeds such as conifers (gymnosperms). The modern classification for angiosperms is Magnoliophytina, so named because the *Magnolia* is a very ancient ovary type seed bearing plant accepted as the 'type' plant for this Subdivision. Below the rank of Subdivision is Class which has two groups known as the Dicotyledons and Monocotyledons, expressive names which are still very much used today. The Dicotyledons embrace all flowering plants except the grasses, the lilies, the orchids and all similar plants which have floral parts in three or multiples of three and which usually do not have stem thickening by cambium tissue. These are the Monocotyledons.

In modern terminology the Dicotyledons became **Magnoliopsida** and the Monocotyledons became **Liliopsida.** There are four Subclasses in Liliopsida, the one which includes **Orchidales** is **Liliidae.**

So Table 4.2 traces the higher taxonomic relationship of orchids from the plant kingdom to seed bearing plants; to seed developed in ovary plants; to monocotyledonous plants; to some plant which we call an orchid in the **Orchidales** or **Orchidaceae.**

The next step and one of some importance for better understanding is to break up the Order and the Family into lower taxa. However, there is no universal agreement that all orchids should be included in the **Orchidaceae.** Some taxonomists, namely Vermeulen (1966) Schlecter (1970-1984) and Rasmussen (1985), prefer an additional family to include the genera *Apostasia* and *Neuwiedia* and call it the **Apostasiaceae.** Vermeulen and Rasmussen carry this a little further by creating the **Cypripediaceae** to include the genera *Paphiopedilum, Cypripedium, Phragmopedium* and *Selenipedium,* but Schlecter avoids doing this. These other two families are then included in the **Orchidales.**

Other taxonomists such as Dressler, Garay, Burns-Balogh and Funk prefer to place all orchids into the **Orchidaceae** and many authors seem to accept, tacitly, this classification. Just as all geraniums are in the Geraniaceae and all roses are in the Rosaceae it seems reasonable enough that all orchids should be in the **Orchidaceae.** Those taxonomists who advocate this do so because they cannot see sufficient reason not to do so. There is after all the Subfamily rank (Table 4.2) where separation can readily be made.

Having accepted that all orchids come within the scope of Orchidaceae we can now examine the Subfamily level. There are six of these although some authorities recognise less or more (up to seven). The grouping of primitive orchids into a high rank like Subfamily is not easy as their lengthy period of evolution has produced very diverse morphology. Similarities of flower structure, the number of anthers, the shape of the column, swollen rootstocks (tuberoids), seed shape and formation are some of the major features used in classification at this level.

The six used here are given below with a brief description of each.

1. Apostasioideae　This includes the genera believed to be the most primitive extant orchids. e.g. *Apostasia* and *Neuwiedia*. These genera have two or three anthers and are generally not familiar to orchid growers.

2. Cypripedioideae　These have two anthers (diandrous); the median anther forms a shield-like staminode (sterile). The pollinia are sticky. This is another primitive Subfamily and includes genera *Paphiopedilum, Cypripedium, Phragmipedium* and *Selenipedium*. Some genera tend to grow on humus-rich rocky ground.

3. Neottioideae　In habit these resemble the Cypripedioideae but are monandrous. Some are saprophytic. There are one Tribe and two Subtribes in this small Subfamily.

4. Spiranthoideae　Monandrous orchids with woody to herbaceous stems, the column is bent or straight, the flowers resupinate or not so. They do not have swollen rootstocks. The characteristics vary widely and they are geophytic. Included are the 'Jewel Orchids' grown for their variegated leaves rather than their flowers.

5. Orchidoideae　Monandrous orchids possessing swollen rootstocks in most Tribes. They are wide spread in southern Australia, South Africa and South America and are represented by *Ophrys* and *Orchis* in Europe.

6. Epidendroideae　This is the largest Subfamily and one of major interest to orchid growers. Because it is so large the growth forms and general morphology are very diverse and there are many Tribes and Subtribes. The genera belonging to these are detailed in Appendix 4.1.

Type specimens

This section describes some aspects of classification and nomenclature which are not normally well known to orchid growers and not used by them. However, if one refers to a Flora or other taxonomic publication issued by herbaria, botanic gardens or similar instititutions, e.g. *Kew Bulletin,* one encounters some unfamiliar terminology.

The ICBN has already been mentioned in relation to higher taxa and approved endings for taxa; this section will deal extensively with Family and below. The primary concept here is the 'nomenclatural type', a sample plant lodged in a recognised herbarium by the person (collector) who proposed its name or its family or genus. If a person (taxonomist) decides that a new family is warranted because he has come across (collected or been given) a plant or plants which do not reasonably fit into an existing family, then a 'type genus' is required to be nominated and lodged with a herbarium. Similarly if a new tribe or subtribe is to be created ('erected' is usually used), a type genus is required. Normally the family name (or tribe or subtribe name) will be derived from the generic 'nomenclatural type' name. As an example, for **Geraniaceae** the nomenclatural type (or type genus) is the genus *Geranium.*

The **Orchidaceae** appears to have derived its name from *Orchis* so named by Theophrastus (370-285 BC) and Dioscorides in the first century of the Christian era. Over the centuries many botanists of the time made small advances in orchid nomenclature, perhaps the most notable being Olof Swartz, the first orchid specialist, and Robert Brown. However, it seems that John Lindley (1799-1865) was the first to use **Orchidaceae.** (For detailed reading on this subject refer to Schweinfurth [1959].)

Similarly if a new genus is to be erected it must have a species as its nomenclatural type. For example the genus *Phalaenopsis* has *Phalaenopsis amabilis* as its nomenclatural type.

In taxonomy there are several 'types' which need defining, these are:

Holotype: A single specimen designated by the author of its name as being the nomenclatural type. Sometimes called the 'voucher specimen'.
Isotypes: These are simply duplicates of the holotype, supplied with the holotype and perhaps sent to various herbaria.
Syntypes: The author of the name may have designated two or more specimens as types rather than a single holotype.
Lectotype: One specimen of the syntypes ultimately selected to form the holotype.
· **Neotype:** A specimen selected to act in lieu of a holotype where this does not exist.

Type specimens are not always truly representative of the genus or family and may even be non-typical, but once the nomenclatural type has been designated it must remain and not be changed because it is non-typical.

Valid publication and priority

In accordance with the rules of the ICBN a plant name is only legitimate (hence recognisable) if it has been validly published in printed matter of recognised standard and available to the botanical world by sale, exchange or gift. The 'recognised standard' is a botanical text of merit normally acceptable to botanists and read by them. This covers a wide range of publications but normally any person wishing to have his/her name suggestion accepted is not likely to publish in a newspaper, gardening magazine or other similar document.

In addition, to be validly published, the name must conform to rules specified for name construction and be accompanied by a diagnosis (description) in Latin or refer to a previously and validly published diagnosis. This latter usually applies to a variety using the published diagnosis for the species with some changes applicable to the variety, but it may also apply to a new species, comparing this with an existing species. Western authors usually add a description in English but are not obliged to do so for valid publication.

Large genera (in the number of species covered) are frequently divided into Sections.

The ICBN requires that the Section in which the type species for the genus occurs must be called by the same name as the genus but without having any author attributed to it. As an example the Section of the genus *Phalaenopsis* which contains the type species for the genus, must be called *Phalaenopsis*. The type species is *Phalaenopsis amabilis*. This can be a little confusing at times if one deals extensively with Sections.

Authority

The author of a name is the authority for it and the author's name (or recognised abbreviation) follows the plant name. There is no standard form of abbreviation but an example of some are given in Table 4.3 and Note. For most modern authors the name is spelt out in full. The author's name may follow a Family, a Subfamily, Tribe, Subtribe, Genus, Genus and species, Section (except as above). For example **Orchidaceae** Ldl. (abbreviation for John Lindley 1799-1865) and genus *Prasophyllum* R.Br. (for Robert Brown 1773-1858).

There are a few variations to this, namely:

1. Sometimes a botanist notes a name onto a herbarium sheet, or elsewhere, but the name is not validly published. Later another botanist validly publishes the same name. This is expressed by the name of the first botanist, the word 'ex' followed by the name of the second botanist.

2. Where a botanist makes a name change for good taxonomic reasons the original author's name is placed in parentheses followed by the name/s of the person/s making the change, e.g. *Encyclia lancifolia* (Lindley) Dressler & Pollard, *Phytologia* 21: 437, 1971. This plant name was changed from *Epidendrum lancifolium* Pavon ex Lindley 1831. Note that in the change to *Encyclia* the gender changes; the same specific epithet has been retained but its gender changes to agree with that of *Encyclia*.

3. The author's name (or abbreviation) is sometimes followed by 'f', e.g. Rchb.f. which stands for the son of (filius) Reichenbach (1824-1889).

4. It is also required that the place of original publication be specified as in the example above. Dressler & Pollard notified their proposed change to the botanical world in Vol. 21 page 437 of *Phytologia* in 1971.

Other abbreviations and terms:

1. When a new species is described the author's name is followed by *sp. nov. (species nova)* or if appropriate for a new genus by *gen. nov (genus novum)*, e.g. *Amesiella* Schltr. ex Garay, *gen. nov.*

2. Sometimes previously published generic names and epithets are used in a new combination notified by the use of *comb. nov. (combinatio nova)*. As an example *Cleisostoma aspersum* (Rchb.f.) Garay, *comb. nov.* in Bot. Mus. Leaflets, Harvard, 23: 4, 1972. In this case both *Cleisostoma* and *aspersum* had been published before but not in this combination.

3. *Nomen novum (nom. nov.)*, a new name, denotes a name not previously published or substituted for one in general use but found unacceptable.

4. *Nomen nudum (nom. nud.)*, a naked name, that is a plant name published without any description or figure and which cannot be allocated beyond doubt to any plant or plant group. *Nomina nuda* are rejected and illegitimate.

5. The symbol ! in the introduction to a citation of the plant indicates that the person describing the plant has seen and examined the specimen rather than relying on second hand information.

6. A basionym is the name upon which a new combination is based. For example, *Cleisostoma suffusum* (Ridl.) Garay, *comb. nov.* is based on the basionym *Saccolabium suffusum* Ridl. in *Journ. Str. Br. Roy. As. Soc.* 44: 189, 1905.

Table 4.3

Abbreviations of authors' names
This is only a small sample of the total to illustrate the method used. Most abbreviations are applicable to early botanists. Those of later vintage usually have their names written in full.

Adanson M.	Adans.
Beccari O.	Becc.
Blume C.L.	Bl.
Candolle A.P. de	DC.
Dockrill A.W.	Dockr.
Eichler A.W.	Eichl.
Holttum R.E.	Holtt.
Hooker J.D.	Hook.f.
Hooker W.D.	Hook.
Jussieu A.H.L. de	Juss.f.
Jussieu A.L. de	Juss.
Linnaeus C. (elder)	L.
Linnaeus C. (younger)	L.f.
Reichenbach H.G.	Rchb.
Reichenbach H.G.L.	Rchb.f.
Schlechter F.R.R.	Schltr.
Teysmann J.E.	Teysm.
Whitmore T.C.	Whitm.

Note There is a 'Draft Index of Author Abbreviations' for authors of botanical names. When this comes into general use it should minimise variations.

References

Bold Harold C., Alexopoulos C., Delavoras T. (1980) *Morphology of Plants and Fungi*, 4th ed. Harper Row.

Burns-Balogh Pamela & Funk V.A. (1986) A phylogenetic analysis of the Orchidaceae: A summary. *Lindleyana* 1(2); 131-139.

Dressler R.L. (1981) *The Orchids, Natural History and Classification*. Harvard Uni. Press.

Dressler R.L. (1983) Classification of the Orchidaceae. *Telopea* 2(4); 413-424.

Dressler R.L. (1986) Recent advances in orchid phylogeny. *Lindleyana* 1(1); 5-20.

Garay L.A. (1972) On the origin of the Orchidaceae. *J. Arnold Abor.* 53; 202-215.

Rasmussen F. (1985) Orchids. pp. 249-274, *The Families of Monocotyledons*. Dahlgren R.M.T., Clifford H.T., Yeo P.F. (eds) Springer Verlag.

Schlecter R. (1970-1984) *Die Orchideen*. Brieger F.G., Maatsch N., Singas K. (eds).

Schweinfurth Charles (1959) Classification of Orchids. In *The Orchids, A Scientific Survey*, Carl L. Withner (ed.) Ronald Press.

Stebbins G.L. (1974) *Flowering Plants, Evolution above the Species Level*. Edward Arnold.

Vermeulen P. (1966) The system of Orchidales. *Acta Bot. Neerl.* 15; 224-253.

Appendix 4.1

The genera allocated to Tribes and Subtribes of Epidendroideae are according to Dressler (1981, 1983 and 1986). This is a widely accepted and popular classification system as it is constantly subject to review and is amended as new evidence comes to hand. It, therefore, differs from older systems which have not been amended in accordance with the continuous stream of information about orchids emanating from many researchers. Only those genera commonly grown are shown below.

Tribe	Subtribe	Genera	Tribe	Subtribe	Genera
Arethuseae	Bletiinae	*Arundina, Bletilla, Calanthe, `Chysis, Phaius, Spathoglottis*	Vandeae	Sarcanthinae	*Aërides, Amesiella, Arachnis, Ascocentrum, Cleisostoma, Doritis, Gastrochilus, Kingidium, Phalaenopsis, Renanthera, Rhynchostylis, Robiquetia, Sarcochilus, Trichoglottis, Vanda*
Epidendreae	Eriinae	*Ceratostylis, Erina*			
	Laeliinae	*Brassavola, Cattleya, Encyclia, Epidendrum, Laelia, Nageliella, Sophronitis*			
	Pleurothalidinae	*Masdevallia, Pleurothallis*		Angraecinae	*Aeranthes, Angraecum, Jumella, Sobennikoffia*
Dendrobieae	Coelogyninae	*Coelogyne, Pholidota*			
	Dendrobiinae	*Cadetia, Dendrobium, Diplocaulobium*		Aerangidinae	*Diaphenanthe, Rangaeris*
	Bulbophyllinae	*Bulbophyllum*	Maxillarieae	Zygopetalinae	*Zygopetalum*
Cymbideae	Cyrtopodiinae	*Ansellia, Chrysoglossum, Cymbidium, Cyrtopodium, Grammangis, Grammatophyllum*		Bifrenariinae	*Bifrenaria*
				Lycastinae	*Anguloa, Lycaste*
				Maxillariinae	*Maxillaria, Scuticaria, Trigonidium*
	Catasetinae	*Catasetum, Cynoches, Mormodes*	Oncidieae	Oncidiniinae	*Brassia, Miltonia, Odontoglossum, Oncidium, Rossioglossum, Trichopilia*
	Stanhopeinae	*Coryanthes, Gongora, Stanhopea*			

5 Energy

Note A more technical description of energy from the sun is given in Chapter 12 on the subject of glasshouse management. Chapter 5 is a simplified version for those not concerned with glasshouse growing. It is given here to enable photosynthesis and other cultural practices to be described adequately.

What has energy to do with growing orchids? Well, orchids are living organisms and all living organisms are complex entities, requiring energy to maintain this complexity which we call life.

Without energy input these organisms die and decay to their fundamental particles. Even stone walls, without an energy input for maintenance, crumble and revert to their mineral constituents. This is a fundamental law of nature, the progression from the complex to the simplistic, or as sometimes expressed, the progression towards chaos.

Except for a few bacteria the sole source of energy for living organisms on earth is the sun; with its surface temperature of about 6000°C, it emits an energy flux of 74 million watts per square metre (W m^{-2}).

By the time this reaches the top of our atmosphere it is about 1360 W m^{-2} (compare this with an electric bar radiator of 1000 watts). Our atmosphere attenuates this by various amounts depending on the season, cloud cover and the turbidity of the lower air. The remainder provides the energy to maintain life on earth.

The part that is useful to us is commonly called the visual spectrum because this contains those wavelengths to which the proteins in our eyes are tuned, just as we may tune into the wavelengths of a radio station. When the radiation energy penetrating the eye excites these proteins our brain receives a message and we see both shapes and colour. Why and how this happens is outside the scope of this Chapter but the important part is that the green plant can also 'see' this same spectrum.

The chlorophyll in the leaves is tuned into some of the wavelengths in this spectrum and is excited by the energy present at these wavelengths and this leads to photosynthesis which is dealt with later on. So instead of calling these wavelengths the visible spectrum, plantsmen use the term 'photosynthetic active radiation band' (PAR band).

Short wave radiation

The 1360 W m^{-2} of short wave radiation from the sun is not all in the PAR band but about half of it is because the sun's surface temperature of 6000°C ensures that its main radiation is in this band. The hotter the radiator the lower the wavelength of the maximum emitted radiation.

It is timely now to put some wavelength figures on to this SW radiation at the earth's surface. Wavelength is measured in metres or parts thereof and we use the micrometre (μm) which is one millionth part (10^{-6}) of a metre, or perhaps it is easier to visualise this as one thousandth (10^{-3}) part of a millimetre.

Those wavelengths smaller than 0.3 μm (extreme and far ultraviolet) are filtered out in the atmosphere by the ozone layer. The near UV of 0.3 to 0.4 μm reaches earth. The visible/PAR band is from 0.4 μm to 0.7 μm and beyond this up to 3 μm we have the infrared.

So conveniently we have the SW radiation from 0.3 to 3 μm with the part of major interest to plantsmen from 0.4 to 0.7 μm. This is frequently called light. It is always difficult to divorce human reactions from natural phenomena. Because we 'see' wavelengths around 0.4 μm as blue we call this 'blue' light whereas, of course, no such thing exists outside our brain. Similarly we call wavelengths around 0.7 μm 'red' light and the part in the middle of 0.5 μm is called 'green'. The other colours we see are arranged in accordance with their effect on the eye proteins.

The effect of wavelength in the PAR band on chlorophyll will be discussed in the chapter on photosynthesis.

Long wave radiation

Energy can neither be lost nor destroyed but it may be converted from one form into another. This conversion is not 100% efficient; some of the energy is converted to heat, for heat is a form of energy.

So the energy from the sun is not wholly concerned with photosynthesis. Most of it goes into warming the earth and all things on it. If this process continued for any length of time it is obvious that the earth and its contents would burn up, so it is necessary to lose some of this heat energy.

This is done by long wave radiation at wavelengths greater than 3 μm. The earth itself, as a sphere, is considered to have a mean temperature of 15° and radiates at a wavelength of 10 μm into the atmosphere and space. All things absorb radiation and re-radiate at a wavelength dependent on their temperatures and this includes leaves and plant parts. Their temperature depends on heat input minus heat output so an understanding of this is important in plant culture. This subject is covered later on.

Energy of radiation

For reasons beyond the scope of this text the energy of radiation is inversely proportional to wavelength so that UV has more energy than the vis/PAR band and is deleterious to plastics, human skin and other substances.

The vis/PAR band energy is sufficient to carry out photosynthesis but the extra radiation energy in the 'blue' end of the band produces some heating in plants.

The infrared is low in energy but this is sufficient to cause heating if it is absorbed. Due to their water content most plants are effective reflectors of infrared and are not greatly heated by it.

Atmospheric attenuation

The atmosphere attenuates the SW band, the degree depending on the impurities present. On a clear, sunny and fairly cloudless day and away from smog the insolation can reach 0.8 of the value present above the atmosphere. Where smog, smoke or other impurities are present this may fall to 0.6 of the value above the atmosphere.

For example, on a clear sunny afternoon in mid-March about 1530 hours the insolation in a busy residential suburb of Sydney was measured as 436 W m^{-2}. The ground was relatively flat. From the known angle of the sun the insolation above the atmosphere was calculated as 672 W m^{-2} giving a transmittance of 0.65.

For a more detailed explanation of radiation refer to Chapter 5 of *The Orchid Grower's Manual* by Gordon Morrison, Kangaroo Press, 1988. Also Chapter 14 of this book gives additional information on light as a form of energy.

6 Carbon Dioxide Entry

It appears to be seldom realised that CO_2 is the major nutrient for plants, possibly because it is free and possibly because one cannot buy it in a packet and tip it on to the plant. Wherever an orchid grows at least half of it is immersed in a fluid called air, so the properties and action of this fluid are relevant to an understanding of plant culture.

The stomata on the underside of the orchid leaf, as shown in Chapter 3, are the entry point for CO_2 and the exit path for water vapour. Writers of early texts on plant physiology used to assert that nature had erred in making the first impossible without the concomitant occurrence of the second, so placing the plant under water stress. Today we understand that nature has not erred and that water vapour loss serves a useful purpose; further, some plants have adapted their physiology to growth in arid conditions.

This chapter deals with CO_2 entry as a lead in to photosynthesis in Chapter 7. The loss of water vapour is dealt with as a separate subject.

I have heard opinions expressed that the air which flows into the leaf via the stomata has the CO_2 extracted from it and the rest of the air flows out again. A little simple arithmetic shows that this idea is hardly tenable. Also air is a mixture of gases, not a chemical compound, and each gas has partial pressure and concentration which act individually on the constitutent gases independently of the other gases. Table 6.1 shows the major components of dry air which is given an equivalent molecular weight of 29 as it is composed largely of the nitrogen molecule N_2 with a molecular weight of 28.

Table 6.1

Composition of dry air at 0°C and 100 kPa, that is at standard temperature and pressure.

gas	molecular weight	density kg/m³	% by volume
nitrogen	28	1.25	78.09
oxygen	32	1.43	20.95
CO_2	44	1.98	0.03
argon	39	1.78	0.93
air	29	1.29	100

Stomata

These are microscopic pores on the leaf undersurface (abaxial) of orchids. The singular of stomata is stoma, a Greek word meaning mouth. Stomata were first observed in 1574 but their function was not understood. Today we understand their purpose but are still in doubt about the mechanisms which open and close the pore in accordance with environmental and metabolic conditions. One factor which keeps stomata closed is a high concentration of CO_2 within the plant. This is discussed in more detail in Chapter 7. Water stress also tends to close up the stomata to make it harder for water vapour to escape.

In orchids the number of stomata vary widely but a figure of 3000 per square centimetre is typical. The central pore of the orchid stoma varies from $3\mu m$ to $28 \mu m$ although $14\mu m$ is fairly common (Goh 1974/75). Orchid flowers also have stomata on the sepals, petals, labellum and column, but these are not functional and are practically closed at all times although they do pass some water vapour outwards from the flowers (Hew, Lee & Wong 1980).

Diffusion of gases

If the stopper is removed from a bottle of scent the odour will escape into the surrounding air because the scent concentration in the bottle is higher than in the air. As the concentration of scent in the air above the bottle increases the odour will diffuse through the air to the corners of the room and eventually throughout the house. This diffusion is driven by the difference in concentrations divided by the opposition or resistance to flow of odour through the neck of the bottle. This may be expressed as

$$\text{flow} = \frac{C_{in} - C_{out}}{\text{resistance}}$$

The flux or flow of CO_2 into the leaf may be compared with this except that the concentration of CO_2 is higher outside than in. Also the resistance is replaced with its three components.

$$\text{flow} = \frac{C_{air} - C_{leaf}}{r_s + r_a + r_m}$$

where the three r terms are respectively for stomata, air and mesophyll. The reason for the latter is that it is not only necessary for the CO_2 to penetrate into the leaf but also for it to enter the cell and chloroplast. The value of r_m is difficult to determine and each species may be different; it cannot be controlled by the orchid grower so is just mentioned here as a contributing factor to total resistance.

The CO_2 concentration in air is about 340 volumes per million or 340 μl per litre. At 25°C it has a density of 1795 grams per cubic metre which gives a calculated concentration of 0.6 grams per cubic metre of CO_2 in air. The value of C_{leaf} is more difficult; for C3 plants (see Chapter 7) it can never go below 50 μl per litre but is more usually around 200 μl per litre which latter calculates to 0.36 grams per cubic metre, giving a difference of 0.15 grams per cubic metre. The concentration of CO_2 in the leaf depends on the rate of photosynthesis.

Sometimes in the tropical forest with damp decomposing litter the CO_2 concentration reaches 550 μl per litre and may even do so in environments where humans are respiring. The adult human at rest exhales 12 to 15 litres of CO_2 per hour so in a closed environment this boosts the CO_2 concentration.

A higher concentration should increase the intake provided this amount can be used up in photosynthesis, otherwise its accumulation within the leaf may cause partial closure of the stomata and the benefit become self cancelling. I know of no quantative measurements on orchids to substantiate whether CO_2 reinforcement is valuable or not.

The control of r_s and r_a

In the foregoing the calculation of the flow due to diffusion has been limited to the concentration difference between the outside and inside of the leaf. The actual values of r_s and r_a have not been given as their calculation is beyond the scope of this text. However, it is pertinent to orchid culture to review the processes which will increase or decrease these two resistances.

The stomatal resistance is largely controlled by plant metabolism but external factors such as loss of water or water stress within the tissue brought about by excessive transpiration in the daytime (C3 plants only) will close or partly close the stomata. This will increase the value of r_s giving a self-limiting action on water loss, but also decreasing the CO_2 flow into the leaf cavity. If this condition persists for long, growth is inhibited.

If the light energy present is insufficient to allow highly active photosynthesis (particularly with CAM plants) the CO_2 usage is slowed and CO_2 concentration increases which gives partial closure of the stomata so increasing r_s. Again this is self regulation, not only by increasing the value of r_s but also by decreasing the driving force for CO_2 entry, that is $C_{air} - C_{leaf}$ reduces in value.

The resistance r_a is controllable to a large extent by the grower. This is the resistance to the diffusion of CO_2 into the leaf offered by the dormant layer of air over the leaf, particularly over the stomata.

Air is a fluid hence it has viscosity which is a measure of the force to be exerted to overcome the 'stickiness' of the fluid across the interface with the surface. Although the viscosity of air is low when compared to liquids it is significant and forms a boundary layer across the surface. See Fig. 6.1.

It is this boundary layer which is responsible for r_a, a thick boundary layer of a millimetre or two creates a high value of r_a. If a turbulent air flow is created close to the leaf surface the eddy currents bite into the laminar flow of the boundary layer and cause it to break up, reducing but not entirely eliminating r_a.

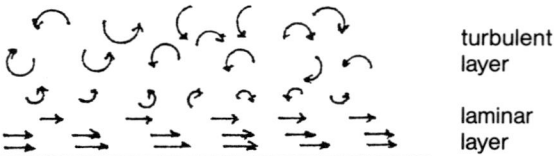

turbulent
layer

laminar
layer

Fig. 6.1 Laminar and turbulent boundary layers in motion near a surface. Note that turbulence is of smaller amplitude adjacent to laminar layer

At the same time this turbulence assists in three other ways:

1. it replenishes the depleted CO_2 concentration around the leaf from where it has been absorbed
2. it removes excess water vapour from around the leaf where it has accumulated during transpiration
3. it removes heat from the leaf by convection of the air.

Items 2 and 3 are dealt with in later chapters on water vapour and leaf temperature.

Air is seldom completely still. It is moved by free convection; as some air warms its density reduces so it rises to be replaced by air at a lower temperature. However the movement is slow, seldom more than 0.1 metre per second and this is insufficient to create turbulence. In nature wind provides forced convection to create turbulence and in glasshouses forced convection can be provided by fans. Probably most orchid growers have some CAM plants (Chapter 7) so turbulence must also be provided at night. Some growers mount a fan near the glasshouse roof and this works 24 hours a day as an effective method of providing turbulence, blowing air downward through the plants.

It takes quite a high wind speed to provide turbulence over a smooth flat plate but leaves are neither smooth nor flat. They have hairs, protruding veins and irregular leaf margins; they are often crinkled, bent or lumpy and are surrounded by other leaves. All of these factors go towards breaking up laminar wind flow and creating turbulence.

As a guide a wind speed of 2 metres per second from a fan is enough to ensure turbulence if the fan is large enough. Increasing this to 10 metres per second reduces the value of r_a to about half of that obtained at 2 metres per second.

While this may appear significant, the value of r_a is usually less than the value of r_s so the latter exercises the major control over the flux. It is not necessary to have a gale blowing across the plants. The size of the leaf has a marked effect on the r_a at a given windspeed; a 100 mm leaf has typically 4.5 times the r_a of a 5 mm leaf, that is the square root of the ratio of leaf size.

References

Goh Chong Jin (1974/75) The anatomy of orchid leaves. *Malayan Orchid Review* 12(2); 14-23.

Hew C.S., Lee G.L. & Wong S.C. (1980) Occurrence of non-functional stomata in the flowers of tropical orchids. *Ann. Bot.* 46; 195-201.

Morrison Gordon C. (1988) *The Orchid Grower's Manual,* Chap. 6 and Topic 3. Kangaroo Press, Sydney.

7 Photosynthesis

Very few non-technical books on orchid culture do any more than just mention this subject and many orchid growers may feel that this is beyond the realms of growing orchids for pleasure or profit. It is true that it is a complex subject but it can be simplified to those essentials needed by the grower, and as this book is intended to provide the essentials for culture, this chapter is included.

The process of photosynthesis is a very old one dating back at least 2000 million years BP (before present) and is considered to be responsible for the accumulation of oxygen in the atmosphere. This shields the earth from severe UV radiation so permitting life to come from the protective sea on to land.

This topic treats photosynthesis purely as an energy-converting system, which changes the energy from radiation (Chapter 5) into chemical bond energy, in which form it may be stored until required by the plant. This energy is then used to produce the simple sugar glucose (6 carbons) at the photosynthetic site.

So the 'photo' part carries out energy conversion and energy storage, and the 'synthesis' part carries out the production of glucose. These two processes taken together may be summarised by the simple equation read from left to right.

$$CO_2 + H_2O + energy \rightarrow glucose + O_2$$

All of this is done in small organelles called chloroplasts, in the leaf cell. There may be from 20 to 50 or so chloroplasts in a cell which is actively engaged in photosynthesis, that is exposed to radiation in the PAR band. The chloroplasts are small elongated bodies typically measuring 5 to 10 μm in one dimension and about 2 to 3 μm in diameter and contain a light-receptive compound called chlorophyll. Radiation in the PAR band of about 0.44 μm and 0.66 μm (the so-called 'blue' light and 'red' light) has just the correct amount of energy to excite these chlorophyll molecules. This excitation energy is subsequently released in small amounts so that it may be stored in the chloroplast.

Just as our TV antenna is cut to size to be tuned to various stations in the TV waveband, so the chloroplasts have antennae, each called a 'light-harvesting antenna', and these are tuned to the wavelengths around the two figures given above. This harvested energy is then transferred to a special molecule in the antenna which ejects one electron for each photon of the appropriate wavelengths absorbed and it is this electron which releases its energy, a small amount at a time, for storage in other compounds. See Fig. 7.1.

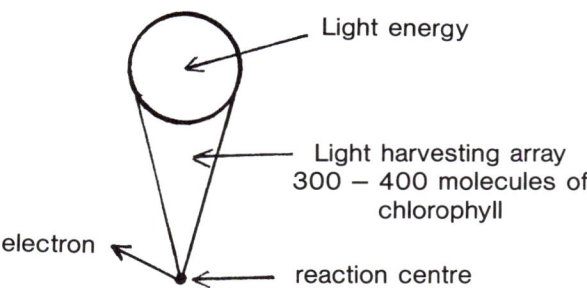

Light energy

Light harvesting array
300 – 400 molecules of
chlorophyll

electron

reaction centre

Fig. 7.1 An imaginative diagram showing light energy exciting the chlorophyll molecules of the light-harvesting array and this energy being funnelled to the reaction centre, which then emits one electron for each photon absorbed

This light-harvesting antenna, consisting of 300–400 chlorophyll molecules placed very close together, less than 0.001 μm (or one nanometre) apart, allows light of low intensity (a few photons) to be put to work and used effectively. As the chlorophyll absorbs the 'red' and 'blue' wavelengths and reflects the mid-wavelength 'green' the eye sees these reflected wavelengths and the photosynthesising plant appears to be green solely due to these chlorophyll molecules.

The photosynthetic process is regarded as complete with the production of glucose in the chloroplast. The glucose is then transported from the chloroplast into the cell cytoplasm, where it undergoes many reactions associated with plant metabolism.

In the foregoing the term energy has been stressed and growers must guard against confusing this with illuminance, the latter being measured in lux (or the outdated foot candle). These are neither physical nor biological units of measurement but are psychologically based on a hypothetical human observer. They are suitable for lighting engineers engaged in illumination for human activities but play no part in plant physiology. A single packet of radiation energy is called a quantum and its energy is very small at 2.84×10^{-19} joules for 'red' light.

When in the PAR band, a quantum is called a photon and the amount of light useful for photosynthesis is the 'photon flux density', measured in micromoles per square metre per second. The derivation of this and further explanation is going beyond the intended limits of this text; the only purpose in mentioning it is to encourage orchid growers to be aware of the meaningless nature of lux measurement in plant culture.

Absorption of energy

When radiant energy falls on a surface, three things and only three things can happen to it. It can be absorbed, reflected or transmitted.

We can say $a + r + t = 1$

In an experiment by Loomis (1965) on four species of plants (not orchids) the total absorption was 82% (all wavelengths in the PAR band), reflectance 10% and transmittance

8%. These figures are given solely to illustrate the magnitude of a, r and t in a typical case. A lot depends on the leaf surface; some leaves have a light coloured surface, are shiny and have a high reflectance.

Chlorophyll is not one simple pigment but a group of related substances and they require light energy for their synthesis, hence plants deprived of light have yellowish leaves and are called etiolated. Conversely some plants receiving a high light energy have yellowish leaves, or at least they are not deep green, and this results from the degradation of chlorophyll. Many orchids are grown in high light levels not only to produce lots of photosynthate but also to promote the production of flowering hormones.

There are several pigments in the plant cell cytoplasm which may absorb various wavelengths, but as these are not in the chloroplast they do not contribute to photosynthesis. However, some xanthophylls and carotenoids are found in the chloroplasts and as these do contribute to energy absorption to a small extent they can be significant for photosynthesis. Perhaps they are able to pass on some of this absorbed energy to the chlorophyll by being closely associated with the light-harvesting array.

A diagram of the absorption spectrum of chlorophyll extracted from plant cells and now in solution is shown in Fig. 7.2. From this one could reasonably assume that mid-wavelength

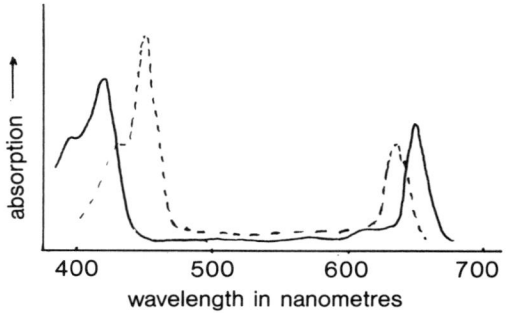

Fig. 7.2 Absorption curves of chlorophyll 'a' (solid line) and chlorophyll 'b' (dash line) in vitro in solvent. The wavelength is in nanometres (10^{-9}m). Divide wavelength figures by 1000 to read micrometres

light from 0.5 μm (500 nm) to 0.6 μm (600 nm) is ineffective in photosynthesis. However, in the intact plant the absorption is rather different and figures given by Loomis (1965) for four plant species (not orchids) are 92% in the blue (0.4 to 0.5 μm), 71% in the green-yellow (0.5 to 0.6 μm) and 84% in the orange-red (0.6 to 0.7 μm). The unexpected 71% in the green-yellow is probably due to carotenes and xanthophylls which absorb in this part of the spectrum.

However, a lot of this absorbed energy may only produce heat unless it can be put to work in the photosynthetic system.

Fig. 7.3 is an action spectrum showing effective photosynthesis over the PAR band, indicating that some mid-wavelength range is partially effective in the photosynthetic process but not nearly as effective as the 'blue' and 'red' wavelengths.

Unfortunately orchids do not appear to be high on the list of plants for investigation. Something a little more common (and cheaper) or having a food value meriting a research grant seems more frequently to be used. One must assume that near similar results will apply to orchids, as most Angiospermae or flowering plants have a common cellular composition.

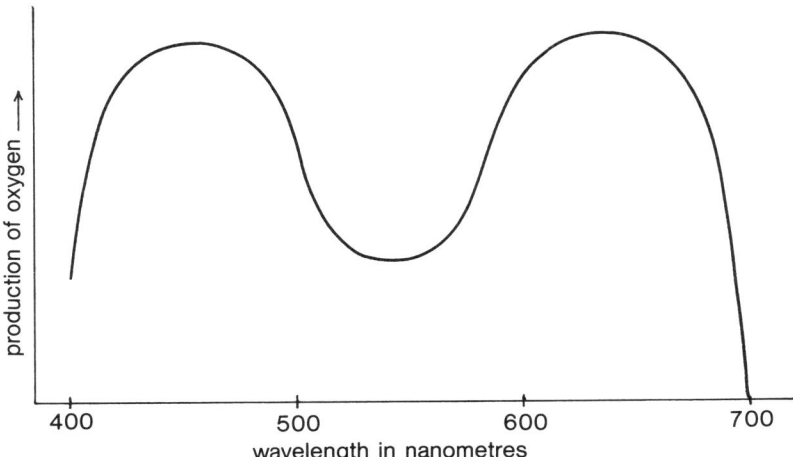

Fig. 7.3 The action spectrum of a typical leaf showing the photosynthetic response the amount of O_2 produced when the leaf is exposed to monochromatic light in the PAR band

Respiration

This is often thought of as reverse photosynthesis so it is appropriate to consider it here. Much of the energy derived from the photons collected by the light-harresting array of chlorophyll molecules is stored in the glucose molecules which are exported from the chloroplast into the cell cytoplasm. Glucose molecules are readily formed into insoluble starch molecules and as such constitute a food and energy reserve stored in the cells against demand.

All parts of the plant, leaf, stem, roots, flowers and fruit, require energy 24 hours a day just to live and grow and the breakdown of this starch into glucose and then into carbon dioxide and water supplies this energy, as well as a carbon skeleton for the construction of tissue. This demand is heaviest at night and in dull weather when little or no energy is being derived from the sun. This process is called respiration and may be represented by the simple equation

$$\text{glucose} + O_2 \longrightarrow CO_2 + H_2O + \text{energy}$$

It will be seen that this is the reverse process of photosynthesis although it occurs in different cell organelles called mitochondria which carry out the breakdown from the complex glucose to the simple CO_2 and water and release energy.

The plant can use CO_2 from outside the plant (exogenous) or the CO_2 from respiration (endogenous) for photosynthesis. The latter acts as a CO_2 reserve in the early daylight and serves to get things going before the stomata open up to admit exogenous CO_2.

Carbon fixation

Chapter 6 described the need to facilitate the entry of CO_2 through the stomata and into the cellular tissue of the leaf. What happens to it then and how it is used play an important role in plant culture and will be discussed in this section.

The incorporation of CO_2 into plant substances is called carbon fixation and there are three types, known as C3, C4 and CAM. Only two of these, namely C3 and CAM, are commonly present in orchids. There is still some doubt about the presence of the C4 method and if present it may only be in a few species.

The designation C3 refers to the first stable compound formed, a 3-carbon organic acid (phosphoglycerate). By a series of further reactions many other compounds including glucose are produced. All of these compounds are produced in the chloroplast from which glucose is exported as the final product of photosynthesis. These other reactions are of no concern here; we are only interested in the input of CO_2 and its fixation and as this differs from CAM it is worthwhile examining it in some detail.

In C3 plants the stomata (Chapter 3 and plates 3A, 3B) are closed at night and open when daylight comes. This allows the entry of CO_2 into the plant cells where, after an initial post-dawn delay, it is combined with a 5-carbon sugar (ribulose biphosphate). The combination of the two is carried out by an enzyme called ribulose biphosphate carboxylase (RuBPase) which is itself activated by light and is dormant during dark periods. The 6-carbon compound so formed is unstable and immediately splits into two molecules of the 3-carbon phosphoglycerate. As long as the plant does not suffer water stress and daylight continues to provide energy, the stomata will remain open and carbon fixation by the C3 method continues. At dusk the photosynthetic energy in the chloroplasts ceases, the CO_2 concentration from both outside and from respiration builds up within the leaf and the stomata close and remain closed until daylight once more allows photosynthesis to recommence. This uses up the CO_2 within the leaf so reducing its concentration and the stomata open to allow the entry of exogenous CO_2.

The C3 process is just what we would expect and is the system present in most plants from tall trees to annual plants. As long as the sun is shining and there is no water stress then photosynthesis proceeds.

CAM is an abbreviation for Crassulacean Acid Metabolism, so called because it was first discovered in the Crassulaceae although it has now been found in 18 families of flowering plants and one fern. Many of the popular members of the Orchidaceae have CAM. So how does this differ from C3 metabolism?

In CAM plants the metabolism is geared towards saving water which gives the clue that they are arid area plants or, like some orchids, they grow where water may be scarce such as in tree tops. To conserve water the stomata are closed during the hot and relatively dry daylight period when the vapour pressure deficit (Chapter 9) is high. At night the stomata open to permit the entry of CO_2 but, as there is no photosynthetic energy available in the chloroplast and RuBPase is not active, glucose is not formed.

In CAM the CO_2 is added to a substance called for simplicity PEP by an enzyme, PEP carboxylase. This produces malic acid which is stored in the vacuole of the cell. The vacuole is a 'tank' within the cell used to store deleterious substances and keep them away from the living cytoplasm. Carbon dioxide fixation goes on all night and a maximum concentration of malic acid is reached at about 0600 hours. As trees are C3 and do not take up CO_2 in the dark, the epiphytic CAM orchids do not have to compete and have the CO_2 to themselves.

At dawn the enzyme PEP carboxylase is inactivated and the malic acid degraded to give up its CO_2 component which is used as a source of endogenous CO_2. The stomata are kept closed by this high concentration of CO_2 which now enters the chloroplasts where it is processed in daylight in the same manner as exogenous CO_2, by the C3 method.

Both night and daylight phases of CAM need to be active. Any lag in photosynthesis during the day previous may not produce enough PEP to combine with the night's intake of CO_2. Also any lag in photosynthesis on the day following results in a high malic acid content remaining, which prevents the stomata opening fully the next night. Therefore, CAM plants usually have a high light requirement.

One method of determining whether a plant is CAM or not is to measure the acid content of the plant in the early hours of the morning, but this requires special equipment and knowledge. Apart from chemical tests on a species, the surest way of forecasting CAM is that the leaf cells have large vacuoles and to contain large vacuoles the cells must be large, which is often detected by thick leaves.

Neales and Hew (1975) tested ten orchids cultivated in Singapore for CAM as well as measuring the mean leaf thickness of several samples of each. They found that five of these with a mean thickness of 1.7 mm ± 0.4 mm had CAM characteristics. These were *Arachnis, Aranda, Aranthera* and *Cattleya,* and the species *Dendrobium taurinum.* The other five had a mean thickness of 0.3 mm ± 0.02 mm and did not have CAM. They included *Spathoglottis, Coelogyne rochussenii, Coelogyne mayeriana* and *Oncidium flexuosum.*

Growers may well use the caliper measurement of leaves to judge whether a given species is CAM. Just because some species in a genus are CAM, it does not follow that all species of the genus are the same. Some genera are very variable in this respect. The only sure method of testing is by chemical or other involved methods.

Net photosynthesis

From the foregoing it is clear that while photosynthesis produces glucose, it is respiration which uses it for 24 hours a day for all parts of the plant. Plants must, at the very least, convert energy from sunlight into sufficient stored chemical energy to last the plant over this period. If this does not occur then the outgoing energy is greater than the incoming energy and once the energy reserves are used the plant will die.

The difference between gross photosynthetic production and respiration is called net photosynthesis. Fig. 7.4 shows this in diagramatic form for a C3 plant under adequate light

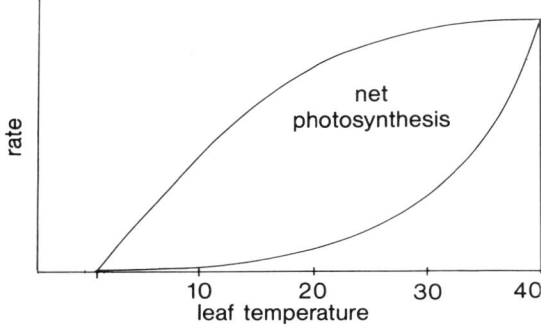

Fig. 7.4 The upper curve shows the photosynthetic rate and the lower curve the respiration rate. The distance between the two curves for any temperature is the net photosynthesis

conditions. Respiration increases markedly with temperature and the photosynthetic rate tends to flatten out. Maximum net photosynthesis occurs where the vertical distance between the curves is maximum. For a C3 plant the maximal band is from 18°C to 30°C, with a maximum at 25°C. Higher or lower leaf temperatures cause a fall in net photosynthesis. Chapter 8 deals with leaf temperature.

For CAM plants there are reports that the optimum temperature is 30 to 35°C although whether this is leaf or ambient temperature is not clear. Neither theory nor experimental evidence is produced to substantiate this. I feel that until these figures are justified in a satisfactory manner they should be regarded with suspicion.

The higher water content of CAM plant leaves would delay the rise (and fall) of leaf temperature under high values of insolation, so maybe some CAM plants will withstand higher ambient temperatures better than C3 plants. Leaf temperature is usually from 2 to 5°C above ambient. (Chapter 8)

Reference

Neales T.F. and Hew C.S. (1975) Two types of carbon fixation in tropical orchids. *Planta* 123; 303-306.

8 Leaf Temperature

Once a seedling has progressed beyond the flask stage and is potted on into the wide world, it is of major importance that it should grow as rapidly as possible otherwise it tends to regress. Growth requires energy and food, both of which are derived via the photosynthetic process.

Energy can be of two types, one which does useful work and one which just produces heat and raises the temperature. In biological systems all energy is derived from the sun's radiation, either directly or from reflection or by re-radiation from other bodies.

Energy is treated briefly in Chapter 5 and photosynthesis in Chapter 7 so this Chapter will be confined to the production of heat and control of leaf temperature.

Many orchid growers seem quite content to allow their plants to become hot as long as the leaves do not scorch. One often sees scorched leaves where both the chlorophyll and protein have been destroyed. This damage is permanent and should have been avoided in the first place. However scorching is not the only result to be avoided. Reference to Fig. 7.4 shows that as the leaf temperature rises so the rate of photosynthesis decreases (upper curve) and the respiration rate increases (lower curve) to a point where the net photosynthesis is zero. This temperature is well below the scorch point, so if the leaves have been allowed to scorch the zero photosynthetic point must have been reached some considerable time before.

Physiological processes such as photosynthesis and protoplasmic streaming within the plant cell tend to break down at 42°C and at 50°C irreversible denaturation of protein occurs. Enzyme activity as shown in Fig. 8.1 is low at low temperatures and increases to an optimum value as the temperature increases, then declines again until it ceases to function due to denaturation or destruction of the enzyme in its active form.

The energy budget

Like all budgets there is an incoming and an outgoing. When energy is the currency, the difference between the two is available to do work and heat the plant. The useful work is photosynthesis and the multitude of other reactions which occur in plants. As this useful work is done by enzymes the maintenance of leaf temperature to give optimum activity

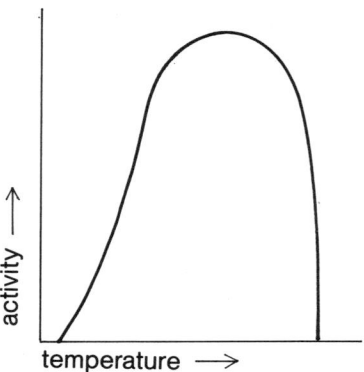

Fig. 8.1 A temperature response curve for a typical enzyme. At low temperature the activity is low but increases to a maximum at an optimum temperature and then falls rapidly as the temperature increases

of the enzymes is desirable (Fig. 8.1). Without heat energy there would be little production, so on cold days and during obscured sunlight it is necessary to maintain adequate leaf temperature for growth to occur.

Although the energy budget emphasises keeping leaves from overheating sometimes it is necessary to warm the leaf, so energy flow can be both ways depending on temperature.

Leaves obey physical principles so there is some compensating response to excessive energy input by an increase in energy output.

Fig. 8.2 shows a typical horizontal leaf and the various energy inputs and outputs to which it is subject. For short wave radiation these are

1. direct radiation from the sun S_A
2. diffuse radiation from the sky S_D; on overcast days this may be the main source of radiation
3. both direct and diffuse radiation reflected from the ground; this is

$$[\alpha (S_A + S_D)]$$

where α is the ground reflectance or albedo (see Table 8.1).

Radiation energy is measured in watts per square metre (W m^{-2}). Just to give some idea of the values involved on a clear day without too much smog, with a high sun angle (warm temperate or tropical) and little cloud we could have

$$S_A = 950 \text{ W m}^{-2}; S_D = 130 \text{ W m}^{-2}; \text{ and } \alpha (S_A + S_D) = 150 \text{ W m}^{-2}$$

The total short wave radiation = 1230 W m^{-2} about half of which may be absorbed = 615 W m^{-2}. Remember that this is the whole SW band and not just the PAR band where the absorptance is much higher than 0.5. It is, however, lower than 0.5 in the near infrared.

Many leaves are not horizontal hence they present a small effective area to direct radiation, although not to diffuse radiation. This means that they absorb much less radiation than a horizontal leaf.

The other energy inputs shown in Fig. 8.2 are due to long wave radiation from surroundings. All things on earth absorb radiation and increase their temperatures and re-radiate long waves in proportion to this temperature; that is, the hotter the body the more heat radiation it gives out in the long wave band from 3 to 30 μm.

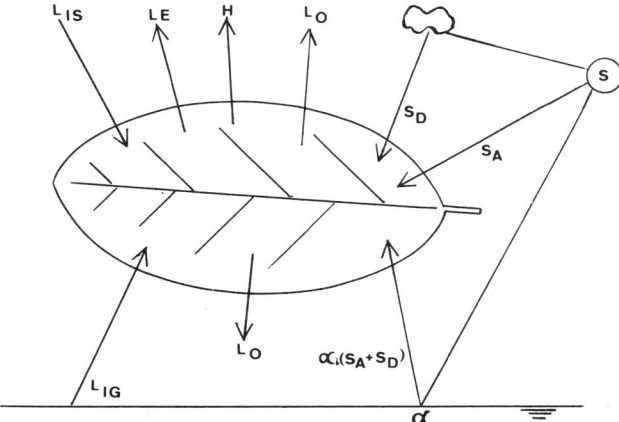

Fig. 8.2 This illustrates the short wave inputs S_A, S_D and $\alpha (S_A + S_D)$ to a horizontal leaf and the long wave inputs L_{IG} and L_{IS} from ground and sky. The output energy is all long wave as L_O due to leaf temperature, H due to air convection and LE due to removal of heat by evaporation of water

Fig. 8.2 shows that there are two long wave inputs to the leaf, L_{IG} being from the ground, benches, walls and other surroundings and L_{IS} from the sky or atmosphere.

Leaves are almost perfect absorbers of long wave radiation and a factor of 0.9 to 0.95 is applicable. For a warm climate some typical values during daylight would be

$$L_{IG} = 400 \text{ W m}^{-2}; \ L_{IS} = 300 \text{ W m}^{-2}.$$

This gives a total long wave radiation of 700 W m^{-2} so allowing for 0.95 absorption this gives 665 W m^{-2}. Add to this the SW radiation absorbed to give a total of 1280 W m^{-2}.

This is quite a high energy value even though it is spread over one square metre, so it clearly needs some output to avoid the leaf being burnt up. Incidentally it is opportune to point out that one watt is one joule per second, so although the energy is spread over one square metre it is at the rate of 1280 joules per second.

If cooling was withdrawn the leaf could reach 85°C with an air temperature of 30°C. This output is all in the long wave band and the radiation emittance factor is again high at 0.95.

Referring to Fig. 8.2, heat loss is due to

1. radiation from both sides of the leaf L_O (long wave out); this forms the major loss
2. the heat flux H due to the convective flow of the air
3. the conversion of water within the leaf into water vapour LE and the exiting of this through the stomata (Chapter 9) on the leaf undersurface.

The energy output from the leaf may be summarised as

$$0.95 \ (2L_O) \pm H \pm LE$$

The $\pm$ sign indicates that the energy flow for H and LE may be from the leaf ($+$), that is cooling, or into the leaf ($-$), warming. When the leaf temperature is below air temperature the negative values of H and LE will apply.

Heat reduction

By cultural methods the input energy can be reduced and the output energy increased. Clearly the reduction of direct solar radiation (S_A) will reduce the input and this can be done by heavy shading but this is likely to reduce the efficiency of photosynthesis, particularly for CAM plants. Decreasing the albedo will also decrease the input and a blue-metal floor will have lower reflectance than clean concrete or brick. See Table 8.1.

Table 8.1

Short wave reflectance (albedo)
The values are typical only and vary with colour, sun angle (should be greater than 30°), vegetation cover and height of canopy where applicable.

surface	reflectance
Dry soil, sand or clay	
light colour	0.3
dark colour	0.15
Most field crops	0.2 to 0.3
Swamp forest	0.1
Orchards	0.15 to 0.2
Asphalt	0.05 to 0.2
Concrete	0.1 to 0.3
Brick	0.2 to 0.4
Glass—sun angle 60° or more	0.08
Glass—sun angle 10° to 60°	0.09 to 0.52
Whitewash	0.5 to 0.9
Desert	0.35
Jungle	0.1

Data collected from various sources.
The sun angle is the angle of the sun above the horizon.

In some plants the leaves hang vertically downward and, as mentioned before, this minimises absorption during the hot part of the day and tends to keep the leaf temperature closer to air temperature. In this case maximum absorption of S_A occurs in the early morning or late afternoon when the path through the atmosphere is longer and the strength of S_A is attenuated.

Heating is also minimised by a waxy reflective surface or by leaf hairs. Diffuse radiation comes from the hemispherical sky-dome from all directions so the leaf angle has little influence on this source.

Other than the natural leaf characteristics above, the more effective way to obtain leaf cooling is to increase the output energy. Nothing much can be done about the $2L_O$ value as this depends on the 4th power of the leaf temperature in kelvin (degrees Celsius + 273 = kelvin). This value can be quite high at about 850 W m^{-2}. Fortunately as the leaf temperature increases so does the value of L_O so there is a compensating effect.

The values of H and LE are more amenable to cultural control although in magnitude the energy lost is not as great as with $2L_O$. The heat flux H is proportional to the difference between leaf and air temperatures, so this is again self-compensating as the greater the difference the greater the heat flux. When these two temperatures are equal the heat flux is zero, so no heat loss occurs.

The major factor here is the wind speed over the leaf as H is proportional to the square root of the windspeed. An increase in windspeed of 9 times would increase H by 3 times, providing the leaf-air temperature difference remained constant. A more likely increase in wind speed as produced by a fan would be 3 times, but even this would increase H by 1.7 times.

Large leaves have a lower value for H, for given conditions, than do small leaves. A leaf 4 times as large (in the direction of wind flow) will have only 0.5 times the value of H. So a leaf 20 cm long will have half the value of H compared to a leaf 5 cm long. This means that large leaves require a cool position as they may burn more easily if exposed to a hot position. The size of large leaves tends to swamp out any increase in wind speed from a leaf cooling viewpoint.

Typical values of H vary between 50 and 200 W m^{-2} for a 5°C difference in leaf and air temperature.

The value of LE (latent heat of vaporisation) is directly dependent on the difference between water vapour pressure within the leaf (at leaf temperature) and the water vapour pressure in the air (at air temperature). This is called vapour pressure deficit (VPD) and is the most meaningful and simplest way of measuring the water loss potential of a plant. This subject is covered in detail in Chapter 9.

As the water vapour exits from the stomata on the leaf surface it is only effective in cooling C3 plants on a hot day. Usually CAM plants have their stomata closed during daylight to conserve water. For C3 plants not under water stress the LE value with leaf temperature of 25°C and an air temperature of 20°C is about 200 W m^{-2}.

CAM plants usually have thick or succulent leaves containing relatively large quantities of water, which, having a high specific heat capacity, heats more slowly than in thin-leaved plants with limited water. However, under continued direct sunlight and usually with closed stomata, these thick leaves reach a higher temperature than others and have a tendency to scorch more easily.

Leaf temperature

The parameters involved in the intput and output energies are sun angle, windspeed, VPD, leaf size, albedo and various temperatures for air, sky, ground and leaf. The values quoted above were calculated from such data but these calculations are beyond the scope of this chapter. It is sufficient that orchid growers appreciate the factors involved and their magnitude.

Davidson (1963) inserted probes into some orchid leaves with the following results. Leaf temperatures were measured on a horizontal *Cattleya* leaf in full noon-day sun. The temperature rose to 50.6°C, 22.8°C above an ambient of 27.8°C. If this had been allowed to persist the leaf would have been damaged permanently. A second leaf at an acute angle to the sun's rays showed a temperature rise to a maximum of 37.2°C which was 9.4°C above ambient air temperature. The *Cattleya* is normally a CAM plant so LE cooling would be minimal.

The temperature of a horizontal *Cymbidium* leaf in full noon-day sun rose to a maximum of 8°C above the 26°C ambient temperature. In shade this leaf temperature was at times 2°C cooler than ambient or sometimes 3°C warmer than ambient temperature. The *Cymbidium* was most likely a C3 plant with LE cooling operating.

All measurements were made outdoors but the windspeed was not specified. This usually fluctuates widely so perhaps the 2°C below and the 3°C above ambient temperature for *Cymbidium* were caused by variation in H due to changing windspeed.

The above examples show that exposure to full sunlight at noon can be damaging to horizontal leaves when the insolation is high. It is also photosynthetically inhibitory to leaves at an angle to the sun's rays and when LE cooling is not present.

In shade the *Cymbidium* leaf at a maximum temperature would be operating within its limits. In full sunlight at noon the temperature would be higher than optimum for a C3 plant.

In nature orchid leaves are not normally exposed to full sunlight for any great length of time (see Chapter 14).

Reference

Davidson O. Wesley (1963) Advances in orchid environmental control *Proc. 4th World Orchid Conference*

9 Water Vapour

Orchid growers and horticulturists generally have little difficulty in measuring and being familiar with temperature but seem to flounder when considering the water vapour content of air and just what this means to plant culture, and the literature is not of much help. The difficulty seems to be the reverence most people have for relative humidity (RH) and the failure to appreciate the meaning of this term.

Relative humidity has its place in plant culture but it is only a minor one. It is particularly applicable in the wild in respect of dew point, that is the settling out of water vapour on to a surface, hopefully the roots, of epiphytic orchids to provide them with moisture. Chapter 14 treats this subject and includes Fig. 14.1 to illustrate the measurement and meaning of relative humidity, vapour pressure deficit (VPD) and dew point (DP).

The main aim of Chapter 9 is to explain VPD and its importance to plant culture, for this is the driving force behind plant water loss. Relative humidity does not show this because it does not take into consideration the water vapour pressure inside the leaf at leaf temperature. In fact in most cases it does not even show the water vapour pressure in the air as the temperature is not quoted along with the RH figure. The meaning of humidity and relative humidity are explained in Chapter 14.

Water vapour

This is the gaseous phase of the water molecule and is indeed pure water. It takes quite a lot of energy to turn liquid water into a gas, the hotter the liquid the less energy required. For example one gram of water at 5°C requires 2489 joules of energy whereas one gram of water at 40°C requires 2406 joules of energy to convert it into a gas. For most horticultural purposes we use the figure of 2450 joules per gram of liquid water. This is near enough for temperatures from 20 to 25°C.

As water vapour is just one of the gases present in moist air it has, like all the other components, a partial pressure. The total air pressure at sea level is near enough to 100 kPa (kilopascals) or, as often expressed in meteorological terms, 1000 hPa (hectopascals). This latter term is a direct equivalent of the older term millibar which is no longer approved under the international system of units.

The partial pressures of water vapour are shown in Table 9.1 for various biological temperatures when the air is saturated with water vapour. These are quite small when compared to air pressure as a whole.

The term saturated means that the spaces between the molecules of air gases are filled with molecules of water vapour and no more can be held therein as a gas. As the air temperature increases the space between the air gas molecules increases and more water vapour can be held, hence its partial pressure at saturation increases as shown in Table 9.1.

Conversely, as the air becomes cooler the molecules in the air gases close up and water vapour is 'condensed out' as liquid water. This is explained in connection with dew point in Chapter 14. When this happens the heat energy input used to change the phase of water to a gas (vaporisation) is given out when the water vapour condenses. This is 2450 joules per gram of water formed and usually heats the surrounding air.

Evaporative coolers work by forcing air past or over water or wet surfaces. The evaporation which occurs is due to this air supplying the needed heat energy to the water. This cools the air being blown through the cooler.

Transpiration stream

This is the name given to the stream of water which passes through the plant from roots to leaves, from where it escapes as water vapour via the stomata. If these latter were simply holes in the leaf, open at all times, high winds would decrease the boundary layer thickness, remove the water vapour surrounding the leaf continually and the plant would soon dessicate, particularly if water was scarce or its water flow rate could not keep up with the loss. Hence the stomata, which open and close depending on water stress and CO_2 concentration within the leaf, give some control over water loss and save the plant from collapse. One frequently sees a plant flaccid in the daytime due to heat and wind causing water loss and lack of turgidity, yet after a night period when the stomata close, heat intput is reduced and the demands of water are lessened, the plant is turgid once more the following morning.

Vapour pressure deficit

This expresses the difference between the water vapour pressure inside the leaf and that in the air immediately surrounding the leaf and as such it is the driving force for the loss of water from the leaf. This loss occurs through the stomata on the leaf undersurface in orchids, so one would expect stomatal resistance and boundary layer air resistance to have some influence on this water loss. This is very similar to CO_2 entry as in Chapter 6.

$$\text{flux of water vapour outwards} = \frac{p_{leaf} - p_{air}}{r_s + r_a}$$

where p is the water vapour pressure and r_s and r_a are the resistances offered by the stomata and boundary layer air respectively.

The intercellular spaces behind the stomata are normally coated with water (assuming no water stress is evident) and the air here is considered to be saturated with water vapour at leaf temperature.

Table 9.1

Saturation vapour pressure of air over water.

temperature of air	SVP in hPa	temperature of air	SVP in hPa
10	12.3	22	26.4
11	13.1	23	28.1
12	14.0	24	29.8
13	15.0	25	31.7
14	16.0	26	33.6
15	17.0	27	35.6
16	18.2	28	37.8
17	19.4	29	40.1
18	20.6	30	42.4
19	22.0	31	44.9
20	23.4	32	47.6
21	24.9	33	50.3

For example, assume the leaf temperature to be 25°C and the air around the leaf to be saturated at a temperature of 20°C. From Table 9.1 the p_{leaf} = 31.7 hPa and p_{air} = 23.4 hPa. This gives a driving force of 8.3 hPa to push water from the leaf. Just how much flows outwards depends on the values of r_s and r_a. For CAM plants with the stomata closed during the daylight the r_s value can be very high at over 3000 seconds per metre (s m^{-1}). This in effect swamps out lower r_a values and very little water escapes. Conversely C3 plants have wide open stomata on a bright sunny day and the r_s value can fall to say, 200 s m^{-1}; so the flux of water vapour is much greater from C3 orchids than from CAM orchids. With this lower value of r_s the value of r_a can make a significant contribution to the total resistance, so if the r_a is reduced to allow increased CO_2 penetration into the leaf, then the water vapour flux is increased in daylight for C3 plants. This action is concominant with the essential CO_2 entry so must be tolerated. But all is not bad news, this outward passage of water vapour from inside the leaf allows more leaf water to vaporise which cools the leaf as described in Chapter 8. It also assists the transpiration stream as outlined above.

In the above example it was assumed that the air around the leaf was at saturation. If adequate ventilation is provided around the plants this should seldom be the case, even in the tropics.

To find the VPD when the air is not saturated we can use Fig. 9.1. This shows the difference between the pressures at saturation and non-saturation. All that is required is a wet and dry bulb thermometer, which many orchid growers possess as part of their relative humidity programme, and a photocopy of Fig. 9.1 hung in a convenient place.

To take an example. If the dry bulb reads 23°C and the wet bulb 20°C then T_{dry} − T_{wet} = 3. Trace along the line marked 3 until the T_{wet} figure of 20°C is reached. This point is marked in Fig. 9.1 by the letter P. Reading horizontally gives a VPD of 6.6 hPa.

This means that the difference in pressures of the air when saturated at 20°C and its present condition is 6.6 hPa.

If we wish to take this further the saturation vapour pressure of the air at 20°C is 23.4 hPa (Table 9.1) so its present vapour pressure is 23.4 − 6.6 = 16.8 hPa. Note that this applies only to the air surrounding the plant and not to the air inside the leaf.

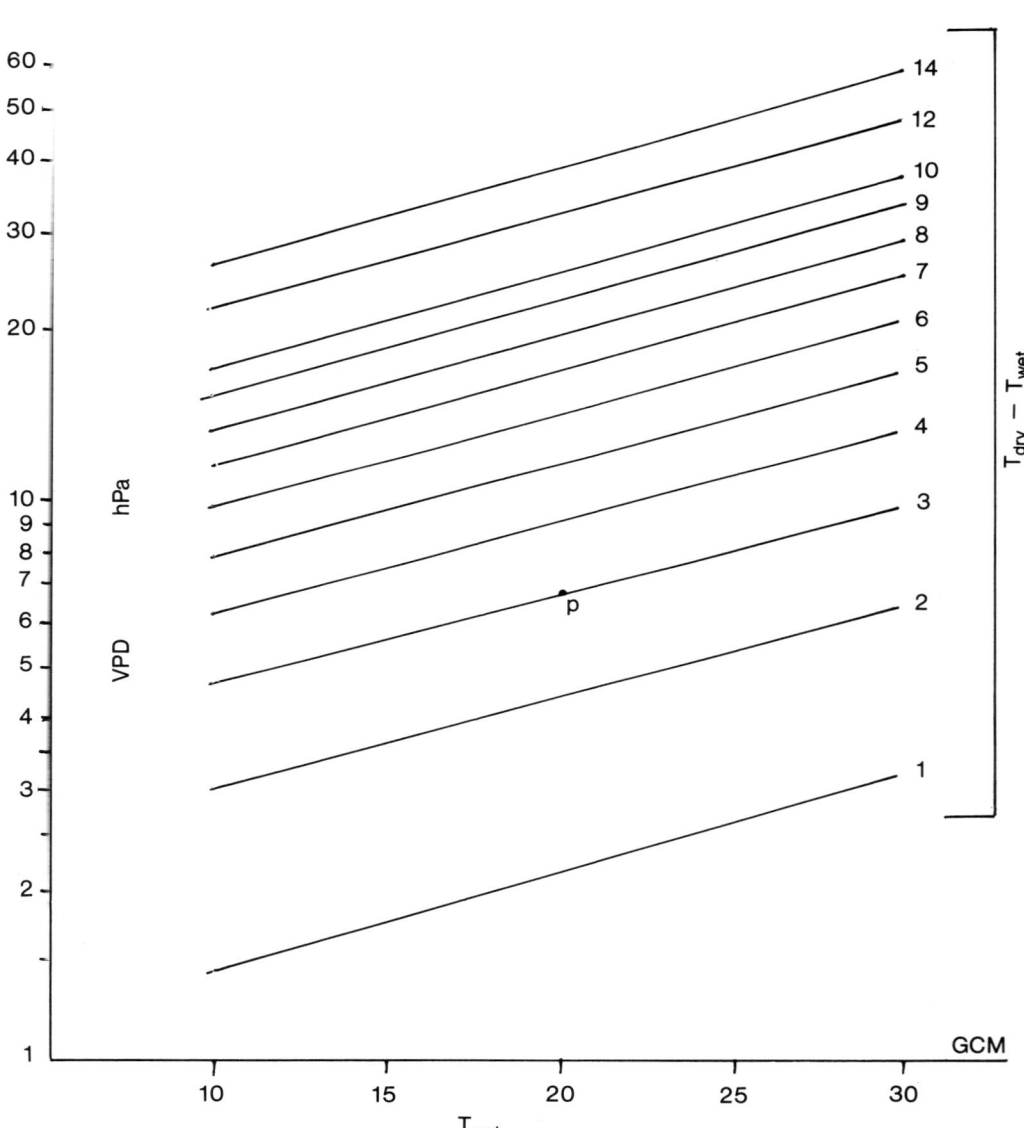

Fig. 9.1 All temperatures are in °C. Point P represents a VPD of 6.6 hPa obtained when $T'_{dry} - T_{wet} = 3°C$ and $T_{wet} = 20°C$

If the leaf temperature is measured or assumed to be 2°C higher than air temperature then, from Table 9.1, the saturation vapour pressure in the leaf spaces is 31.7 hPa; so the difference is

$$VPD = 31.7 - 16.8 = 14.9 \text{ say } 15 \text{ hPa}$$

which is now the force available to drive the water vapour from the leaf.

It is important when using a wet and dry bulb thermometer to use only distilled water in the wet bulb tank as all calculations are based on pure water and not upon salt solutions.

Reduction of r_a was mentioned previously. While the calculation of this is beyond the intended scope of this text it should be clear that r_a for water vapour can be reduced by decreasing the thickness of the laminar boundary layer which clings to any surface due to the viscous property of air.

Some data showing how the thickness of this layer varies with leaf size and wind speed are given in Table 9.2. This shows that larger leaves tend to have a greater thickness of laminar air, hence lose less water per unit area than smaller leaves, but will also have less cooling so tend to be hotter than small leaves under the same conditions.

Table 9.2

Laminar boundary layer thickness for water vapour, as length of leaf and wind speed vary

length (cm)	windspeed (m s⁻¹)	layer thickness (mm)
2	2	0.3
2	10	0.14
10	2	0.7
10	10	0.3
20	2	1.0
20	10	0.4
30	2	1.2
30	10	0.5

Note The length of the leaf refers to its dimension in the direction of wind flow. For circular leaves use 0.7 of the diameter as the length.

Most orchid growers will not be able to measure leaf temperature so this must needs be estimated. Generally with good culture this will be between 2°C and 5°C above ambient air temperature during periods of high insolation and with good ventilation around small leaves. Larger leaves may be 10°C higher than air temperature. Some examples are given in Chapter 8.

There is very little information on the VPD requirements of C3 orchids except for *Paphiopedilum*. Williams, Grivet and Zeiger (1983) found that at an ambient temperature of 20°C, maximum net photosynthesis occurred up to a VPD of 5 hPa but dropped sharply by 33% when the VPD increased to 10 hPa. Other C3 plants may behave similarly. In my glass house I always try to keep the VPD below 10 hPa. Plants having CAM open their stomata at night when temperatures are lower and the T_{dry} and T_{wet} are low enough to give a low VPD. As CAM plants keep their stomata closed during daylight hours the ambient VPD is of little consequence except under the following conditions.

If the vacuoles in a CAM plant are depleted of malic acid during the daylight period due to either a low photosynthetic rate the day before and/or a high photosynthetic rate today, the reduction of endogenous CO_2 allows the stomata to open. This may occur in late afternoon, whereupon exogenous CO_2 is taken in and the plant adopts C3 metabolism. At this time of the day the leaf is probably still quite warm so water loss could be a problem if the climate around the leaf is dry. In such a case the VPD can become important.

The temperature of air is difficult to measure in many situations. Air is a poor conductor of heat and pockets of air tend to localise and heat up. These rise and cold air replaces them, so the thermometer readings tend to vary. To obtain a reasonably true reading of air temperature, thermometers, particularly wet and dry bulb types, should be aspirated, probably by a small fan as wind speed, although helpful, is not consistent. Air movement is very necessary for correct wet bulb readings. Also all thermometers should be shielded from radiation, both direct and diffuse, as much as possible, but without inhibiting air flow. Use only distilled water in the wet bulb tank.

Refer to Chapter 12 for further data on this subject.

Reference

Williams William E., Grivet Cyril and Zeiger Edwardo (1983) Gas exchange in *Paphiopedilum. Plant Physiol.* 72; 906–908.

10 Propagation

The following broad definitions will serve to introduce the subject.

Sexual propagation is the germination of seeds produced by pollination of the stigma and subsequent fertilisation of the ovules.

Asexual propagation simply means not sexual and covers the production of progeny by any means other than seed. It is sometimes called vegetative propagation because somatic cells are used.

Self pollination occurs when the pollen of a flower is placed onto the stigma of the same flower or perhaps a flower of the same plant (that is the same genotype) but is not extended further than this. Even with this restricted system of pollination the resulting progeny can be quite different either as genotypes or phenotypes. Species may be sufficiently stable to reproduce both genotypically and phenotypically. Hybrids are usually unstable and any type of progeny may result.

Cross pollination occurs when the pollen of one flower is placed on to the stigma of a flower of a different plant (a different genotype) even though of the same species or variety. If the process goes beyond this it is usually called hybridisation although the cross may not be fertile. The term is used rather loosely.

Asexual propagation

Competency in this is essential for all orchid growers to control that *Cattleya* or *Coelogyne* or whatever which is climbing out of its pot and becoming too difficult to handle. Before recommending that large plants be broken up the other point of view should be mentioned. Many plants having small flowers and compact growth make splendid specimen plants if allowed to grow undivided, year after year, in a saucer-type container. Such a specimen is a sight when in full flower. Examples taken from the Australian native collection are *Dendrobium kingianum, Dendrobium gracilicaule* and *Sarcochilus hartmannii* but doubtless many other species will respond equally well.

When dividing a plant which has been given a cultivar name be sure that this name is attached to all of the pieces which are to be grown on.

Sympodial growth

In this type of growth pseudobulbs arise in succession from a rhizome and in many cases three or four pseudobulbs may overhang the pot and these may be conveniently cut off and used as one division. Never try to propagate from less than 3 pseudobulbs (four are preferred). A lesser number may be used but the plant takes years to develop if it ever does. The time to take the 'cutting' is when a new growth is evident, about 2 cm long, but new roots have not grown. If this is an epiphyte and is destined to grow in a pot place it on *top of the pot* with the new growth to the centre and the cut edge against the pot rim. Do not bury the rhizome or pseudobulbs; most of the old roots may be cut off, leave just a few to assist anchorage in the pot. New roots will grow but any shifting of the plant in relation to the potting mixture will easily damage these; hence firm staking is necessary.

Keep the potting mixture slightly damp which will ultimately encourage root growth to enter the mix. To protect the plants from excess water loss keep in a cool shady place and mist spray the leaves and pseudobulbs twice on sunny days. When potting epiphytic plants into a medium or large size pot it is a saving in the substrate if an unbroken clay pot is placed in the bottom of the new pot in an inverted position. Clay pots of 7.5 cm and 10 cm are most useful.

If an entire orchid plant is to be subdivided it is useful to cut through the rhizome in several places to give 3- or 4-pseudobulb divisions, and leave it in the pot undisturbed until new shoots appear. The several plants may then be removed and potted as described. This procedure can only be done with those plants having a sufficiently long interval between pseudobulbs.

Monopodial growth

New plants may arise from offshoots coming from near the base of the plant. If it is desired to propagate these do not attempt to do so before the new growth has sent out one root, preferably two roots or more. A sharp knife will separate the young plant from its parent.

Phalaenopsis at times produce young plants from the flower stems instead of flowers. Do not separate these from the plants too early. Young orchid plants are not easy to raise so the more robust they are when forced into an independent existence, the better.

Most monopodials can be cultivated on cork slabs which ensures that the roots are well drained. If pot culture is necessary the root tips are very delicate and should not be forced into pots or allowed to rub against charcoal or bark. Firm staking is essential, with misting and shading until the roots have decided where they will go and what they will adhere to. It is very easy to lose a young plant if this point is not watched carefully.

While monopodials can be grown into specimen plants, some offshoots will fairly rapidly produce another offshoot and then refuse to go any further, neither growing nor flowering. If this condition persists for a year, separate the two growths if both have roots and at least one should then show progressive growth; the original offshoot may not grow and can be discarded.

Paphiopedilum

These multiply by sending out new growth from the base. It is very inadvisable to remove these at any stage. Apart from this a full pot of *Paphiopedilum* in flower is gratifying to everyone. After many years the plant may grow too large in which case it can usually be split into just two or three good size divisions, repotted and grown on.

Aerial offsets (keikis)

These are very prevalent on *Dendrobium* and may be allowed to remain on the stems and grow. They will eventually flower just as well as the main stem flowers. If it is desired to remove these to grow on, this should not be done until the keiki is about 15 cm long. The roots tend to cling to the main stem so may be damaged on removal. If the young plant is to be grown on a cork slab remove the keiki and part of the old stem to which the roots are clinging and secure the lot on to a slab.

Deflasking

Growers who do not wish to be involved in the cost and labour of sexual propagation by hybridising and sowing their own seed may purchase flasks of seedlings. These young plants may be deflasked easily and grown on to increase one's collection.

As this is asexual propagation as far as the purchaser is concerned the process of raising these seedlings is described here.

Young orchid plants pass through three stages in their life before becoming adult flowering plants. These are:

1. The flask stage from seeds.
2. The community pot stage from the flask.
3. The 5 cm pot stage from the community pot.

Plants may be purchased at any of these stages and the purpose of this chapter is to cover the removal from the flask or bottle, i.e. deflasking and planting into community pots and their care.

Flasked plants come in two types:

1. Those in which the seed was sown.
2. Those in which the plants have been transplanted from the seedling flask.

For the home orchid enthusiast the second type is preferred. The number of plants in a transplanted flask is less than the original seedling flask but quite sufficient to satisfy the needs of the home grower. Also the plants are more uniform after transplanting and the discards will be fewer.

Before plants are removed from the flask prepare the community pots. These can be ordinary 12 to 15 cm pots, squat type preferred, or seed flats used by commercial growers for garden seedlings. The orchid roots are going to cling to the material used in the pots and may be broken on removal if the material is too large and heavy. Very fine bark with pieces no larger than 0.5 cm and some finely chopped up sphagnum moss may be used as a substrate. Some small pieces of charcoal can also be advantageously mixed in with the bark. The charcoal holds moisture in its crevices and ensures some humidity around the roots even when the bark dries out.

This substrate should be pasteurised a few days before use. This can be done by steaming a small amount in a pressure cooker or steamer using a shallow container. Usually steaming at 100°C for 20 minutes is sufficient, it being unnecessary to pasteurise under pressure. Another method is to wet the substrate thoroughly and place it on a flat tray in an oven set to 110°C for 20 to 30 minutes.

As an alternative some growers are satisfied with drenching the substrate thoroughly with a fungicidal solution, making sure all particles are wet, and then allowing this to drain and dry out. If heat is used the substrate material should be ventilated at room temperature for several hours with occasional stirring with a clean fork. At all other times keep the substrate covered to minimise re-infection.

If the flasks have arrived in good condition there is no need for immediate deflasking. The flasks may be placed in a cool shady spot. Although some light is required too much may burn up the seedlings. If the contents of the flask look a mess, due to rough transport, deflasking should be done at once.

Some bottles and flasks have a wide mouth allowing a knife blade to be slipped into the flask and the seedlings lifted out. For narrow-necked bottles one needs a piece of stiff wire with the end bent into a U to hook out the seedlings. They are fairly tough despite their delicate appearance.

The seedlings should be scooped, hooked or otherwise removed from the flask directly into a basin of water, not too cold, about 22 to 25°C does nicely. Here they are washed to remove all of the agar gel. Leaving this on the roots will only promote fungal growth. Several changes of water may be needed to ensure clean plants.

If the seedlings are from a non-transplanted flask they will be very variable in size and need to be sorted into large, medium and small sizes in three bowls of water. Never let seedlings dry out. Sorting is preferred at this stage rather than later on in the community pots, where it is desirable for all seedlings in a pot to progress uniformly.

Before planting, the seedlings are immersed in a fungicide solution of your choice and then planted immediately into the community pots. This is a tiring task so you may decide to use only the large plants or large and medium, discarding the small sizes.

The pots should be filled to one third of their depth with drainage material, such as clay crocks, and the seedling substrate added and the whole lot wet and allowed to drain.

Commence sowing near the rim of the pot or back edge of a flat using a pencil or similar device to make a hole in the substrate. Insert the seedling without breaking the roots and cover with the substrate. Keep the junction of the root and stem just above substrate level. Some roots will fit into the hole easily, others will want to go anywhere but the desired place. Let them do so even if they are on top of the substrate. Place seedlings 2 or 3 cm apart, depending on size, and work around the pot edge gradually towards the centre.

After sowing, spray with a very dilute water soluble fertiliser using enough to cover a 2 cent piece to four litres of water. Make out a label and insert into the pot.

Plants grown in flasks have not developed a cuticular covering on the leaves so water loss occurs very readily. Place the plants in a clear plastic bag or into a box having a clear plastic or glass top. Ideally a minimum night temperature of 16°C is needed for good growth, so an electric blanket or other heater should be arranged to maintain this temperature.

At first the seedlings need low light intensity, similar to a living room. Strong light will be detrimental at this stage so use a shade cloth over the box if necessary. After a few months, depending on the growing season, increase the light intensity twofold. The cover on the box should be lifted during part of the day to ensure air change. The seedlings must be made to grow. If they remain static they are likely to reverse growth and die off. Raising young orchid seedlings is not always easy. To promote growth by maintaining humidity, mist spray every day to wet the plants and the container, perhaps twice on a hot dry day when the lid is open. Fertilise as above once a week and as the plants grow increase the fertiliser concentration by 2.

Fungal attacks can still occur and if the young plants are seen to keel over at soil level or look brown, remove the pot, pull out the dead or sickly plants and douse the pot with a fungicide solution. The use of several pots instead of a single seed tray has the advantage of confining any fungal attack to a few plants rather than letting it rampage through the lot.

Snails and slugs are a real pest but if the pots and flats are properly boxed up with a well fitting cover these are not a serious problem. However, some Baysol around the seedling box is a worthwhile precaution.

After spending a year in a community pot the small plants are ready to be individually potted into 5 cm pots. However, this should not be done until early spring or summer as it is unwise to disturb the plants when growth is minimal.

The plants are still young, only two to three years of age, and so require some coddling, particularly at first. Treat them in just the same way as they were treated in the community pots. A somewhat coarser substrate may be used; larger pieces of bark or charcoal for epiphytes, for others use a substrate as given in Chapter 11. Depending on the time of the year when transplanting was done, these young plants will take six to twelve months to establish. After this period and with new growth commencing, they may be treated a little less carefully.

Many people may prefer to buy their plants already established in 5 cm pots at a modest price. This saves one or two years of delicate growing time. One does not obtain as many plants but perhaps one or two of each will meet your needs.

Points of interest

It has been reported that seedling growth is much accelerated by watering with one millilitre of 'Formula 20' placed in one litre of water to which is added seven grams of sugar. This is applied every two weeks to seedlings which have been established in community pots for a month. Growers may care to try out this procedure on a few plants to test its efficacy. The sugar will most certainly act as a carbon source for fungal growth, but whether you have good or bad fungi present is open to chance.

Some 20 years ago a report came from Indonesia that beer, fed to seedlings once per week for six weeks at the rate of 5 ml per pot, greatly encouraged growth. As an alternative spray the seedlings twice per week with a mixture of beer and water at a 1:1 ratio for a period of six weeks. The significance of the six week limit is not understood.

Further experiments made in Malaysia using diluted beer as a foliar spray appeared to be very effective and many local party goers may like to use the left overs to advance our knowledge of fertilising adult orchid plants.

More on asexual propagation

There are two other methods of asexual propagation, tissue culture and protoplast culture. Neither of these is covered here in detail as both require expensive biochemicals and equipment, including a pH meter and a balance which will read to 0.1 gram. Many amino acids and plant hormones are added at less than 1 milligram per litre and these quantities are obtained by making more concentrated solutions and taking aliquots. If you are really competent in biochemical and bacteriological procedures and you simply must carry out tissue culture, then by all means try it.

Prepare and maintain a laboratory notebook to record all that you do, successes and failures. There will be many of the latter and a record of what went wrong is valuable information. Purchase a book on tissue culture of plants in general or of orchids in particular. *Cymbidium, Cattleya, Phalaenopsis* and *Paphiopedilum* all have their own likes and dislikes.

If you are not well versed in such procedures and/or are a bit short of cash, I suggest you pass your tissue across to a recognised micropropagation centre.

Although this is vegetative or asexual propagation there is no guarantee that the resulting plantlets (they are clones not seedlings) will be true reproductions of the parent tissue. Firstly cultivation techniques of clones must be better than good and mutations will probably occur. Some of the plants flower poorly or not at all, others have distorted flowers with twisted parts or even more parts than a flower should have.

A still more expensive and difficult task is to culture and grow protoplasts into plants. Protoplasts are somatic cells with the outer wall of cellulose removed. The cells are thus separated and each one is a potential plant. The big aim here is somatic hybridisation where two somatic cells join. In some cases the nucleus on one cell disappears but the two cytoplasms fuse. This becomes a 'cybrid' cell rather than a hybrid. This is essentially a research programme and not recommended for use outside research laboratories. It is mentioned here to complete the picture. For those interested in tissue or protoplast culture I recommend *Experiments in Plant Tissue Culture* by Dodds and Roberts, Cambridge University Press.

Sexual propagation

It is not essential for every orchid enthusiast to be able to raise orchids from seeds. Some people do not desire to do so, others have neither the equipment nor the time. There are some very experienced growers who hand their seed over to other persons to sow into a flask on their behalf rather than go to the trouble of acquiring all the chemicals, apparatus and know-how to do the job themselves for just a few seed capsules per year, and this approach really makes sense.

Before embarking on the project of growing orchids from seed or even of producing seed for someone else to grow, think carefully about it. Is the seed you have or anticipate, going to be worth growing on? If it is a hybrid seed you will indeed be lucky to get really worthwhile plants. Good hybrids are bred from carefully selected stock by persons who have had much training and experience in this field. Often this requires repeated crossbreeding and the weeding out of thousands of useless plants. Many growers just do not have the time, premises and equipment for this type of activity. Breeding new plants can be fun, if it is fun you want, but lots of labour goes with it, as plants take three years or more to show whether anything worthwhile has eventuated.

Many enthusiasts and commercial growers support the concept of conservation of plant species, both exotic and native. As a practical gesture they self-pollinate many species and grow and sell these seedlings rather than strip plants from the jungles and bush. Flasks of these may be purchased and contain between 6 and 30 plants each.

So instead of seed sowing techniques this section will deal with pollination and fertilisation of the orchid flower, as this activity is worth attempting just for experience and learning more about the anatomy of the plants.

Chapter 1 described the anatomy of the flower, however hours of studying paper work will not replace some practical experience, even if you do not intend to grow the seed formed.

A toothpick is an excellent tool for pollination and a large magnifying glass, about ×3 or ×5, helps a lot unless your eyesight is keen.

Obtain an orchid flower, the larger the better for a start, and set it in a secure and stable position; place a small white card under the column to catch falling pieces. Lift the anther cap with the point of the toothpick. This will show the pollinia inside, which will probably be in groups of 2, 4 or 8. The number of pollinia forms a very useful method of differentiating between genera, for example between *Cattleya* and *Laelia* and between *Dendrobium* and *Eria,* so the practice of lifting out and examining pollinia has some use other than pollinating flowers.

In some species any probing under the anther cap will result in the pollinia sticking to the toothpick by a sticky (viscid) disc attached to the pollinia stalks. In other species, e.g. *Dendrobium,* the pollinia are quite free and may tend to fall out and get lost easily. In this latter case, touching the tip of the toothpick on to the stigmatic surface which is sticky, and then on to the pollinia will help to secure them. Press the pollinia on to the stigmatic surface of the flower destined to become the female parent, where they will be covered with the sticky substance. The rest is up to the plant.

Fertilisation is not immediate; orchids are rather slow and it takes some time for the pollen tubes to grow down the column into the ovary, find the ovules and inject the gametes (sex cells) to fertilise the embryo. An orchid capsule may contain a million or more possible embryos and just how the pollen tubes and gametes find these and mate with them defies imagination. Not all seeds are fertile, usually those closer to the top of the ovary and the flower receive better attention from the pollen than those lower down.

The following list gives some idea of the time taken between pollination and fertilisation of some species.

Orchis (a geophyte — many geophytic orchids are very quick to fertilise)	2 weeks
Paphiopedilum insigne	14 weeks
Dendrobium species	10 to 14 weeks
Vanda sauvis	26 to 40 weeks
Cattleya species	6 weeks
Bulbophyllum species	8 weeks

However, the sepals and petals will wilt quickly or change colour and may be removed, leaving only the flower stalk topped by the ovary and column.

Storing pollen

For those who wish to cross hybridise it may be necessary to store the pollinia until the desired female parent flowers. Pollen may be stored and is usually viable for at least six months. It should be placed in a small sealed specimen bottle (3 cm × 0.7 cm). Dipping the sealing cap end of the specimen bottle in melted paraffin wax and letting solidify is a good method of sealing around the plastic cap. The specimen bottle(s) may then be placed in a larger jar, e.g. a jam jar, for storage and safety. No dehydrating agents, such as silica gel or calcium chloride, should be added as this causes the germination percentage to fall rapidly. Storage at about 7°C is advisable, particularly if the pollinia are to remain viable for 12 months. Storage temperatures of up to 20°C are satisfactory for most short term (6 months) storage, but if facilities are available, the bottom shelf of the domestic refrigerator seems a preferable storage place.

Obviously pollen should never be mixed with other pollen and only one set of pollinia should ever be placed on the one stigmatic surface. Always wait for the flower to mature before pollinating it, this is usually after it has been open for a few days.

Many epiphytes and geophytes will indulge in self-pollination so it may be necessary to remove the pollinia of these flowers as soon as they can be reached. However, this may cause immediate wilt and no further development of the flower, so some experimental work is needed.

The fruit

The time for the development of the orchid fruit, which is a capsule not a pod, varies with the genus. Some geophytes become ripe and burst open in a short period, others take 2 to 4 months and some, such as *Phalaenopsis,* much longer.

At some stage in the development of the fruit, when the seed is still not ripe, it may be removed from the capsule under sterile conditions and sown in nutrient medium. This 'green-seed culture' has two advantages in that the seed does not have to be sterilised, which does nothing to improve its viability, and the grower does not have to wait so long for the capsule to ripen. As a rough guide the capsule is ready for culture in about half the time taken to fully ripen. There are also two disadvantages: all the seeds must be used at the one sowing so distribution is limited and the risk of failure is high should the capsule be harvested before fertilisation of the ovules occurs.

If allowed to remain on the plant the capsule will eventually open up and disperse the seed.

A plant which is required to nurse fruits to maturity puts a lot of effort into this task to the detriment of new growth; therefore, unless you require the seeds, it is better to cut the old flower stem and fruits off the plant so that it can break into new growth.

The Seeds

When the orchid fruit splits open it releases thousands of seeds not all of which are viable. A *Cypripedium* is alleged to contain 28 000 seeds while a *Cycnoches* may contain three million.

Most plants produce seeds which contain a reserve food supply sufficient for storage and subsequent germination of the seed. An orchid seed has no such food reserve except for an oil droplet which is sufficient to maintain life for a while but not sufficient for germination. The orchid seed, therefore, needs to be supplied with nutrients from an external source until it can germinate and produce its own biochemical products and energy.

In nature, this external source has long been considered a symbiotic fungus. A French botanist, Noël Bernard, was the first to recognise the purpose of this fungus although it had been seen before (Arditti 1979). Others had considered it to be parasitic.

It was Lewis Knudson who experimented by growing orchid seed (around 1920) without the presence of a fungus (asymbiotic germination). He added simple sugars to an existing plant culture substrate and the germination and raising of orchid seedlings *in vitro* was born. Arditti (1990) traces the life and work of Knudson. See also Chapter 14.

Unfortunately asymbiotic substrates are also excellent for growing fungi of all sorts so careful sterilisation of the seed, glassware and substrate is necessary.

The Knudson C formula, useful for the germination of many orchid seeds, is given in Table 10.1 simply to illustrate the type of mixture used. For those who wish to pursue this subject refer to Arditti (1977) for greater detail and also other substrates for various genera.

The life of seeds depends on the species and their storage conditions. Most seeds lose viability if stored at room temperature, but if dried and stored over a desiccant at low temperature (refrigerator) their longevity increases.

Table 10.1

The Knudson C formula for seed raising

ingredient	milligrams per litre of solution
Monobasic potassium phosphate K_2HPO_4	250
Calcium nitrate $Ca(NO_3)_2$	1000
Ammonium sulphate $(NH_4)_2SO_4$	500
Magnesium sulphate $MgSO_4.7H_2O$	250
Ferrous sulphate $FeSO_4.7H_2O$	25
Manganese sulphate $MnSO_4.H_2O$	7.5
Cane sugar	20 gram
Agar	12 gram
Distilled water sufficient to make up the solution to 1 litre	

References

Arditti Joseph (1977) *Orchid Biology Reviews and Perspectives II.* Appendix on orchid seed germination and seedling culture. Cornell Univ. Press.

Arditti Joseph (1979) *Advances in Botanical Research* Vol.7 Ed. H.W. Woolhouse.

Arditti Joseph (1990) Lewis Knudson (1884-1958) his science, his times and his legacy. *Lindleyana* 5(1) 1-79.

11 Substrates and Culture

There are, perhaps, no two subjects which excite more discussion and argument among a group of orchid growers. Whatever they say, most are correct; which does not make the others incorrect. Although many growers tend to be very dogmatic about what is the best and only method of growing orchids, the newcomer should try out various substrates and culture methods.

The most important thing to remember is that a plant responds to total environment made up of factors such as temperature, light, humidity, carbon dioxide, water and fertiliser. The experienced grower integrates all factors and adjusts each one for optimum results. Growing plants of any kind where they do not grow in nature is a compromise and he who provides the best compromise meets with greatest success.

The guide lines given in this Chapter are only starting points for further experimental work by you. Plants can accustom themselves to a given environment but any rapid change in this usually has a deleterious effect on them. For example, if a plant has been growing in mottled shade conditions, moving it to full sun in spring/summer is a rapid change. The plant should be placed in full sun in late autumn/winter to become more accustomed to high light intensity. With few exceptions, such as the so-called 'jewel' orchids and some of the mottled leaved *Paphiopedilum*, orchids are not grown for the appearance of their foliage and often the more 'beat-up' and degenerative the plant looks the better it will flower.

In their natural environment many orchids are stress tolerant plants coping with dry conditions, lack of adequate mineral nutrients or poor light. It is this stress tolerance which allows them to be grown under all sorts of conditions different from their natural environment. However, it should not be assumed, as is often done by writers, that where an orchid is growing is its optimum position and that growing conditions are perfect. As anyone who has collected orchids from the jungle knows quite well, the plants will most likely do better in the collector's glass-house than they ever did in nature.

The substrate

The substrate is whatever the plant is growing on or in. It may be the bark of a live tree, a piece of picket fence, a piece of cork or a pot full of bark, charcoal or other material.

With very little exception the orchid plant needs a substrate which will not become sodden and which will allow good penetration of air. The prime example is a piece of hardwood to which the roots will cling; when doused with water the excess immediately runs off leaving the wood and roots to dry out.

If orchid roots are anchored into a substrate such as a potting mix or bark this will in time decompose to form the gardener's delight—beautiful humus produced by fungi and bacteria growing, multiplying and dying within the substrate. This is rich in nutrients but inhibitory to the free air circulation and good drainage necessary for orchid roots, so the orchid is repotted into fresh substrate and the old material thrown on to the garden where it will do some good.

All fungi and most bacteria are not autotrophic, that is they cannot photosynthesise and produce carbon molecule skeletons from CO_2 as a green plant does. They need another carbon source and this is usually obtained from a complex carbohydrate such as starch or cellulose, sugar alcohols or even free sugars, lipids and sundry other organic compounds which can be broken down by enzymes secreted by these microorganisms. The wide range and availability of these carbon sources mean rapid growth of the microorganisms if they can secure sufficient nitrogen, which is required in abundance, for their growth. Their carbon/nitrogen (C/N) ratio varies from 6/1 to 10/1 which is much lower than for green plants. A leguminous plant which can obtain nitrogen from the atmosphere via the root nodule bacteria associated with it has a C/N ratio of about 20/1 while in other soft tissue plants this is greater, being 30/1 or 40/1. The highest C/N ratios occur in wood, for example sawdust has a C/N ratio of about 200/1; so any woody substance used in or as a substrate provides plenty of carbon for the molecular skeleton but insignifcant nitrogen for either microorganisms or plants to grow.

If one is growing in a predominantly bark substrate the recommendation is to use pot fertilisers high in nitrogen in the hope that after the microorganisms have satisfied their needs there will be some left over for the plant. Like many fertiliser regimes described in orchid journals this is all rather vague, particularly with regard to units of measurement. Is it by gram weight of the element, gram weight of the compound or atomic weights or moles? Also there is seldom any evidence presented that the results obtained were better than 'control' or that the results were such that they did not occur by chance or that some other environmental factor was not responsible for the improvement, if any.

One solution, of course, is not to confine the roots to pots but allow them to grow and function in the open air. However, this is frequently inconvenient, requiring a humid atmosphere and feeding by spraying at frequent intervals as may occur in nature.

This is particularly applicable to monopodial orchids which are grown in wooden slat containers, called 'teak baskets'. The roots of the plant soon outgrow the basket which may be hung by wires near the glasshouse roof, leaving the roots to grow and cling to anything they can find. A constantly humid atmosphere is required for success.

Morrison (1973) investigated the use of charcoal as substrate, one that lasts for ever and avoids root disturbance as repotting is not required until the plant outgrows the pot or the pot disintegrates due to damage by UV radiation. The surface of charcoal has an abundance of cavities which give it a high water-holding capacity and the roots cling to this surface. At the same time there are large air spaces between the charcoal pieces giving excellent drainage and aeration. The retention of nutrients relies more on the physical porosity, that is, the cavities, than cationic exchange capacity and it is comparatively easy to flush out any excess nutrients from it.

Two major advantages of charcoal is that one has almost complete control over fertilisation and that any nutrients absorbed by the bacteria are available when these die, either for the production of more bacteria or absorption by the plant; one is not concerned with C/N ratios and breakdown of substrate.

Some growers use a mixture of both bark and charcoal. Some even toss in extras like Perlite to increase the air spacing; others use a wide variety of inert or organic substances. If organics are used one should be cognisant of the C/N ratio and of any toxins which may be washed from them.

If bark or charcoal or a mixture of both are used for a substrate, the size of the components should be commensurate with the thickness of the roots. *Vanda*, for example, should be grown in large pieces of bark or charcoal or even in pieces of broken up clay pot.

Natural cork slabs are also used. The plant should be tied tightly to the slab so that movement is not possible. The roots should be tied in contact with the cork and not separated from it by a pack of sphagnum moss although this latter may be placed on top of the roots to provide a moisture reservoir. This pad of sphagnum moss may be kept in place by a small piece of chicken wire placed over it. The same technique should be used when securing plants to a live tree.

Some orchids, e.g. *Paphiopedilum*, tend to grow better in a slightly alkaline substrate. I have seen them growing quite well with marble chips (calcium carbonate) as the sole substrate in the pot.

Substrates for geophytes will vary according to their natural conditions. A good commencing mixture is peat moss, sand and soil in the ratio of 3:5:2 by volume. The addition of some fine gravel or perlite will give extra drainage if needed. Adding a mulch of broken up leaf litter to conserve evaporation of moisture from the surface is an added advantage if this is needed. Some blood and bone fertiliser can be mixed into the substrate at a rate of 1% fertiliser (by volume). Geophytes grow in such a wide variety of places, from high limestone to semi-arid, that it is impossible to specify one substrate for all genera and growers need to do their own research to establish the optimum mixture.

Nutrition

An important part of culture is nutrition. While CO_2 is the major nutrient of plants this has been considered in Chapter 6 and nutrition is normally meant to cover the inorganic elements plus the forms of nitrogen. The elements necessary for plant nutrition are given in Table 11.1 together with the uses to which the plant puts these elements. Notice that there is nothing so naive as phosphorus for the roots, nitrogen for leaves and potassium for health, wealth or wisdom or anything else the author can think of. Nutrition is not that simplistic. The terms used in Table 11.1 are rather beyond the level of this text, but they are factual and indicate the complex nature of plant nutrition, hopefully minimising the chance of the orchid grower becoming swayed by over-simplistic statements.

Just how much fertiliser should an orchid receive in order to maximise growth, minimise cost and avoid toxicity? There is no simple answer to this. Fig 11.1 shows a curve of growth verses the concentration of the fertiliser element. When the concentration of this latter is low in the substrate, growth will be low, that is the slope of the curve is slight as the applied fertiliser is being consumed by microorganisms in the substrate or actually living on the roots. As the applied concentration is increased the needs of the microorganisms are satisfied

Table 11.1

This provides a quick reference to the main mineral elements required for plant nutrition and the use to which they are put.

Element	Use
Nitrogen as NO_3^- and NH_4^+	A constituent of amino acids, therefore protein and enzymes; a constituent of chlorophyll and of the bases that are in the DNA and RNA molecules.
P as $H_2PO_4^-$ or HPO_4^{2-}	Part of the DNA and RNA molecules; ATP and NADP; phospholipids in membranes; the phosphoralisation of sugars in respiratory steps.
K as K^+	An activator of enzymes: providing a cation to neutralise anionic charges; changing osmotic potential, such as opening stomata. Potassium is a non-toxic cation except at high salinity concentrations.
S as SO_4^{2-}	Sulphur is a constituent of amino acids as —S—H groups and plays a major part in the configuration of the protein when it is twisted into shape. The sulphur atoms which are close together form S—S bonds.
Ca as Ca^{2+}	This element has low mobility in plants and is chiefly used in the 'glue' between cell walls.
Mg as Mg^{2+}	This is a very active element in plant metabolism. It is a constitutent of chlorophyll. Importantly it is the activator of ribulose-biphosphate carboxylase, the enzyme initiating CO_2 fixation in photosynthesis. It activates many enzymes.
Mn as Mn^{2+}	An element needed only in small quantities and used in the water splitting process of photosystem II. It can also function in enzyme reactions in a manner similar to Mg.
Fe as Fe^{2+} and Fe^{3+}	Fe^{2+} is the reduced state which can be readily oxidised to the Fe^{3+} state. Its principal function appears to be its ready oxidisation/reduction ability. This occurs in photosynthesis and in the electron transport chain of respiration. Fe is also a major activator of enzymes.
Cu as Cu^+ and Cu^{2+}	Cu^{2+} is easily reduced and this element is in the photosynthetic electron transport chain between photosystem II and photosystem I in photosynthesis. It is also a component of several enzymes most of which react with O_2 and reduce it to H_2O_2 or H_2O.
Zn as Zn^{2+}	This element is very prominent in enzyme structure and function. Zinc deficiencies in plants can have drastic results such as lack of chloroplast development. Nucleic acid and protein synthesis, as for example its necessity in DNA and RNA polymerases.
Mo as MoO_4^{2+}	Although an element required in small quantities (about 1 part per million in dry weight tissues) molybdate is a weak acid and even large amounts of it are not toxic to plants. It is known principally as a component of nitrate reductase in roots and shoots.
B possibly as $B(OH)_3$	This is rather a mystery element; no enzyme is known which requires it and our knowledge of it is based entirely on deficiency symptoms. Perhaps it is in some way connected with hormonal control.
Cl as Cl^-	This is essential for O_2 production from isolated chloroplasts but a universal need for it *in vivo* is still to be confirmed. It is possible that it is tied with Mn in the splitting of water in PSII. It could be useful as an anion to counter rapid changes in K^+ to maintain turgor in the cells.
Na as Na^+	This has been included as there is some evidence of it being required by plants in arid areas. CAM plants also tend to grow better with a small addition of sodium but I know of no evidence to date supporting this for CAM orchids.

Fig. 11.1 A generalised diagram showing the growth rate against fertiliser element applied. The growth commences slowly as the substrate microorganisms take up most of the fertiliser element. As more fertiliser becomes available the plant growth increases until the critical zone (CZ) is reached. After this, moderate increases result in luxury living where the fertiliser elements which cannot be used for growth are stored in the stems. Increasing the fertiliser concentration further is detrimental to the plant metabolism and the growth rate decreases. The dash line shows that the margin for error in overdosing with trace elements is very small. If this occurs the growth rate diminishes rapidly and the plant is likely to die. The actual amount of fertiliser represented by the abscissa will vary with each element. The relative amounts are shown in Fig. 11.2

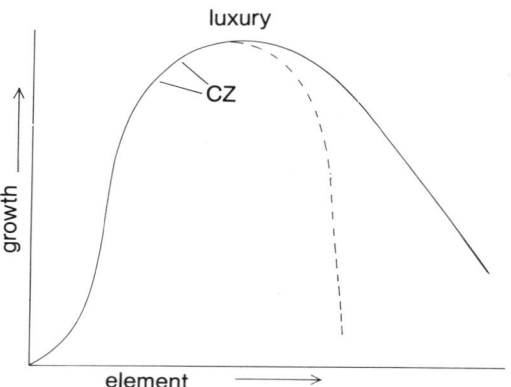

and there is some available for the plant, so the growth increases at a more rapid rate. Eventually the critical zone (CZ) is reached where growth is maximum for a given concentration. Beyond this zone the plant is 'luxury living'; excess fertiliser is stored in the tissue and growth is not promoted further. If more fertiliser is added the plant enters a decline phase, the sharpness of which will vary for each element. Too much fertiliser becomes toxic and the prime offenders here are the trace elements boron, zinc, copper and manganese. These cause a very sharp decline (dashed line) after the luxury-living level.

The most difficult part is determining the difference between insufficiency of any of the elements where the plant is on the upward growth curve and a surplus when it is on the downward path, except for the evident toxicity represented by the dash line in Fig. 11.1. While the shape of the curve remains substantially constant for all elements the concentration along the abscissa will have different values for each element.

Fig. 11.2 is an octagon of plant nutrition showing the relative quantities of nutrient elements, represented in moles, required for a typical plant. Molybdenum (Mo) is required in the smallest quantity and has been given a value of unity and all other elements related to it. Each arm of the octagon represents an increase of one magnitude (10 times) travelling in a clockwise direction. *Note:* A mole is the unit for the amount of a substance and 1 mole equals the atomic weight of the element expressed in grams, e.g. atomic weights are $Mg = 24.3$, $P = 31$, $Mo = 96$. So for every mole (96 grams) of molybdenum needed, the plant needs 5×10^4 moles of phosphorus or $5 \times 10^4 \times 31 = 155 \times 10^4$ grams. In fertiliser applications the quantities are more manageable if we use millimoles instead of moles. This simply means stating the weight in milligrams rather than grams, that is 96 milligrams and 155×10^4 milligrams gives the ratio of the respective fertilisers to be used. For every milligram of Mo used by the plant we need 1.6×10^4 milligrams of P.

As a first consideration it would appear that a chemical analysis of the plant tissue would be a sure-fire way of determining the quantity of each element needed by the plant and some fertiliser regimes are based on such analyses, which is probably better than having no basis at all. For orchids, much has been made of the analyses by Poole and Sheehan (1973, 1974) for *Cattleya* and *Phalaenopsis*. The plants used in the analyses had been well fertilised glasshouse-grown plants, so could have been in the luxury living class in respect of some elements. The results of these analyses are given in Table 11.2. The authors consider that the high potassium content of *Phalaenopsis* tissue could have been due to this genus

Fig. 11.2 The octagon of plant nutrition. This shows the relative quantities of nutrient (fertiliser) elements, expressed in moles, required for a typical plant. Molybdenum (Mo) is the element required in the smallest quantity and it has been given a value of unity and all other elements related to it. Each arm of the octagon represents a 10 times increase. The term mole is described in the text

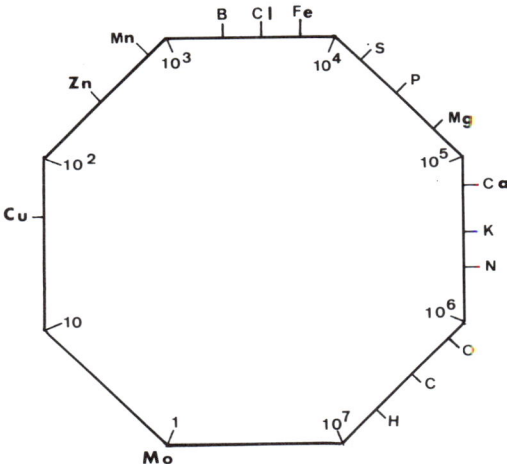

Table 11.2

Suggested ranges of dry weight mineral composition of new leaves, 1 to 2 years old, of *Cattleya* and *Phalaenopsis* for regular tissue analysis. Adapted from Poole and Sheehan (1973 and 1974).

Element %	*Cattleya*	*Phalaenopsis*
Nitrogen	1.5 — 2.5	2.3 — 2.7
Phosphorus	0.1 — 0.2	0.16 — 0.2
Potassium	2.0 — 3.0	4.5 — 6.0
Calcium	0.4 — 1.0	1.2 — 2.4
Magnesium	0.3 — 0.6	0.7 — 1.0

Element ppm		
Iron	50—100	100—140
Manganese	40—80	200—400
Zinc	60—100	60—100
Copper	30—50	15—30

accumulating the element rather than really requiring it. Too much reliance should not be placed on one-off nutrient tissue analysis, particularly on well grown advanced plants. One should commence at the seedling stage and plot the growth rate for each fertiliser element concentration change until the graph climbs towards the critical zone. Then we might know the answer for one species. But to do this requires a very closely controlled environment for all measurements to ensure that light quantity and quality, CO_2 concentration and water content do not vary.

Foliar feeding

There has been considerable controversy over the years about foliar fertilisation, that is the absorption of nutrients through the leaves. As far as I am aware Sheehan (1966) was the first to demonstrate (using orchids) that radioactive P could be absorbed through the leaves. He used sixty plants of *Cattleya* Trimos: twenty were subject to foliar spray on the second mature leaf, twenty received a root drench and a further twenty received a root drench to plants with a cut rhizome between the 3rd and 4th pseudobulbs. Various parts of the plants were sampled after 0.5 hours, 2 hours, 12 hours, 24 hours and 120 hours. The P had been absorbed through the second leaf and after the first 24 hours the concentration in the second pseudobulb was high (probably indicating storage). The second highest concentration was in the roots after 12 hours. Other leaves and pseudobulbs, the 1st and 3rd, also gave a positive reading of radioactive P.

The 50 ml of soil drench of radioactive P was also absorbed, this increasing with time, and was in greatest concentration in the pseudobulbs, so it is quite likely that these do act as storage organs, which again raises the question of validity in assessing the plant's needs by tissue analysis.

The application of potting medium drench of P to the plants with cut rhizomes is also interesting. It indicated that old roots behind the cut (which are frequently cut off plants when repotting) can absorb P just as well as young roots in front of the cut. Sheehan also states that the movement of N, K and Mg are similar to that of P so it is assumed that these elements can also enter the plant via foliage.

One of the major points used by doubters of the efficacy of foliar feeding is the nature of the cuticle. This is a non-living non-cellular membrane covering the leaf surface, the outer layer being composed of cutin and wax (see SEM photographs in Chapter 3). As the leaf grows so does the cuticle, but growth ceases when the leaf no longer increases in size. The major barrier to nutrient passage into the leaf is the wax surface; below this the cutin layer is rather more hydrophilic and the proteins and pectins within it absorb water. However, there are pores penetrating the cuticle and leading to the epidermal cell walls (Miller 1985). The pores link up with canals consisting mainly of pectin.

The waxy leaf surface is highly hydrophobic and water collects on this in near-spherical droplets. To maximise penetration into the leaf a detergent or surface tension reducing agent should be added to the foliar nutrient spray; this is commercially available under the name of 'wetting agent'. The water droplet then flattens out over the leaf surface coming into close contact with it over a much larger area than a spherical droplet, so being more likely to cover a cuticle pore.

Entry of the nutrient ions across the cuticle is by diffusion. The nitrogenous substance urea seems to enjoy preferential transport across the cuticle, and this increases the rate of penetration of other ions co-present with it (Yamada, Wittwer, Bukovac 1965). So it seems advantageous to have both a surfactant (wetting agent) and urea present in any foliar spray.

For many fertiliser compositions the use of 'chelated iron' is advocated, largely because it prevents unwanted reactions between iron and phosphates and the oxidation of Fe^{2+} ions to insoluble Fe^{3+} complexes. Chelated iron is a much larger molecule than Fe^{2+} obtained from $FeSO_4$ and as a result the former penetrates more slowly through the cuticular pores. Fe^{2+} is one of those ions whose absorption is promoted by urea.

Once the nutrient solution has passed the cuticle it enters the apoplast of the epidermal cell walls and has relatively free access to the plasmalemma. However, the apoplast forms a continuum within the leaf, estimated at about 3 to 5% of the total leaf volume, varying with species (Crowdy & Tanton 1970) and solutes within the leaf can take either the apoplastic or symplastic pathway to reach the vascular tissue for translocation within the plant.

When nutrients are absorbed by roots they are transported in the xylem tissue by transpiration pull and move towards the leaf tip. In foliar application the nutrients can move in either direction; but movement out of the leaf is opposite to xylem flow and occurs towards the petiole where the nutrients then enter the phloem tissue travelling towards the roots along the same pathway taken by photosynthates (Marshall and Wardlow 1973). Possibly those nutrients which reach the roots are transferred to the xylem and re-circulate within the plant in the same manner as those taken up by the roots.

It is now quite well established that foliar feeding by aqueous sprays is possible and practicable; the cuticle is not so impervious to water penetration as one might think. The converse is also true of course; those plants which are exposed to rain or to frequent misting in the glasshouse can also lose nutrients via the cuticle pores, hence such plants may require additional and more frequent feeding.

Pridgeon (1981) investigated the leaf trichomes in the Pleurothallidinae which contains some 3000 species in 30 genera, including *Pleurothallus, Stelis, Masdevallia* and *Lepanthes*. All 18 genera and 120 species studied contained glandular trichomes on both leaf surfaces, the diameter of the apical cells of the trichome being 25 to 30 micrometres. The apical cell is supported by a stalk cell. The longitudinal walls of the stalk cell become covered with cutin but the transverse wall between the stalk and the apical cells does not. As the leaf matures the apical cells rupture leaving a 'water-proof tube' from the surface to the cells below the epidermis. These trichomes are apparently absorbtive devices allowing penetration of water from the leaf surface down into the apoplast of the leaf. Pridgeon reports that other authors have found similar trichomes in 58 orchid genera while he has also noted trichomes on genera outside the Pleurothallidinae.

Perhaps it can be assumed that mineral uptake by these trichomes takes place but this has yet to be proven. The assumption is made on the basis of *Tillandsia usneoides* uptake of P and the fact that the trichomes of both *Tillandsia* and Pleurothallidinae are similar.

Nitrogen source for seedlings

This chapter is not oriented towards the nutrition of seeds and seedlings as there are many good papers on the subject, for example Arditti (1967) or Arditti, Clements, Fast, Hadley, Nishimura and Ernst (1982). However this latter reference does not cite Raghaven and Torrey (1964) so some mention should be made of this here.

These authors investigated the useful nitrogen sources for *Cattleya* hybrid seedlings and the results may well be useful for other genera and are given here for the information of those readers who may be involved in raising plants from seed.

When either NH_4^+ or NO_3^- is absorbed by a plant the nitrogen component is used to form amino acids and subsequently proteins or other nitrogenous products. This is done by converting NH_4^+ to NH_2 or the more involved reduction of NO_3^- to NH_2. This latter function is initiated by an enzyme 'nitrate reductase'. In the young seedlings of *Cattleya* (and probably other orchids) this enzyme is lacking and 20 to 40 day old seedlings cannot carry out nitrate reduction even though the nitrate is absorbed from the nutrient medium and detectable in the tissue. Even 60 to 80 day old seedlings did not grow as well on the $NaNO_3$-containing medium as those growing on NH_4NO_3-containing medium. Other nitrates, e.g. KNO_3 were also poor nitrogen sources.

The authors suggest that NO_3^- is not used by the plants if NH_4^+ is present and that nitrate reductase may well be an 'induced' enzyme. Periods of 12 to 14 weeks of growing on $NaNO_3$ were necessary to obtain measurable nitrate reductase activity with the assay methods used.

Solid fertilisers

While most orchid growers seem to favour fertilisers in liquid form, i.e. in solution, some growers advocate solid or lump fertilisers as being suitable for pot culture. I have always regarded this as a chancy business which requires great care to be successful. If the substrate containing such fertilisers dries out to some extent, i.e. less water, then the concentration of the fertiliser in the remaining water will increase to such an extent that ex-osmosis is possible; the root tip adjacent to this concentration of salts loses water, blackens and dies. Water flows from a point of high water concentration (i.e. low salt concentration) in the root towards a point of low water concentration (i.e. high salt concentration) in the substrate, rather than in the usual direction of into the root from the substrate.

However, no serious work seems to have been done on suitability for orchids in various substrates of pelleted solid fertilisers which give very slow release of nutrients. I have tried these to a limited extent qualitatively only and so far without any deleterious results, but this requires some quantitative work, particularly as their efficacy must be influenced by environmental conditions.

pH

In general terms pH is often stated to be a measure of acidity or alkalinity of an aqueous solution. Nature is not cognisant of the terms acidity or alkalinity; these are two man-made terms used for convenience. Metabolic systems recognise the number of hydrogen ions (H^+) present in solution and react accordingly. In order to measure these the pH system was devised and, as stated above, it relates only to aqueous systems; that is, we cannot have the pH of a solid such as soil, bark or the kitchen table. We are really speaking of the soil solution, which again is a misnomer as the soil does not go into solution but only the water soluble salts in it.

Water is well known as being H_2O which may be written as H—OH. A small part of water ionises or develops an electrical charge to give two ions, H^+ (cation) and OH^- (anion). Pure water has an equal amount of each, that is, in our terms it is neither acidic nor alkaline and is called neutral. This corresponds to a pH of 7 which is not an arbitrarily chosen figure but is derived from the measured electrical conductance of pure water, where only the ions can carry electrical current. The value of the ionic product is 1×10^{-14}. As there are equal amounts of H^+ and OH^- in pure water there are 10^{-7} H^+ ions and 10^{-7} OH^- ions. By definition the negative sign is eliminated so giving a neutral solution of pH of 7. The term acid or acidic is used to refer to solutions which have a pH from 0 to 6.9 and alkaline is used to refer to solutions with pH from 7.1 to 14.

Substances which are able to donate a H^+ to a solution are called acids or sometimes just proton donors as H^+ is a proton. An example is hydrochloric acid (HCl), so if a small amount of HCl is added to pure water the H^+ content increases and the pH decreases. Many growers find this confusing and need to commit it to memory, but the reason for it is not difficult. The value of 10^{-7} is 0.000 000 1 whereas 10^{-5} is 0.000 01 which is 100 times larger than the former value. The other obvious point here is that a change of two pH units is 100 times so a change of one unit (10^{-7} to 10^{-6}) is equal to 10 times, or the change is logarithmic to the base of 10.

Sodium hydroxide (NaOH) is an alkali and when added to pure water removes H^+ ions. The value of 10^{-7} may become 10^{-9} which is 100 times less than 10^{-7} so leaving a deficiency of H^+ ions. In considering pH it is fruitful to consider H^+ ions only; in acid solutions there are more than in a neutral solution and in alkaline solutions there are fewer than in a neutral solution There is no need to become involved with OH^- ions.

Much is made of pH values for substrates in orchid culture; perhaps a little too much as the pH measured today may be quite different from the pH of the same substrate next week. It depends on the buffering capacity of the substrate and generally this is poor. A buffer solution is one which resists change in pH when placed under the influence of conditions which can change the pH, that is it is self compensating although this action has its limits. So how is pH measured? This is fairly well established for soils. A sample of the soil is mixed with a small volume of recently boiled and cooled distilled water using either 1.5 or 2.5 times the volume of water to the volume of soil. Various laboratories have their own standards for this; the general procedure is to use as little water as possible. To obtain the pH of the solution around bark is more complex. As little water as possible should be used, say a 1:1 ratio.

Many people are puzzled by the fact that distilled water does not have a pH of 7 but is about 5.3. This is due to dissolved CO_2 in the water; hence the need to boil this to remove the CO_2 which is more soluble in cold water than hot. The water is then bottled to exclude as much air as possible and allowed to cool before use.

The measurement of pH can be done by 'indicators' or by a pH meter. For those concerned with nutrient solutions for seed growing or tissue culture a pH meter is recommended. This needs to be calibrated at intervals, particularly if there are long periods between use, by using two buffer solutions. The formulation of these and some guidance on the use of a pH meter are given in Appendix 11A.

For general use pH indicators are sufficiently accurate. Appendix 11A gives some useful indicators and more than one is necessary to have an overlapping range. Avoid 'universal indicators' having a wide pH range; these are too coarse and only serve to indicate which of the indicators in Appendix 11A should be used for final determination. Just a few millilitres or even drops of the solution to be measured are all that is needed. This is placed on a white tile or equivalent and a drop or two of indicator added. Under normal circumstances substrates can be expected to show a pH from 5 to 7.5. A reading above 7.5 can result in decreased availability of the fertiliser elements iron, manganese, zinc and copper. A reading less than 5 can reduce the availability of phosphorus, potassium, calcium and magnesium.

References

Arditti Joseph (1967) Factors affecting the germination of orchid seeds. *The Bot. Rev.* 33(1); 1-84.

Arditti Joseph, Clements Mark, Fast Gertrud, Hadley Geoffrey, Nishimura Goro and Ernst Robert (1982) Orchid seed germination and seedling culture. In *Orchid Biology Reviews and Perspectives II.* Ed. Joseph Arditti, Cornell.

Crowdy S.H. and Tanton T.W. (1970) Water pathways in higher plants. *J. Exp. Bot.* 21; 102-11.

Haas Norbert F. (1975) in *Z. Pflanzenphysiol. Bd.* 75; 427-35.

Khaw Cheng Haw (1982). Mineral nutrition of orchids. *Malayan Orchid Review* 16; 34-39.

Marshall C. and Wardlaw I.F. (1973) *Aust. J. Biol. Sci.* 26; 1-13.

Miller R.H. (1985) The prevalence of pores and canals in leaf cuticular membranes. *Ann. Bot.* 55; 459-71.

Morrison G.C. (1973) Charcoal as a compost. *Aust. Orchid Review* 181-85.

Poole Hugh A. and Sheehan T.J. (1973) Chemical composition of plant parts of *Cattleya* orchids. *Amer. Orchid Soc. Bull.* 42; 889-95.

Poole Hugh A. and Sheehan T.J. (1974) Chemical composition of plant parts of *Phalaenopsis* orchids. *Amer. Orchid Soc. Bull.* 43; 242-46.

Pridgeon Alec M. (1981) Absorbing trichomes in the Pleurothallidinae. *Amer. J. Bot.* 68(1); 64-71

Raghaven V. and Torrey John (1964) Inorganic nitrogen nutrition of seedling of the orchid *Cattleya. Amer. J. Bot.* 51; 264-74.

Sheehan T.J. (1966) Fertilisation of orchids. *Proceedings of Fifth World Orchid Conference.*

Yamada Y., Wittwer S.H., Bukovac M.J. (1965) Penetration of organic compounds through isolated cuticular membranes with special reference to [14]Urea. *Plant Phys.* 40; 170.

Appendix 11A

Useful indicators to measure pH

indicators	pH range	colour at range limits
Bromophenol blue	3 to 4.6	yellow—blue
Bromocresol green	3.8 to 5.4	yellow—blue
Methyl red	4.4 to 6.3	red—yellow
Chlorphenol red	5 to 6.6	yellow—red
Bromothymol blue	6 to 7.6	yellow—blue
Phenol red	6.8 to 8.4	yellow—red

Notes
1. The indicators are solids and come in 1, 5 or 10 gram packets.
2. There are many indicators; only a few have been chosen to cover the pH range useful to orchid growers.
3. Indicators are usually prepared by dissolving a small quantity (a pointed knife-tip full) in a few cm³ of water (or methylated spirits) and making up to 30 cm³. Store in a clear glass 30 millilitre pipette-type dropping bottle fitted with an Ansell teat. Adjust colour to mid-point of range by adding dropwise very dilute acid (hydrochloric will do) or dilute alkali (a pellet of sodium hydroxide, caustic soda, in some 250 cm³ of water).
4. The colour at the mid-point of the range can be found by using two small clear glass vials of water, making one acidic and the other alkaline (as above). Add 1 or 2 drops of indicator, the same amount to each. Hold the vials together and look through both one behind the other, at daylight. As an example bromothymol blue appears to be green at the mid-point.
5. When estimating pH add a minimum quantity of indicator. As this depends on H^+ for its action too much indicator may give an incorrect reading.
6. Note that a pH beyond either end of the range does not change the colour, e.g. bromothymol blue is still blue at a pH of 8 and still yellow at a pH of 5.

Buffer solution for calibrating pH meters

Usually two buffers of pH 4 and pH 6.8 are sufficient. The quantities of solutions are in cm³ (millilitres).

pH	solution A	solution B	indicator
4	38.5	61.5	Bromophenol blue
5	51.5	48.5	Bromocresol green
6.8	77.2	22.8	Bromothymol blue
7.6	93.6	6.4	Phenol red

Notes
1. The quantities must be measured accurately using pipettes. E.g. 61.5 may be measured by three times use of a 20 ml pipette plus 1.5 ml from a 0–5 ml calibrated pipette. Alternatively a burette may be used. Measuring cylinders are not accurate enough for the purpose.
2. To prepare solutions use distilled water which has been boiled for a few minutes to remove dissolved CO_2, cool to about 60°C (just too hot to hold for more than a few seconds), bottle and cork to cool. Fill the bottle if possible to exclude air.
3. Soda glass bottles tend, over a period of time to make the contents alkaline. Although buffers resist change of pH it is advisable to rinse the bottle with three washes of dilute HCl, swirling it around for some minutes, then with three washes of distilled water to remove the HCl; drain thoroughly before use.

Solution A
Weigh out 35.6 grams of disodium hydrogen phosphate $Na_2HPO_4.2H_2O$ and treat as in Solution B. This is a 0.2 molar solution.

Solution B
Weigh out accurately 21.01 grams of citric acid $C_6H_8O_7.H_2O$, dissolve in a little water and make up the volume to one litre with boiled distilled water. This is a 0.1 molar solution.

Note
Analytical grade reagents must be used. These have the formula on the bottle label for easy checking. The H_2O part is the water of crystallisation and it is important to use the solids which have this amount of water attached to their crystals.

The pH meter

The glass electrode of the pH meter is permeable to H^+ ions and made of very thin glass, usually 0.05 mm thick. It is therefore very fragile. The bulb on the electrode, when not in use, should be immersed in distilled water and should be washed every time after use by a jet of distilled water (from a plastic wash bottle). It should be blotted dry with facial tissue but never wiped.

New or dry electrodes should be soaked in water at about pH 7 for several hours.

When calibrating the meter with buffer solutions ensure that the temperatures of the buffer solutions are near the temperature of the solution to be measured (usually room temperature). When inserting the electrode into a liquid swirl it around prior to taking a reading. Unless specifically designed to do so, the glass electrode does not give accurate readings above pH 9 or 10. Solutions of metal salts, e.g. fertilisers, do not affect the reading but should be washed off thoroughly with a water jet after use. Do not plunge the electrode into a pot full of soil or compost.

12 Glasshouse Management and Equipment

In this text glasshouse means a structure having the main part of its cladding consisting of glass. Nevertheless, there are several other plastic type coverings used which may have similar or different characteristics to glass, and most of this chapter can be related to enclosed transparent structures of all sorts used to grow orchids. The single span only type has been considered, and that generally of the gable and inverted V roof type, but again the general principles expounded here are applicable.

The type of glasshouse used will depend on many factors such as the climate of the location, latitude, topography, altitude, proximity to lakes or sea, genera to be grown, capital cost of glass house, running expenses, degree of automation required and ingenuity of the constructor. With this multitude of factors for consideration it is little wonder that the glasshouses of amateur orchid growers vary in style and it is impractical here to do more than generalise.

In the southern hemisphere with its vast tracts of ocean there can be few orchid growers south of latitude 45°S, but in the northern hemisphere with its large land mass the latitude 50°N is approximately the boundary between the USA and Canada, so that the whole of Canada and a large slice of Europe are above this latitude. The cold winters, snow and frost must influence the style of glasshouse used in these areas for orchids if we allow for a minimum temperature of 10°C.

In England the typical glasshouse seems to have vertical or near vertical sides with gable roof and a complete surround of glass. Where the climate is overcast for much of the time the radiation is diffuse, coming from the sky dome from all directions and angles; very little direct radiation is received for a large part of the year. Hence it is desirable to use all-round glass for maximum energy penetration.

In more temperature climates, e.g. Mediterranean, this style of glasshouse has also gained favour, but here there is more direct radiation for most of the time and the glasshouse needs to be shielded from excess radiation energy in summer by shadecloth. Perhaps the substitution of solid walls for some of the glass would minimise temperature hikes and enable humidity to be kept at a more equable value.

It will be seen later that considerable heat can be lost through glass and some aerated concrete walling is advantageous in minimising heat loss in winter and heat gain in summer.

Size and location

For the small time amateur orchid grower a glasshouse measuring 5 metres by 3 metres is quite a good size, is fairly economical to heat and will contain quite a lot of plants. The door and the gable end are at the 3 metre width dimension. Although a glasshouse can be extended to accommodate more plants it is more economical to erect another house and heat this to a lesser degree than the former house, say one at 15°C and the other at 10°C minimum temperatures. In England it was not unusual for the amateur grower to have three small glasshouses, the cold, the intermediate and the warm. This allowed genera to be placed in the near optimum temperature range for winter growth and avoided the costly heating of one house, of equivalent area, to the warm temperature.

It is also well known that some genera will not grow and flower if not exposed to some low temperature weather. This is a difficulty experienced by some growers with one house, particularly if the outside weather is too cold to allow growing outside the house.

Glasshouses which have a low height to area ratio are difficult to maintain at a stable temperature, they heat up and cool down very quickly. The wall height should be at least 2 metres with a gable ridge height of 3 metres for a modest-sized house. Where glass is not required to ground level some form of brick/concrete wall 60 to 75 cm high below the glass part will assist in maintaining a stable temperature and moist atmosphere.

There has been much discussion over the years whether a glasshouse is better with the long axis (the gable ridge) running N-S or E-W. Table 12.1 shows the results of some experiments on this subject made in the northern hemisphere for single span houses. Table 12.1(a) for a latitude of 50°N shows that the E-W orientation is far better in mid-winter. In spring there is little to choose between the two and in summer the E-W position may be considered somewhat better as less summer sunlight penetrates. Alternatively, if summer sunlight is at a premium, then the N-S orientation may be better.

As the latitude becomes less, Table 12.1(b) for 36°N, the E-W orientation gives a somewhat better light penetration than N-S, but this is not so pronounced as for 50°N. From this it may be inferred that for latitudes less than 36° there is very little difference between E-W and N-S orientation. The results shown in Table 12.1(c) confirm the findings for a high latitude.

Table 12.1

Percent transmittance of direct sunlight
(a) and (b) taken from Kozai *et al.* (1978)

(a) *For 50°N latitude*

Date	NS	EW
1 Jan	34	72
1 Mar	55	67
10 Apr	62	62
1 July	66	58

(b) *For 36°N latitude*

Date	NS	EW
1 Jan	52	67
1 Mar	62	65
10 Mar	63	63
1 July	69	60

(c) *Other results from England*
    (unknown source)

	NS	EW
mid-summer	64	66
mid-winter	48	71

Some simple physics for the glasshouse

Whether the orchid grower has a glasshouse or some alternative, the physical factors of radiation, heat and humidity are relevant to good management. The effect of these factors on plant physiology has been covered in other Chapters. In this chapter the object is to provide an understanding of these factors and their interdependence in relation to the glasshouse.

Radiation

This may be divided broadly into two types, that from the sun called short wave radiation and that from cooler objects, e.g. the earth, called long wave radiation. Only SW radiation is dealt with in this section; it provides the source of energy to run the biological world. The surface temperature of the sun is about 6000°C and it emits about 74×10^6 watts per square metre irradiance. This produces about 1360 watts per square metre above the earth's atmosphere which is divided (by man) into various wavebands: the ultraviolet, the visible (called light) and the infrared. The visible band is also called the PAR band (photosynthetic active radiation band) and about 45% of the total radiation is in this band, which at the lower wavelength end is 0.4 μm (400 nanometres) and at the long wavelength end is 0.7 μm (700 nanometres). A micrometre (μm) is one millionth part of a metre, a nanometre is 1000 times smaller. The very short and harmful wavelengths of the UV are filtered out in the upper atmosphere, largely by ozone. The SW band at the earth's surface is conveniently regarded as from 0.3 μm to 3 μm.

As stated in Chapter 7 the wavelengths in the PAR band are needed for plant growth, hence it is essential that whatever cladding is used in the glasshouse minimum attenuation should occur over this band and in particular the wavelengths around 440 and 660 nm (0.44 and 0.66 μm). These are often designated 'blue' and 'red' wavelengths respectively for convenience as these are the colours registered by the human brain when these wavelengths impinge on the human eye. Glass is the best material for minimum attenuation, but many plastics are also suitable and have a transmission factor of 85%.

Greenish materials should be avoided as these appear green only because they have absorbed energy in the 'red' and 'blue' wavelengths vital to photosynthesis. So it is not only light quantity which is needed but also light quality in that the appropriate wavelengths must reach the plant leaves.

Plants grow because there is an energy input from SW radiation at the appropriate wavelengths. This energy input is in the form of quanta, more often called photons when in the PAR band, and it is this photon energy which is absorbed by chlorophyll in the plant and turned into a form of chemical energy which is retained to do work. The amount of energy in a photon depends on the wavelength and only those photons having a critical amount of energy can be used by chlorophyll to form chemical energy. This is the reason why only certain wavelengths are suitable for photosynthesis. It is easier to conceive wavelengths than it is to conceive parcels of energy or photons and the wavelengths absorbed are easier to measure, hence the term 'wavelength' has predominated in literature. This is acceptable providing one realises it is a substitute term for the photon energy and that only certain wavelengths are useable for photosynthesis. Photon energy can be measured but the equipment is currently rather expensive.

The orchid grower must guard against the trap of measuring the illuminance in lux as an indication of photon energy. Lux is a measure of candela $\times$ steradians per square metre and is part of a photometric system of psychologically derived units based on the judgement of a hypothetical standard observer. It is fine for lighting engineers concerned with illumination for humans but it is neither a physical nor a biological system and has no place in plant culture. The lux is only given some respectability by having the candela included as a basic unit in the International System of Units.

Although the SW radiation above the atmosphere is 1360 W m^{-2} this is attenuated by the gases, dust and other particles in the atmosphere, such that the noon radiation on a clear day with the sun near overhead can be 1000 W m^{-2}. About half of this, say 500 W m^{-2}, is in the PAR band giving a photon flux density (PFD) of 2130 μmol m^{-2} s^{-1}. It is beyond the scope of this text to explain this more fully; those interested should refer to Morrison, Chapter 5 (1988).

SW radiation may be direct sunlight (called irradiance) and also from the sky dome on both clear and cloudy days (diffuse radiation). This diffuse radiation is caused by scattering of the SW radiation. Very small molecules of gas scatter shorter wavelengths (blue) about nine times more effectively that longer (red) wavelengths and this causes the clear sky to appear blue. Larger particles such as pollutants, water droplets and ice crystals also scatter SW radiation. Generally this is not wavelength selective and the sky appears whitish. Dust particles are more effective in scattering the 'red' wavelengths and this gives a redness to the sky.

It is diffuse radiation which gives some light to shaded areas, and this radiation increases with a solar elevation up to 30 degrees but after this remains constant. At sea level in tropical and temperate zones the diffuse radiation varies between 100 and 200 W m^{-2} depending on atmospheric turbidity. As the altitude increases the amount of diffuse radiation decreases below 100 W m^{-2}. This radiation is very important for places of high latitude where low solar elevations reduce the direct solar energy due to a thicker atmospheric passage, hence more absorption. In England diffuse radiation may contribute between 50 to 100% of the total SW radiation. This has produced a glasshouse which has the maximum amount of glass in walls and roof to transmit this omni-directional radiation.

SW radiation is also reflected from the ground and other surfaces. The reflectance or albedo for various surfaces is given in Table 8.1. If the glasshouse floor is of dark bluemetal with an albedo of 0.15 it will reflect both direct and diffuse radiation and the total reflected radiation is 0.15 of the sum of these. This can also be between 100 and 200 W m^{-2}. A brick floor with an albedo of 0.4 would give a much higher value. Of course the whole floor does not reflect all of the direct sunlight; there are shadows caused by benches, plants and other fittings.

Heat

Heat is a form of energy and it is this energy which is converted into kinetic energy to move the atoms and molecules in a substance. Temperature is a man-made label used to indicate the degree of this kinetic energy which ceases only at zero degrees absolute. This is called zero kelvin and is -273.15°C. All bodies above zero kelvin have some kinetic energy and will radiate heat, however small this may be.

This is called long wave radiation and for convenience it is regarded as being from 3μm to 30 μm. The wavelength of maximum radiation is dependent on the temperature; for the earth, with a mean temperature of 15°C, this wavelength is about 10μm. It so happens that there is an atmospheric window at this wavelength where none of the gases, except water vapour, absorb much energy, so allowing the excess heat of the earth to escape into space. If it was not for this window the earth would 'cook up'.

The temperature of a body must not be confused with the amount of heat in it, its heat capacity depends on its mass. For example 10 kg of water at 50°C has 10 times the quantity of heat in it compared to 1 kg of water at 50°C. In glasshouse management it is customary to use the degree Celsius (°C) although at times when studying the physics of heat it is necessary to use kelvin or absolute temperature. The relationship to °C is quite simple, 0°C = 273 kelvin so 27°C = 300 kelvin (300K).

The unit of energy is the joule (J) and it takes 4.18 kJ to raise 1 kg of water (1 litre) through 1°C. The specific heat capacity of water = 4.18 kJ per kg per °C or 4.18 kJ kg^{-1} °C^{-1}. The use of containers of water for a heat storage source in the glasshouse allows us to calculate the amount of heat energy stored. The specific heat of water is defined as unity and the specific heat of other substances related to it. All common solids and liquids have a specific heat of less than unity, e.g. aluminium has a specific heat of 0.212. If this is multiplied by the specific heat capacity of water, as above, then the specific heat capacity of aluminium is 0.887 kJ kg^{-1} °C^{-1}; so aluminium may be heated to the same temperature as an equal quantity of water with much less energy.

Heat which is felt by the senses (or instruments) is called sensible heat and the degree of sensible heat in a body is measured by a thermometer; the addition or withdrawal of sensible heat varies the body temperature.

When water changes from the solid state of ice to a liquid state and then to a gas (water vapour) it is said to change in phase. At the point where these phase changes occur water absorbs (or gives out) heat which is not measurable by a thermometer, that is there is no change in temperature; this is latent heat. It takes about 335 kJ to change 1 kg of ice at 0°C into water and about 2442 kJ to change 1 kg of water at 25°C into water vapour.

The latent heat of vaporisation plays a very important part in glasshouse temperature control. An evaporative cooler evaporates water as air is forced through the cooler; the heat energy required to turn liquid water into a gas is taken from this air which is cooled. This action is also important in leaf cooling as described in Chapter 8.

Heat energy may be transferred by three methods, namely by conduction where the objects are in contact either directly or indirectly, e.g. the two surfaces of glass are in contact through the body of the glass which then transmits heat by conduction; by convection where transfer is by movement of the fluid molecules (air is a fluid); and finally by radiation which is by electromagnetic waves which require no medium through which to make the transfer.

It was once considered that the glasshouse became hot inside because SW radiation readily penetrated the glass and increased the heat energy in the floor, benches, plants and fittings and these radiated in the long wave band which could not pass through the glass, hence was trapped inside as heat energy. This is only partially correct. The inside surface of the glass is also heated and glass is not a very good insulator at the thickness at which it is used; although it does block LW radiation it does conduct heat to the outside atmosphere. Also trapped inside is hot air which accounts for the rise in temperature. If we wish to keep the glasshouse at about ambient outside air temperature then something like half the roof would need to be removed plus part of the wall to allow free convection air currents to flow.

The ability of a substance to insulate against heat loss is often referred to as its R value where R = d/k, the higher the R value the better the insulator. The material thickness is d and k is its thermal conductance (Table 12.2).

Table 12.2

List of thermal conductances where K is in
$W\ m^{-1}\ °C^{-1}$

Substance	k
Aluminium	240
Iron-steel	67–80
Brick	0.63–0.83
Glass	0.8–1
Water	0.6
Plant tissue	0.4 variable
Dry soil	0.17–0.33
Wet soil	1.2–3.3
Wood light	0.08
Wood dense	0.2
Non-aerated concrete	1.5
Aerated concrete	0.08
Cork	0.05
Rock wool	0.04
Still air	0.025
Turbulent air	> 100
Polystyrene	0.03

Consider a pane of glass where $d = 3$ mm or 0.003 m and $k = 0.8$ W m^{-1} °C^{-1}.

So $R = \dfrac{0.003\ \text{m}}{0.8\ \text{W m}^{-1}\ °\text{C}^{-1}} = 3.75 \times 10^{-3}$ m^2 °C per watt, a rather low figure.

As an alternative consider rock wool as an insulator where $d = 8$ cm and $k = 0.04$.

$R = \dfrac{0.08}{0.04} = 2$ (units usually omitted) which is quite a good insulator.

R values of material in series are additive, so for double glazing with 5 cm of air spacing between two layers of glass with the k of air = 0.024

$R = \dfrac{0.05}{0.024} = 2.1$ The insulating value of glass is so small compared to R = 2 it may be ignored.

An alternative to double glazing is the use of clear reinforced plastic material inside the glasshouse under the roof. This can provide quite deep air space (5 to 10 cm) between the plastic sheet and the glass, so giving a high R value. If the plastic is UV inhibited it lasts quite a long time. Additionally the plastic sheet may be used to cover a wall to the south or north of the glasshouse, depending on the hemisphere, to further reduce the loss of heat. If this inside roof cover is left in place in summer it diffuses the direct sunlight and so may obviate white-washing the glass or some other form of shading.

Materials

A fairly new material available is aerated concrete with a low k value of 0.08 which is nearly as good as cork but has the strength to form into a wall. Retailing as 'Supablocs', it comes in various widths from 75 mm to 200 mm. So even 100 mm blocks have an R value of 1.25 which provides good heat insulation for the lower 0.6 to 0.8 m of the glasshouse. They need a good concrete or masonary foundation and can be joined either with a 'Gluemortar' or ordinary mortar. However, for glasshouse use both external and internal walls need to be sealed and several commercial paints and sealers are available for this purpose. A data sheet on this material is available from landscaping and building sale yards. I have not used this material but have it earmarked for the construction of my next glasshouse; it should be ideal for a base wall about 0.8 m high upon which to stand the glass-holding framework.

An aluminium or steel framework with a k value of 67 to 240, although strong and long lasting, does constitute a 'heat-hole' in the house. It is interesting to calculate just how big a heat hole is, or would be, in your glasshouse using a metal framework, yet practically every glasshouse is constructed of such materials. This makes it almost mandatory, unless you are very rich, to have a special plastic liner inside the house to provide a poor man's double glazing to conserve heat. In some countries long thick plastic strips are available to fit externally over metal glazing bars to protect these from contact with cold air.

In the cold climate of Canada many glasshouses use wood, presumably light wood, for all structural members (perhaps they do not have termites there). This timber appears to be 50 mm × 150 mm on edge so as to obstruct the entry of light as little as possible. The 150 mm dimension gives strength and allows 600 mm glass panels to be used. As shown in Table 12.2 light wood has a k value of 0.08, similar to that of aerated concrete, but by building the whole house from timber the heat loss is reduced to a minimum. In Canada growers maximise their limited low angle radiation by sloping the roof to be normal to (i.e. at right angles to) the sun's rays for the major part of the daylight period. Often the north (shaded side) of the house is partly buried in an excavated hillside, and if the earth is kept dry by adequate drainage near the wall, the k value of 0.25 helps to conserve heat.

I have used, at latitude 35°, a glasshouse using a concrete block base to 0.6 m with a wooden framework for the walls holding double glazing and found this quite superior to the metal frame glass-down-to-the ground type in respect of humidity, temperature control and heat loss. As there are no kits for this type of house it requires some planning, time and ability to construct, but is worthwhile if forward planning is possible.

Opening and closing vents can become tiresome and require the presence of someone to do this at inconvenient times, so fitting auto-vents should be considered. These are about twice the price of manual vents but are worth the cost. They open and close by a heat sensitive gas in a cylinder and may be set to close tightly at a desired temperature, say 15°C. For the 5 × 3 m house three vents are usually sufficient: one high in the gable end opposite the door to clear away the hot air just under the roof and two below the benches to allow the entry of cool air. A fan, blow-in or exhaust, fitted high up in the opposite gable end, assists in removing the hot roof air as the temperature increases.

Heat conservation will be improved if the house is properly sealed. When there is a difference in air pressure between the inside and outside of the glasshouse a stream of air flows in or out through any holes, so we either lose warm air from the inside or admit cold air from the outside. Air entering a hole one cm in diameter will slow to 20% of its initial velocity when 20 cm inside the house and is by then well mixed with the inside air.

A hole equivalent to a missing pane of glass, say 40 cm square, could feed in cold air for a distance of 8 m before becoming mixed with house air and spread out over a width of 3 m. This could subject a large number of plants to an unacceptable blast of cold air. This would be typical of an open vent in winter. As cold air blowing on to a plant can cause leaf drop the additional cost of an auto-vent can be worthwhile.

In contrast to the above the air flow from the house to an opening such as an exhaust fan is quite different. The air flows from all directions at once and at a distance of one fan diameter from the fan inlet the air is moving at about 12% of the exit velocity. However, exhaust fans do not create turbulence as the air movement over the plants is very slow. A blow-in fan is needed to produce forced convection in the house, to replace CO_2 expended air and to bring in cooler air.

Cooling

There are several methods of cooling but all depend on the latent heat of vaporisation of water. The most popular is the evaporative cooler, which may replace one of the vents and the blow-in fan. Domestic models having a motor of 350 watts or more are large enough for a 5 m × 3 m house. These are relatively cheap and are mounted in a suitably sized wall gap (say 0.6 m wide and 0.4 m high) near to ground level. The other vent should be positioned so that the cooled air must circulate around the house before it exits. Evaporative coolers work best when the outside air is warm and dry. Theoretically they can drop the temperature of the air flow down to the wet bulb temperature of the outside air but in practice this is never attained. Table 12.3 shows the cooling ability of the device for various temperatures of outside air.

Table 12.3

The cooling capacity of an evaporative cooler

Outside air temperature		RH	Incoming air cooled to
dry bulb	wet bulb		
35	24	0.4	26
35	28	0.6	30
40	22	0.2	24
25	21	0.7	23

All temperatures are in °C.
In the last example the low temperature and moist air are satisfastory.
Opening the door would give sufficient cooling.

The use of an evaporative cooler poses a problem similar to manual vents. Some-one needs to be present to monitor the water level and fill the tank when it empties, so some auto system is advantageous. I use a small magnet attached to the water level indicator arm protruding through the front of the unit. As this arm falls the magnet operates a magnetic reed switch (as used in burglar alarms). This closes a 24 volt water solenoid which opens and supplies water to the tank via a hose. After about 15 seconds sufficient water enters the tank to raise the magnet and the flow stops. It is a sort of electrical ball and cock system and a circuit diagram is given in Fig. 12.1. It is simple to construct and cheap; anyone with some radio or electronic know-how can construct it.

A simple alternative to the evaporative cooler is a blow-in fan fitted in front of a below-bench vent with two misting jets located in the air stream. Both the fan and the misting jet solenoid can be controlled by separate thermostats set, as a suggestion, at 22°C and 28°C respectively. Even on hot days this system can control the temperature in the glasshouse to below 30°C. Domestic fans seldom have enough power for glasshouse cooling and a 25 cm or 30 cm commercial type fan is recommended.

Some growers try to control temperature solely by the use of shade cloth and open vents. If the shading is heavy enough this may prevent leaf burn in summer but it generally permits the leaf temperature to exceed the optimum for maximum photosynthesis. Additionally, the heavy shading limits the light available for photosynthesis and many orchids are 'high light' plants.

Another method of cooling is to spray a fine mist from misting jets in the top of the glasshouse and let this fall through the air and over plants. This mist is controlled by a water solenoid and by a thermostat set, say, to 30°C, but it is necessary to have a timing device, usually electronic, in the circuit to allow 10 seconds misting and 30 seconds off. The misting will occur only when the temperature reaches 30°C (or whatever) and if this temperature persists for some time the glasshouse will not be flooded due to the duty cycle of the timer. These timing devices are commonly used for a variety of purposes and are easily constructed. Refer Fig. 12.2. Also many thermostats have a high differential and take quite a fall in temperature before they turn off, so the timer tends to overcome this difficulty.

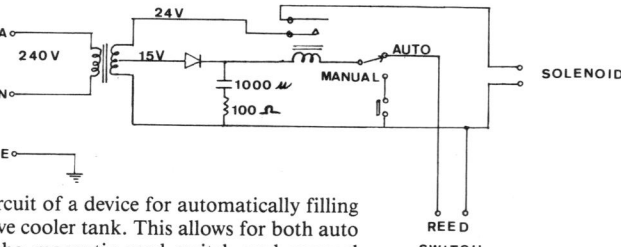

Fig. 12.1   Circuit of a device for automatically filling the evaporative cooler tank. This allows for both auto control via the magnetic reed switch and manual control via a push button. This device operates from mains voltage and should only be constructed by a person experienced in electrics

Fig. 12.2   Timing circuit for mister control. The time may be increased by increasing the value of the capacitor. The LED lights when 555 pin 3 is + and relay opens. The LED indicates a lock-out of the misters. The relay contacts are normally closed and supply 24 v power to the misting solenoid via the thermostat

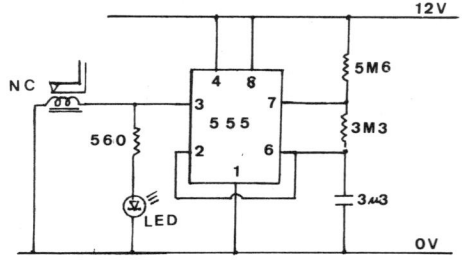

Heating

All heating costs money either through direct outlay or in capital expenditure, so it is good economics to minimise heat loss. Heat holes due to metal glazing bars and imperfect sealing have already been mentioned in respect of heat loss. Plastic liners inside the glasshouse conserve warmth as explained earlier.

So called solar houses have become popular where the incoming heat from radiation during the daytime is stored in water contained in many 5 litre black plastic jars or even in 50 litre black plastic drums. Both of these must be placed to receive full sunshine during the daylight period. When the glasshouse temperature falls heat is released from the water into the air, probably assisted by a fan. An alternative system is to duct the hot air from under the glasshouse roof, via a fan, into a rock pile (using 25 mm stones) housed in a concrete block structure above the ground and used to support a bench or two, or buried under the floor. At night another fan exhausts the warm air into the glasshouse. If the rock pile is to be buried into the ground it is desirable to avoid heat loss by surrounding the concrete block structure with thick batts of styrofoam material 50 mm or greater in thickness.

In some cases it may be convenient to excavate the ground and build the base part of the glasshouse into the ground, so protecting part of the structure from heat loss due to wind. The excavation should be large enough to fit styrofoam batts on the external surface of the concrete blocks before back-filling with earth.

By far the most efficient and clean method of heating is by electricity, whether by a fan-heater or a hot water tank of 300 litres capacity located in the glasshouse. If this latter can be heated at off-peak rates more than once per day (as allowed by some electrical authorities) it is very economical. The hot water is circulated by a pump through 4–5 cm pipes (copper preferred) under the benches and the pump is controlled by a thermostat. This type of system will usually maintain a modest glasshouse at 13°C in moderate winter temperatures. A lot depends on leakage and wind temperature and strength around the house. To avoid hot spots an internal fan should blow air over the pipes. This system at least provides basic warming which may then be supplemented by a fan heater (2000 watts) which comes on if the temperature falls below that required from the hot water system.

As an alternative a fan heater alone may be used. For a 5 m × 3 m glasshouse a 2000 watt heater specifically made for glasshouse use, such as the 'Maxi-Grow' Turbo-Aire 2000 made by Ridgehaven Electrical, St Agnes, South Australia 5097, is suggested.

Do not attempt to heat the glasshouse with domestic bar radiators; all they do is produce hot spots and cold spots. Single bar water heaters do much the same, hence the need for forced air movement to distribute heat. The fans in domestic fan heaters are usually not powerful enough to heat any but the smallest of houses.

Measuring glasshouse temperature

Air is a poor conductor of heat. If four thermometers are placed in the glasshouse four different readings are likely, even allowing for the disagreement of readings when all four are immersed in a flask of water. Commercial mercury-in-glass thermometers have poor accuracy. As a standard, use a good 0 to 50°C laboratory thermometer having an accuracy no worse than 0.5°C. If one has an accurate, well made wet and dry bulb thermometer the dry bulb may be used to read glasshouse temperature provided that it is aspirated and shielded from the sun. In any case it is necessary to aspirate the wet bulb to obtain accurate

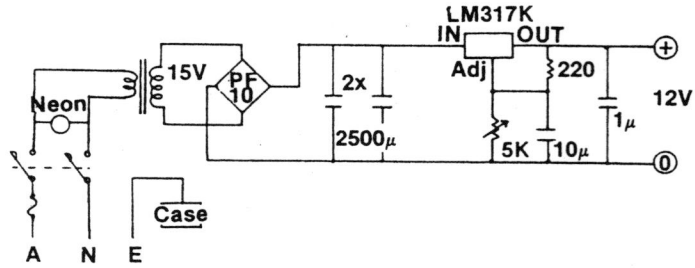

Fig. 12.3   The LM317K is fitted with a heat sink

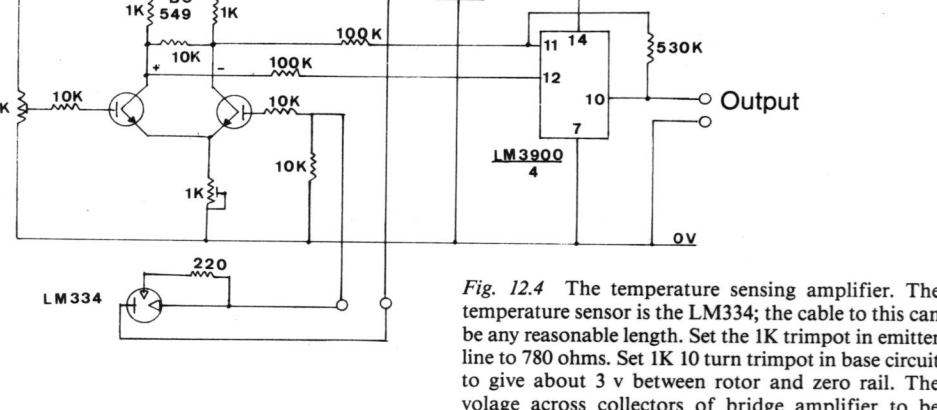

Fig. 12.4   The temperature sensing amplifier. The temperature sensor is the LM334; the cable to this can be any reasonable length. Set the 1K trimpot in emitter line to 780 ohms. Set 1K 10 turn trimpot in base circuit to give about 3 v between rotor and zero rail. The volage across collectors of bridge amplifier to be between 0.5 and 1.5 v depending on temperature. Ensure that polarity of collector voltage is as shown

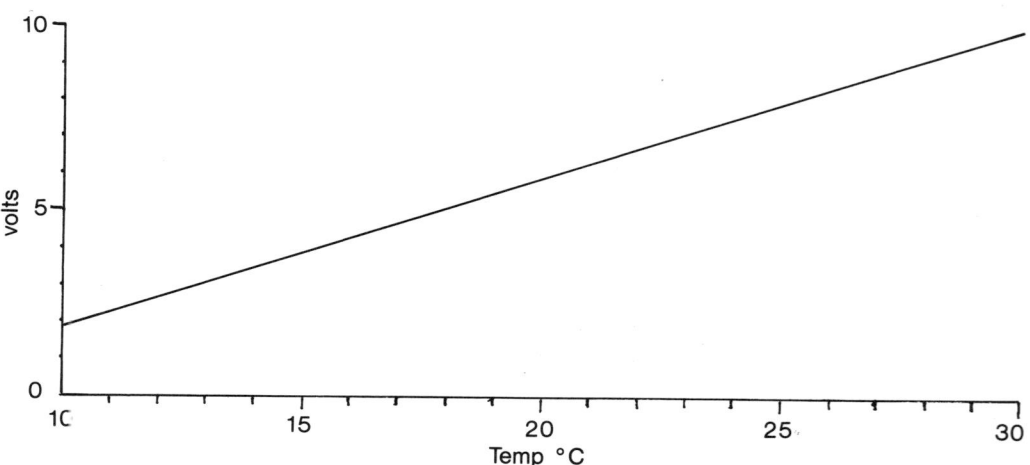

Fig. 12.5   Measure temperature at LM334 accurately and from graph determine desired voltage at output of LM3900. Adjust 1K trimpot in base of BC549 to give this voltage

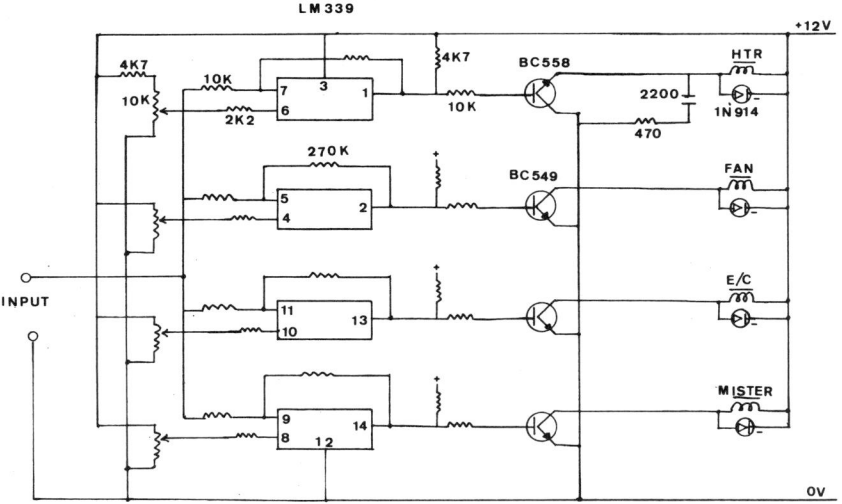

Fig. 12.6 The comparator circuit. If a misting on-off timer is used (Fig. 12.2) pin 3 of 555 may be connected via a diode 1N914 (not shown) to pin 8 of LM339 in lieu of using a relay. Rising volts on pin 9 turns mister relay to on, but application of 12 v + to pin 8 from pin 3 (555) will lock off this comparator section

readings. Aspirating air should be at 3 m s⁻¹ and to provide this I find a 240 volt fan made for cooling small computers is ideal. It runs continuously, consumes 11 watts and is only 8 cm square (Tandy part number 273-9542). When this is housed in white plastic storm water piping (10 × 8 cm rectangular and 9 cm round) it provides adequate aspirated air flow for the wet and dry bulbs, for the 0–50°C mercury thermometer in the piping and the electronic thermostat sensor element adjacent to the mercury thermometer.

Position this assembly at some convenient place, usually in the centre of the glasshouse at eye level, and make this your measurement centre. As far as possible all thermostats should be placed at the measurement centre so they will react to aspirated air, but there is a problem. Thermostats are often large and this grouping is difficult. For those who wish to use electronic temperature sensing and control I have added here the circuitry for a four unit thermostat using just the one sensor which can be aspirated without difficulty. No constructional details are given as it is intended that only a person who can read the circuitry should build this equipment. The captions give a few tips on adjustment.

I use a fan heater, a fan, an evaporative cooler and a mister as the four items controlled, but this may be changed to suit your needs. The differential between on-off is from 0.2°C to 0.5°C which is quite good for a thermostat.

Wind

Fig. 12.7 shows how the warm air inside the glasshouse becomes colder near the glass. The difference in temperature between the inside and outside of the glass is very small (say 1°C). In conditions of no wind the temperature outside the glass pane decreases slowly with distance.

If there is a wind the air outside the glasshouse is removed more rapidly than occurs with free convection alone. This results in a sudden lowering of the temperature at the outside of the glass and an increase in heat loss through the glass. This is equivalent to having a lower outside temperature and is called the wind chill factor. For example if the actual outside

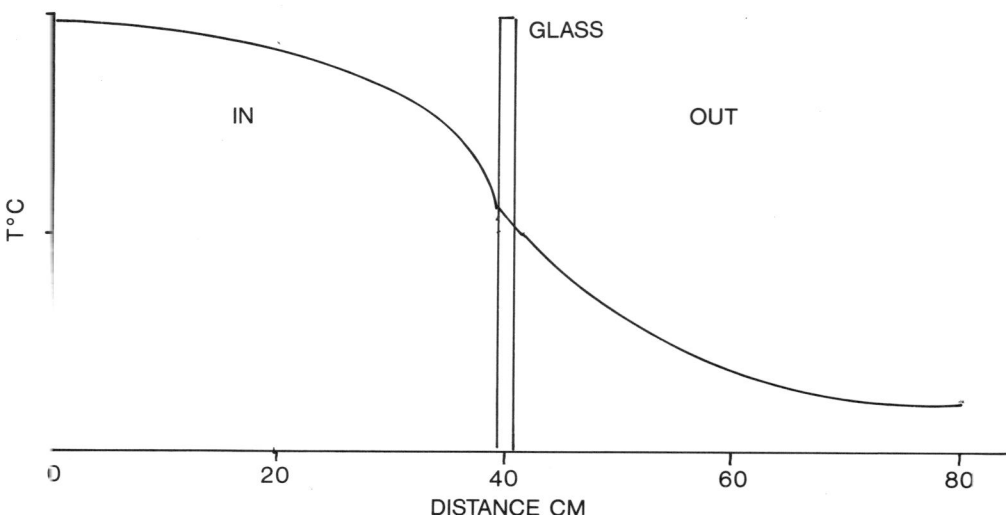

Fig. 12.7 Generalised diagram showing temperature variation in and outside a glasshouse in a no-wind condition. The glass, at the thickness used, is a poor insulator and the temperature drop across it is very small. If wind occurs, the effective temperature outside the glass panel drops sharply in response to both wind temperature and wind speed

temperature in calm conditions is -10°C, a wind of only 5.5 m s^{-1} will reduce this to an effective temperature of -20°C.

Even moderately cold winds at moderate speeds will reduce the air temperature outside the glass and this has led to the use of blankets or curtains mounted externally against the glass walls. These trap the layer of air between the glass and the curtain and prevent the rapid heat loss through the glass which occurs when forced convection due to wind is present. At present this curtain has to be manually closed at night and opened in the early morning but it seems inevitable that it will eventually be motorised and actuated by a light sensitive device via an electronic circuit. One difficulty in this respect is to seal the gap at the top of the curtain, between it and the wall, as free convection occurring through this space will admit more cool air.

Other equipment

Every glasshouse should be equipped with a minimum-maximum thermometer to read and record these temperatures while you are not present. The push button type where blue markers descend by gravity is recommended and it should be hung near the measurement centre. Also one hung outside the glasshouse in the shade is useful.

An inside/outside thermometer is also valuable as it gives an instantaneous reading of how good the heating, cooling and sealing of the house may be.

Chapter 14 mentions a wind speed indicator, made in the USA and marketed in Australia by Dick Smith Electronics. This is useful to measure the wind speed provided by fans and the evaporative cooler.

Solar trapping houses

For those who wish to experiment with solar trapping houses it is necessary to know the angle of the sun above the horizon at noon for a mid-winter day (21 June in southern hemisphere and 22 December for northern hemisphere). This may be calculated for all practical purposes by using the following formula.

Noon sun elevation = 90 – latitude – sin t(23.5)

whre t is the number of days since the last equinox (21 March for southern hemisphere and 23 September for northern hemisphere).

As an example for latitude 42½ S.
21 March to 21 June = 91 days = t
sin t = 0.99 so 0.99(23.5) $\doteq$ 23.5
hence the noon elevation is 90 – 42.5 – 23.5 = 24° above horizon.

Those who have some knowledge of trigonometry will realise that this angle will remain within 2 or 3° from 26 May to 19 July, which covers 54 days over mid-winter. The sloping roof will be normal to (at right angles to) the sun's rays at noon so the roof slope should be 90–24 = 66° to the horizontal.

The term 'noon' has been used here rather loosely. Strictly solar noon is meant, which can be quite different from clock noon, but solar noon calculation is beyond the scope of this text. In any case it does not matter as solar noon will probably occur somewhere between 1100 hours and 1300 hours and the sun angle remains substantially constant over this period.

Naturally, with heating at a premium all previous comments about minimising heat loss are important.

Reference

Kozai T., Goudriaan J. and Kimura M. (1978) *Light Transmission and Photosynthesis in Greenhouses.* Centre for Agricultural Publishing and Documentation, Wageningen.

13 The Origin and Dispersal of Orchids

This chapter has the elements of a detective story. One possesses certain facts, some theories and a good deal of speculation and a little conjecture. Speculation is based on the individual's interpretation of facts and theories and this interpretation often differs between individuals, nevertheless it is usually fruitful to hear the views of others and a great deal of scientific progress has been the outcome of speculation. Conjecture arises when one is obliged to fill in gaps in our knowledge because sufficient factors and theories do not exist. Conjecture often proves to be incorrect, but occasionally intelligent guessing gives a lead to some-one else to whom this viewpoint had not occurred.

The contents of this paper rely heavily on many disciplines but it is not a dissertation on any one or more of these, hence the authorities are not quoted for all of the statements made. The discussion is kept at a general level to give orchid growers an appreciation of origin and dispersal. Some floristic regions are suggested and defined so that orchids can be allocated to these to show distribution, however, it is not possible to define these regions by use of orchids alone, one must rely on the evolution and distribution of many genera of flowering plants.

The movement of land masses over the last 140 million years is an important factor for plant origins and dispersal so some weight has been given to this. The regions we now call India, Southeast Asia, New Guinea and Australia are important orchid areas and the movement and juxtaposition of these over the millenia make fascinating reading. The whole question of land mass movement is given a general treatment sufficient for an understanding of the subject by the non-specialist. A list for further reading is also given for those readers who wish to pursue this subject further.

The effect of mankind cannot be ignored. Many plants, including orchids, had some value to early man, probably either decorative or medicinal or for food (Lawler 1981) and were doubtless dispersed by man either deliberately or accidentally. This is conjecture as there is no definite evidence of this, although it appears likely.

The Angiospermae

Within the plant Kingdom seed bearing plants form a Division called Spermatophyta. This is subdivided into those plants bearing naked seeds, i.e. not encased, the Gymnospermae, and those bearing seeds in a case, the Angiospermae or flowering plants. The word angiosperm is derived from the Greek *angeion,* a container, and *sperma,* a seed, so the seeds are packaged into a case. This gave the angiosperm improved fecundity over naked seed plants by minimising predation and dessication, thereby enabling the Angiospermae to reproduce in a climate becoming drier. The orchid plant is an angiosperm so the history of these is of some importance when tracing orchid development.

In 1903 Charles Darwin wrote of the mystery surrounding the apparent sudden appearance, in abundance, of the flowering plants in the fossil strata of the Cretaceous Period (Table 13.1) and the lack of fossil evidence that proto-angiosperms existed prior to this period.

Table 13.1

Geological time scale
Derived from composite data from various sources.
The times are quoted as millions of years before present.

Time	Era	Period	Epoch	
0	↑	Quaternary	Recent	
			10 000 years	
2.5			Pleistocene	
	Cenozoic		Pliocene	7
		Tertiary	Miocene	26
			Oligocene	38
			Eocene	54
65	↓		Paleocene	65
	↑	Cretaceous		
140	Mesozoic			
		Jurassic		
200	↓			

Angiospermae fossil remains are in the form of leaves, fruits, flowers and pollen and cannot always be attributed to extant families or genera of flowering plants. However, in the past plant fossils fell into disrepute partly due to the propensity to publish 'identifications' on very meagre evidence, so that today's paleobotanists tend to disregard this early material. Pollen is very resistant to decay and from an evolutionary point of view very conservative, so its identification is more definite; however, pollen is easily dispersed and finding it at a site may simply mean it has been transported over a distance. Likewise absence from the fossil record is no indication that some plants did not form part of the vegetation. We can never hope to have a complete picture of the vegetation existing at any period of time; perhaps the plant did not fossilise or we have not yet found the fossils.

Orchid plants are singularly devoid of fossil remains so their origin and dispersal is even more speculative than for trees and shrubs. The following reasons have been advanced for lack of orchid fossils although some of these are not too convincing. For example, the epiphytic habit removes orchids from the aquatic conditions conducive to fossilisation. Firstly, not all orchids are epiphytes and if they are surely when forest trees die and fall their epiphyte loads are just as much on the moist ground or swamp as the tree. Other reasons given are 1) the wet tropics are areas of rapid decay, 2) herbaceous habit, 3) production of pollinia rather than individual pollen grains and the disposal of pollinia by animal vectors, 4) minute seeds, easily degradable (Schmid & Schmid 1977). Obviously not all orchids grow in the wet tropics, other herbaceous plants are fossilised and not all pollinia are carted away by animals.

The most likely orchid fossil is *Protorchis monorchis* showing three leaves and fibrous roots attached to a tuber, found in Italy and attributed to the Eocene 54–38 million years BP (before present). One tropical botanist expressed the opinion that this sterile specimen, (i.e. no flowers or fruits) might be any tuberous plant with juvenile leaves and that the specimen is hardly evidence for the fossil record of the Orchidaceae. His comment seems well founded.

The origin of the Angiospermae is still not resolved. They are usually thought to be monophyletic, i.e. derived from a single ancestral stock. Because some basic features are common to all angiosperms it is difficult to conceive that identical evolutionary development should have taken place more than once. Other authors have considered them to be polyphyletic, i.e. from more than one ancestor or of mixed ancestry. If this is correct the question arises, what caused the ancestors to produce angiosperms almost simultaneously?

The Angiospermae has two Classes, the monocotyledons (Liliopsida) and the dicotyledons (Magnoliopsida), and many authors have regarded the monocotyleons (to which orchids belong) as being of later evolution than the dicotyledons. There seems little evidence to substantiate this. Monosulcate pollen (having one groove) is a primitive characteristic and is found in monocotyledons and some Orders of dicotyledons regarded as primitive because of several features, i.e. Magnoliales and Nymphaeales. This seems to give support to the idea that monocotyledons arose early and monosulcate pollen has been found in sediments dated to 127 million years BP.

Land mass movement

In this section the papers of Powell, Johnson & Veevers (1981), Keast (1981) and others are used to explain the southern continental disposition. Northern land mass movement is taken from various authors mentioned in 'further reading'.

In the late 1960s and 1970s a scientific revolution occurred: global plate tectonics was accepted by geophysicists. Plant geographers were quick to show their appreciation of this new outlook which replaced their land bridges by moving land masses. Land bridges between continents and islands had always been a doubtful explanation and their non-existence in modern times could only be accounted for by their sinking beneath the sea. This philosophy was handicapped by no one being able to find such bridges. Some botanists had the place of origin of plants distributed over areas which today are in close proximity but in the Cretaceous and early Tertiary were vast distances apart. Plate tectonics has virtually made these places of origin untenable.

The mapping of the ocean floor, deep sea drilling, magnetic anomalies, fracture zones and paleomagnetism have all contributed to our knowledge of land mass movement (continental drift) to such an extent that the overall pattern is known. As the subject is vital to understanding plant distribution, a broad outline is given here. This leads on to the possible area or origin of the orchids and the delineation of floristic regions so that extant orchids can be grouped into these.

The maps shown in this section are not meant to be geographically accurate. Their form is only such as to enable land masses to be identified with those currently existing. Where doubt may exist, such as with islands, these are identified by suitable lettering. The outlines of modern continents are for convenience only as the plates upon which they stand are much larger.

The earth has a radius of 6370 km and consists of an inner and outer core, both metallic and molten. This is surrounded by the Mantle which is about 2900 km thick, comprising 83% of the earth's volume, and consists of red-hot rock. The outer surface of the Mantle is cooler rock but is still soft enough to have fluidity. This is the Asthenosphere upon which the outer crust of cold solid rock floats. This latter is the Lithosphere which varies in thickness from 30 to 40 km under continents or even thicker under mountain ranges to 5 to 10 km under oceans.

The Lithosphere is fractured into 10 large plates of rock, several smaller ones and fragments broken from the larger plates. These plates jostle one another and move around on the Asthenosphere by forces within the Mantle and sea floor spreading from upwelling of magna from within the Mantle. Each large plate has a constructive edge and a destructive edge. At this latter the plate is being subducted or pushed down into the Mantle, sometimes to a depth of 700 km, where it loses its identity and becomes part of the Mantle. The subduction rate varies from 5 to 10 cm or more per year and occurs at ocean trenches, which abound in the ocean floor as any good ocean topographical map will show. These subduction zones are unstable and form the major earthquake and volcanic zones of the world.

The constructive edge of the plate occurs along the ocean ridges. These form an under-ocean mountain range totalling 40 000 km in length and which winds through all the oceans; it is the longest mountain range in the world. It is at these ocean ridges that new rock material, molten from the Mantle, is added to the plate; hence the name constructive edge. The rate of plate movement is around 10 km or greater each million years, as measured from the upwelling in the mid-ocean ridge to each constructive plate boundary. There is some doubt whether the plates are pulled into the subduction trench and the ocean ridge upwelling closes the gap between plates, or whether this upwelling at the constructive margin pushes the plate into the subduction zone at its destructive edge.

The continents and islands sit upon these plates or fragments and slowly shift about as the plates move into the subduction zone and are built up at their opposite edge. The above explanation is introductory to the main consideration, namely the position, proximity and movement of land masses from the time flowering plants appeared to the present time.

Some 200 million years BP or even earlier the total land mass of the earth was gathered together into one supercontinent named Pangaea (all lands) which covered 200 000 km² or 40% of the earth's surface. The remaining surface was covered by the ancestral ocean, Panthalassa, which also filled a large bight between Africa and Eurasia named the Tethys

Sea. Map 1 is constructed as a composite of several ideas on the shape and fit of the land masses of Pangaea and for our purposes it is adequate. Panthalassa became the Pacific Ocean and the Tethys Sea became the Mediterranean.

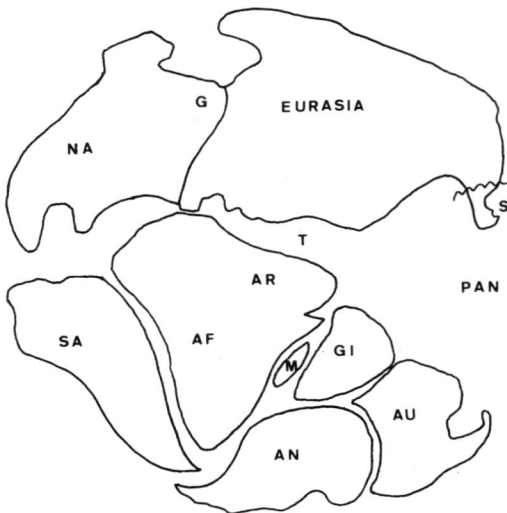

Map 1   The universal land mass of Pangaea separated 180 million years ago into the northern supercontinent of Laurasia containing North America (NA), Greenland (G) and the present continent of Eurasia. Sunderland (S) was attached rather indeterminately, as shown by the wavy line, to Eurasia which was rotating clockwise.

The southern supercontinent of Gondwanaland was composed of South America (SA), Africa (AF) with Arabia (AR) attached, Greater India (GI), Antarctica (AN) and Australia (AU). This latter is shown with the southern part of New Guinea attached to the tip of Cape York. Madagascar (M) is sandwiched between Greater India and Africa.

The continents of Gondwanaland are joined at their plate margins thus closing the spaces shown between them.

The Tethys Sea (T) became the Mediterranean Sea when the clockwise rotation of Laurasia closed the gap. The ancestral ocean Panthalassa (PAN) covered the remainder of the globe.

Gondwanaland drawn from data by Powell *et al.* (1981). Laurasia drawn from data from various sources.

About 180 million years BP, still in the Jurassic period, rifting occurred which broke Pangaea into two land masses, Laurasia in the north and Gondwanaland in the south. The rifting rotated North America and its Europe-Asia neighbour in a clockwise direction, opening up to the sea the present Gulf of Mexico and the east coast of the present USA which now lay in an east-west position. The only point of contact between Laurasia and Gondwanaland occurred at the peninsula, now Spain, and the coast of Africa. The rotation of Laurasia reduced the size of the Tethys Sea until about 65 million years BP it was closed to form the Mediterranean. This clockwise rotation of Laurasia is important for it ultimately brings the area marked Sunderland down to the equator. About 135 million years BP rifts appeared which separated Greenland and Europe-Asia from North America.

Gondwanaland consisted of the continents we now call Antarctica, South America, Africa, Australia and India, with other smaller parts like Madagascar and New Zealand. Antarctica formed the link between all the other continents, but it was not the Antarctica we know today; it was not ice covered and at least had vegetative cover around its coastal region prior to 37 million years BP. As late as the mid-Paleoene epoch (58 million years BP), oxygen isotope ratios suggest a mean annual sea surface temperature of 18° to 20°C for the Campbell Plateau to which New Zealand is attached (Kemp 1981). Antarctica did not develop ice cover until the mid-Eocene (45 million years BP) and this cover was limited to regions around the South Pole, so the angiosperms arising somewhere in the early Cretaceous (140 million years BP) would have been able to migrate to other continents via Antarctica. Drake's Passage between South America and Antartica opened 23 million years BP in the Oligocene, allowing circumpolar oceanic circulation and climatically isolating Antarctica. The temperature of the waters of the Campbell Plateau dropped to 6° to 7°C. In the Miocene (7 million years BP) ice cover of the Antarctic was complete.

The earliest break-away from Gondwanaland occurred in the western section during the Cretaceous about 110 million years BP when South America began to move westward away from Africa, the southern part of South America moving first. The rift between the continents developed and movement continued at 5 to 10 cm per year, so for a long time the continents were in close proximity. The final separation occurred at the Angola-Guinea basin off the west coast of Africa. Africa appears to have moved northward separating from Antarctica about 90 billion years BP.

South America continued to be tied to Antarctica, despite its break-away from southern Africa, by the Scotia Ridge, which today includes the Falklands, South Georgia, Southern Sandwich and the Southern Orkney Islands. This ridge was also close to the southern tip of Africa during the early phase of separation until the middle Cretaceous. The break between South America and Antarctica did not occur until 30 to 40 million years BP.

Madagascar was located some 15° north of its present position against Tanzania-Kenya and Africa was 15° south of its present position. A rift developed which carved Madagascar away from Africa some time after 80–90 million years BP.

As well as Antarctica being a connecting land mass between continents, there was also a land connection from the west coast of Australia, as far north as Exmouth Gulf, across Greater India and Madagascar to Africa during the early Cretaceous. About 125 million years BP Greater India broke free from Antarctica and drifted very slowly northward (at a rate of 3 to 5 cm per year). During this period the west coast of India remained in contact with Madagascar and Africa. For the next 45 million years the latitude of India changed by only 10°. The rift which separated India from Antarctica and Australia also caused the slow movement of Australia southward to a latitude of 40 to 60° (Johnson, Powell & Veevers 1976).

Australia began to move northwards leaving Antarctica 53 million years BP, although direct migration between Antarctica and Tasmania may still have been possible via the South Tasman Rise until 38 million years BP when separation was complete.

At this point we leave both India and Australia drifting northward and look further eastward to a land mass which today contains New Zealand and islands to the north. Whereas Australia was joined to Antarctica at Wilkes Land in east Antarctica the New Zealand mass was joined to west Antarctica at Marie Byrd Land. Around 80 millon years BP the land mass containing the Campbell Plateau, New Zealand, Lord Howe Rise and Norfolk Ridge broke away from Antarctica. The Campbell Plateau foundered and the above-water lands today are New Zealand, Lord Howe Island, New Caledonia and Norfolk Island, all of which have been isolated from Australia for a long period of time.

That part of the Eurasian plate called Sunderland was coming southward due to the clockwise rotation of the Eurasian plate and at the same time being pushed westward by the Pacific plate. Map 2 shows Sunderland as it is today located on its own section of plate. It has been proposed by McElhinny, Haile and Crawford (1974) that the Malay Peninsula was not firmly attached to mainland Eurasia in Cretaceous times and occupied a low latitude of 15° north about 140 million years BP, undergoing a 70° clockwise rotation while at this latitude.

In the early Paleocene (65 million years BP) Greater India broke contact with Madagascar and continued to drift northwards, this time at a fast rate exceeding 20 cm per year. During this travel the continent scraped alongside the western edge of Sunderland until finally, 55 million years BP, it collided with the southern margins of Asia. After Greater India lodged against Asia the islands of Sunderland continued westward across the ocean track of the northeastern coast of Greater India.

During this time Australia was drifting northward. The latitude for the last 58 million years of one easily identifiable point, the tip of Cape York peninsula, is shown in Table 13.2. The northern edge of the Australian plate was over 600 km further north and carried a small land mass north of Cape York. This is now identified as southern New Guinea from about 138°E to 144°E longitude.

Table 13.2

Northward movement of Australia
Measured at tip of Cape York Peninsula.

million years BP	latitude S
58	40°
37	30°
30	25°
20	20°
0	12°

New Guinea is of special interest as it carries a large orchid flora and is of composite structure; the southern part from the Australian plate while the central and northern parts come from the Bismarck plate. Both the Bismarck and Solomon Island plates are thought to be fragments from the Pacific plate.

In the early Tertiary the Bismarck plate lay parallel to the north Queensland coast but was pushed north and west by the moving Pacific plate and made a 90° anticlockwise rotation coming to rest against the top of the Australian plate at what is now southern New Guinea (Audley-Charles, Carter & Milson 1972). The now northern edge of the Bismarck plate was submerged, but continued northern movement of the Australian plate raised this above sea leavel and possibly contributed to the mountain range in central New Guinea. This provided a whole new land area, previously uninhabited, from the mid-Miocene to which both tropical sea-level flora and temperature mountain flora could migrate. The adjacent Solomon Island fragment followed the Bismarck plate and became an extension of the latter.

A near collision between the Australian plate and Sunderland was averted by the latter moving westward out of Australia's way by 15 million years BP. Between this time and 10 million years BP the northern margin of the Australian plate, now including New Guinea, collided with the Lesser Sunda Islands in the Banda Sea and pushed these northward by an estimated 800 km and rotated some of them. These islands became the Sunda Arc and include Lombok in the west, Timor and Tanibar in the east, Sulawesi, the Halmahera, Ceram and assorted small islands in the north. They are separated from and have no long term connection with Sunderland. The well known Wallace Line separates the Sunda Arc from Sunderland by passing through the Makassar Straight and southward between Lombok and

Bali. A counterpart to this line has been proposed in the east, separating the Australian plate and New Guinea from the Sunda Arc (Mayr 1944). These lines are shown dashed on Map 2.

To the east of the Southwest Pacific Margin of New Zealand and New Caledonia there is Oceania consisting of Fiji and many other islands. Fiji is considered to have evolved in Tertiary and Quaternary times from volcanic eruption built up on part of the Pacific plate. The origin of the other islands is not clear. Perhaps they once lay closer together and have been separated by ocean floor spreading.

It now remains to bring North America and South America into contact again. After the rifting of North America from Greenland and Eurasia, the North American plate and the South American plate underwent some significant relative movement and remained separated until the late Tertiary. There was considerable volcanic upwelling to form part of Central America. South America moved northwards from 38 to 9 million years BP to join with North America. The geology of Central America and the Caribbean is difficult to resolve but it is probable that this area is comparatively young.

Origin and dispersal

In discussing the possible origin of the Orchidaceae the following ground rules are accepted and apply.

1. The concepts of continental drift and plate tectonics have moved from the domain of theory to accepted fact. A plant geographer cannot be on tenable ground by retaining theories not reconcilable with these concepts. Therefore, it is not possible to uphold theories which involve sunken land bridges proposed by early biogeographers or centres of origin which extend across areas at present in close proximity but in the Cretaceous were widely separated.

2. The above in no way negates later dispersal across island arcs, e.g. the Scotia Ridge, particularly where shallow sea depths occur and maximal ice accretion, especially in the Arctic, lowered sea levels and exposed land.

3. Flowering plants, the Angiospermae, first appeared in the early Cretaceous 140 million years ago. This chapter is only concerned with these plants in that orchids are part of the Subdivision Angiospermae, so orchids could not have preceded this Period.

4. The Orchidaceae is the largest family of flowering plants, having a nominal 700 genera and a nominal 25 000 species. This appears to indicate a high evolutionary rate over a long period since the early Cretaceous.

5. The geophytic orchid is universally regarded as being more primitive than the epiphyte which evolved in later times. The epiphyte is not simply a geophyte that went to live in trees; it required a much more pronounced evolutionary change for this to occur. Most geophytes seem to possess food storage organs below ground level. These are commonly called tubers but initial examination shows that they are probably swollen root stocks similar to those of *Dahlia,* as the roots and shoots are derived from one end of the root stocks. These roots commonly possess root hairs to extract nutrients and water from the soil. Many epiphytes possess food storage stems rather than root stocks which have now disappeared.

The roots are covered with velamen rather than root hairs; the velamen soaks up water and provides a heat-reflecting surface and an effective boundary layer against water vapour loss from the root.

While a monophyletic origin of the orchid is assumed here there seems to be little reason why the epiphytic mode of life could not have arisen independently in several places. Many epiphytes are morphologically different: some have pseudobulbs (so called), others just have long stems, others have minimal stems and thick leaves, and yet others consist of roots only arising from an insignificant stem point.

6. The seed of Orchidaceae has been considered highly dispersable but unlike other seeds which are endowed with considerable endosperm, the orchid seed needs its complementary fungal symbiote. Fortunately for dispersal this fungus is not species specific except in rare cases. It is ubiquitous, occurring naturally over a wide geographical range. Some have asserted that the orchid seed's small size and light weight enables dispersal by the wind which can also disperse fungal spores. I feel a lot of dispersal can be by birds, either in the soil clinging to their feet or by electrostatic attraction to the keratin of their feathers. For dispersal over continents the feet of reptiles and other animals could also be relevant.

Short distance dispersal by these methods is clearly possible. The re-vegetation of the island Krakatoa is a modern example. The vegetation on this island was destroyed by a massive volcanic eruption in 1883, but by 1896 three orchids, all geophytes, were found there. The first epiphyte was a fern found in 1906; by 1928 23 epiphytes were present, 13 of these being orchids. By 1933 the orchids growing there had increased to 17 epiphytes and 18 geophytes. The fungus must also have been transported to the island, presumably by wind-borne spores or by birds. By 1913 there were 30 species of land and freshwater birds inhabiting the island. Krakatoa is about 50 km from both Java and Sumatra which minimises the time taken for dispersal and both of these islands are rich in orchid flora.

Long distance dispersal is another matter and is scorned by some plant geographers. However, one cannot deny the existence of vegetation on Hawaii and Fiji, which are roughly the same size. The Hawaiian Islands have never been anywhere near any continental mass. They have been produced *in situ* by the Pacific plate moving over a 'hot spot' volcano penetrating deep into the mantle. This volcano exists today as Kilauea, possibly the most studied volcano in the world.

The 1729 species and varieties of plants on Hawaii can be traced back evolutionary-wise to 272 ancestral immigrant species (Fosberg 1963). This would require only one successful new immigration each 37 000 years (Smith 1982). The Hawaiian vegetation is Indo-Pacific 40%, Austral 16.5%, American 18%, Pan-tropic 12.5% and the remainder obscure (Gillett 1972). The number of orchids is just three.

Compare this with Fiji which has 451 genera, but these islands are closer to New Guinea and the Solomons so the distance for dispersal is not so great. There are 113 species in 38 genera of orchids in Fiji (taken from Williams 1938, compiled from collections made in Fiji and from specimens in various herbaria).

In 1960 Garay proposed that the origin of the Orchidaceae occurred in the 'Asiatic Tropics', possibly Malaysia, in the Cretaceous on the basis that the most primitive extant orchid, *Neuwiedia,* occurs there. It also grows in Sumatra and Java. No mention was made of plate tectonics and moving land masses, but in 1960 this had not been accepted fully by geophysicists let alone by biogeographers, so it was a reasonable speculation that this was the area of origin.

The area known today as Sunderland, which includes Malaysia, was somewhat loosely and indeterminately attached to the eastern part of the Eurasian plate as described earlier, so in the Cretaceous and early Tertiary the orchids would have had a vast and precarious distance to migrate to the continents of Gondwanaland which they have done so well. There is a certain weakness in using extant primitive species to determine the place of origin of a family. These species may exist in a given location because the climatic and edaphic factors are conducive to the plant's well-being. I believe that some other criteria are needed, although we are not likely to have support for any location until some unequivocal fossil data are discovered. In the meantime we can only speculate on the origin by using facts and theories known to us at present.

Once again accepting the Gondwanaland configuration of Powell *et al.* (1981), I speculate that orchid origin occurred in the subcontinent of Greater India during the early Cretaceous. At that time the east coast of Greater India touched the Western Australian coast from the southwest corner as far north as the Exmouth Gulf, and the west coast of Greater India was in contact with the southeast coast of Africa. Madagascar was north of its present position adjacent to Tanzania-Kenya and sandwiched between India and Africa. This gave something like 5 to 15 million years for geophytic orchids to spread from Greater India to the fynbos in Africa and the Kwongan in Western Australia. Both areas are similar in nature and even today there is a morphological similarity between some geophytic orchids in both provinces.

The Kwongan (or sandplains) is located in the southwest corner of Western Australia, forming roughly a right-angled triangle with the hypotenuse extending from Shark Bay in the north to a point on the southern coast 480 km east of Esperance (Pate & Beard 1984). This area is rich in orchids, with 120 geophytic species.

The South American geophytes could have been derived from the Kwongan via Antarctica over a period of 70 to 80 million years, for both continents were attached to Antarctica for a long period. There is quite a similarity between plants of temperate South America and temperate Australia, more so than between those of South America and Africa.

India separated from Madagascar and East Africa about 65 million years BP, but they remained in contact for 60 million years, giving ample time for orchid migration and speciation. The climate of Greater India in the early Cretaceous was temperate and fairly dry. As the break-up of Gondwanaland occurred the ratio of sea surface to land surface increased, resulting in a moister climate. The temperature still remained warm until some time in the middle Miocene when ice accumulated in Antarctica. By this time both Australia and Greater India were drifting northward and the climate became drier over part of the continents.

There are several reasons why plant evolution is relatively rapid in arid and semi-arid regions, as explained by Stebbins (1952). In areas with limited moisture, local terrain and soil have a greater effect on the flora than in moist regions. Semi-arid climates divide large size populations into smaller isolated units which may exchange genes via pollen vectors occasionally. In dry climates vegetative structures change to either store water when it is available or to minimise water loss, such as becoming deciduous, or any combination of these. Axelrod (1972) agrees with Stebbins but believes that the steep-sided mountains, ridges and mesas provide dry edaphic sites in proximity to tropical and temperate rain forests.

The steep gradient of decreasing moisture at these sites has provided environmental opportunities for speciation. These dry sites are not conducive to fossil formation.

As Greater India drifted northwards into the tropics it became a gigantic floating flora Noah's Ark for 10 million years. During this northern flight Greater India scraped alongside the western edge of the westerly moving Sunderland, giving ample opportunity for the migration of orchids into this land. Finally Greater India collided with the southern part of the Eurasian plate. In both cases a vast new area was made accessible for further migration to occur.

Just when some orchids transformed from geophytes to epiphytes is impossible to determine but there appears to be no reason why this could not have happened on many occasions on different continents, possibly via rupicolous intermediates. There are some epiphytes which are sympodial or monopodial and some with and without pseudobulbs.

Any consideration of orchid evolution must involve their insect pollinators. Orchids are largely entomophilous and the insect Orders which pollinate plants are Coleoptera (beetles), Diptera (flies, midges and gnats), Hymenoptera (bees, wasps and ants) and Lepidoptera (moths and butterflies). Insects as a Class are very old and except for Lepidoptera have their origins well before the Cretaceous, although bees are thought to have originated in the lower to middle Oligocene. Lepidoptera first appear in the fossil record about 38 million years BP. Some orchids by accident developed scents attractive to insects, so giving these orchids better fecundity than others, hence a better chance of survival and dispersal.

Many naturalists in the past have believed strongly in the dictum *Natura non facit saltum*, that is nature does not favour leaps from one structure to another but change is done by slight successive variation. Evolution is progressive adaptation and nothing else. This philosophy is much favoured by zoologists.

Most plant people are aware of 'sports' developing on plants, examples of saltatory evolution producing change by large leaps. But whatever the cause of this, climate or nutrition, the change will only occur within the potential of the genome to produce such forms. Also living within the genome potential is the ecological capacity of the plant. Some will not withstand tropical locations except in the highlands, others will not withstand the cold or low or high insolation. Often the genetic system produces unexpected results, possibly by part of this system becoming 'uncovered' in the chromosomes and expressing itself morphologically or environmentally. There is more genetic material in a chromosome than is used to direct the growth of the plant, but the suppression and release of this is beyond the scope of this chapter.

The tropical forests harbour a large number of species, not only of orchids but of all plants, that is, speciation is apparently high; but whether competition limits the number of plants of each species and whether these species have originated close by (as suggested by Axelrod 1972) and have sought 'the good life' of the moist forest is not known.

Floristic regions

The floristic regions suggested here are based on plate tectonics and the movement of land masses since the origin of the Angiospermae. These regions should not be confused with areas of botanical study or interest created for convenience, e.g. Australasia and Malesia are two terms commonly used for this purpose, nor should they be confused with botanical provinces. There are several to many floristic provinces within these regions, each determined by the biophysical ecology of the province and edaphic factors.

1. The India-Burma region.
2. The Sunda region embracing Thailand, Laos, Vietnam, Cambodia, Malaysia, Java, Sumatra, Bali, Borneo and Palawan.
3. Wallacea being that area from the Wallace Line in the west to its complementary line in the east (Map 2) and including the islands of Lombok, Sumbawa, Flores, Sumba, Timor, Sulawesi, Ceram, Tanibar and the Halmaheras, plus associated small islands of the Flores sea, Banda sea and Molucca sea.

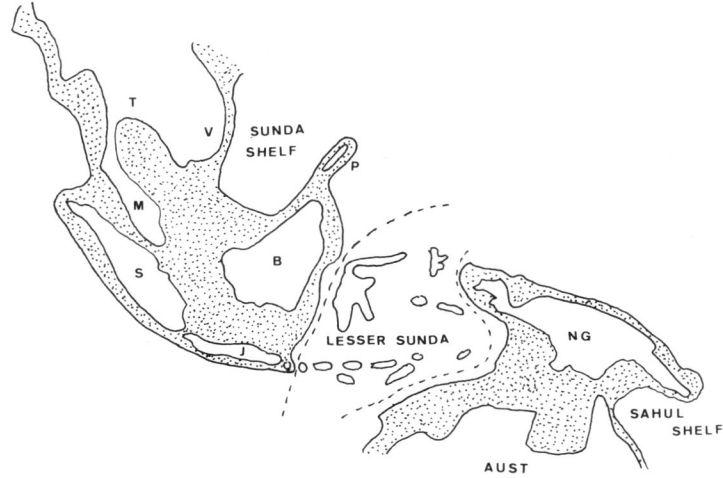

Map 2   The present-day position of Sunderland showing countries located on the Sunda Shelf: Thailand (T), Vietnam (V), Malay peninsula (M), Sumatra (S), Borneo (B), Java (J) and Pelawan (P).
  The Lesser Sunda Arc is bounded by the Wallace Line to the west and its complementary line to the east. New Guinea and Australia are shown joined by the Sahul Shelf.

4. The Bismarck region being the entire island of New Guinea, the Bismarck Archipelago and Solomon Islands.
5. The Southwest Pacific Margin consisting of New Zealand, Lord Howe and Norfolk Islands and New Caledonia.
6. The Australian region consisting of the Australian mainland and Tasmania.
7. The Oceanic region comprising the area from Fiji to the Tuamotu Archipelago in the east.
8. The African region.
9. The Madagascar region.
10. The South American region.
11. The North American region.
12. The Eurasian region.
13. The Philippines region. The delineation of this presents some difficulty and needs further study. It appears to have recent linkage with the Sunda Arc in the south and Taiwan in the north and even with the southern Ryukyu Islands. Part of eastern Eurasia has been submerged and uplifted during geological history and associations are doubtful.

References

Audley-Charles M.G., Carter D.J. & Milsom J.S. (1972) Tectonic development of Eastern Indonesia in relation to Gondwanaland dispersal. *Nature Phys. Sci.* 239; 35–39.

Axelrod Daniel I. (1972) Edaphic aridity as a factor in Angiosperm evolution. *Amer. Nat.* 106; 311–320.

Fosberg F.R. (1963) Plant dispersal in the Pacific. In *Pacific Basin Biogeography.* Ed. J.L.Gressitt, Bishop Museum, Honolulu.

Garay Leslie (1960) On the origin of the Orchidaceae. *Bot. Mus. Leaflet,* Vol.19, No. 3. Harvard Uni. Cambridge Mass.

Gillett George W. (1972) The role of hybridisation in the evolution of Hawaiian flora. In *Taxonomy, Phytogeography and Evolution.* Ed. D.H. Valentine, A.P.

Hoffman Noel & Brown Andrew (1984) *Orchids of Southwestern Australia.* Uni. of W.A. Press.

Johnson B.D., Powell C. McA. & Veevers J.J. (1976) Spreading history of the Eastern Indian Ocean and Greater India's northward flight from Antarctica and Australia. *Bull. Geol. Soc. America.* 87; 1560–1566.

Kemp Elizabeth (1981) Tertiary paleogeography and the evolution of the Australian climate. In *Ecological Biogeography of Australia,* Vol.1. Eds. Allen Keast, W. Junk.

Keast Allen (1981) Origins and relationship of Australian biota. In *Ecological Biogeography of Australia,* Vol.1. Eds. Allen Keast, W. Junk.

Lawler Leonard J. (1981) Ethnobotany of Australia: Orchids. *Proc. Orchid Symp.* 13 Bot. Congress, Sydney 1981.

Mayr E. (1944) Wallace's Line in the light of recent zoogeographic studies. *Quart. Rev. Biol.* 19; 1–14.

Pate J.S. & Beard J.S. (1984) *Kwongan, Plant Life in the Sandplain.* Uni. of W.A. Press.

Powell C. McA., Johnson B.D. & Veevers J.J. (1981) The Early Cretaceous break-up of eastern Gondwanaland, the separation of Australia and India and their interaction with Southeast Asia. In *Ecological Biogeography of Australia,* Vol.1. Eds. Allen Keast, W. Junk.

Schmid Rudolf & Schmid Marvin J. (1977) Fossil history of the Orchidaceae. In *Orchid Biology, Reviews and Perspectives.* Ed. J. Arditti, Cornell Univ.

Schuster R.M. (1972) Dispersal of land plants. *The Bot. Rev.* 38; No. 1; 3–86.

Schuster R.M. (1974) Plate tectonics and its bearing on the geographical origin and dispersal of Angiosperms. In *Origin and Early Evolution of Angiosperms.* Ed. Charles Beck, Columbia Uni.

Smith J.M.B. (1982) An introduction to the history of Australian vegetation. In *A History of Australian Vegetation.* Ed. J.M.B. Smith. McGraw-Hill.

Stebbins G.I. (1952) Aridity as a stimulus to evolution. *Amer. Nat.* 86; 33–44.

Williams Louis O. (1938) The orchids of Fiji islands. *Bot. Mus. Leaflets,* Vol.5, No. 7. Harvard Univ.

Further reading

Continents Adrift and Continents Aground. Readings from *Scientific American.* W.H. Freeman and Company.

Seed morphology and classification of Orchidaceae. *Phytomorphology,* Vol.19, 1969. H.T. Clifford and W.K. Smith.

The Way the Earth Works. Peter J. Wyllie, John Wiley & Sons.

14 The Ecology of Orchids

Ecology is defined as 'the relationship between organisms and their physical, chemical and biotic environment'.

The physical factors are edaphic and climatic, to be considered in more detail later. The chemical factors relate to toxic substrates, nutrient availability and acidity. The biotic factors include intra- and inter-specific competition, intergeneric competition, fungal symbionts, bacterial and fungal saprophytes, the distribution and abundance of the species.

While these factors may be tabulated separately as above and described separately as below, it is abundantly clear that they cannot be treated as isolated subjects; e.g. the mineral nutrient availability is dependent both on a climatic factor, namely rainfall, and the decomposition or leaf litter by saprophytic organisms. The ecology of orchids is dependent, therefore, on the integration of all the above factors at some time in the life of the plant.

I do not claim that this subject can be covered so comprehensively as to include all possible configurations of the ecology of orchids nor is there sufficient space available in a general book on orchids to do so. The aim of this chapter is to give the orchid grower an appreciation of the natural surroundings of the plants in the wild and the factors which control their growth. Many writers in orchid journals emphasise the need to study the natural conditions under which orchids grow and try to duplicate these as far as possible.

Orchids are very accommodating plants and often grow in captivity under a variety of conditions, but some are quite fussy and insist upon being close to their natural environment. However, some orchids seen growing in the wild are near the limits of their required environment and the observer should be cognisant of this possibility when assessing the habitat of a given stand or clump.

Habitat

This is often confused with 'niche'. One often hears that there must be a niche (empty space) for a species to establish itself, but once established the niche disappears. Alternatively a niche is used to mean 'the role that an organism plays in the ecosystem' or the 'requirements of a species to establish itself'. I suggest the word niche be avoided and the word habitat used to indicate a place where the orchid grows. The habitat may be described by listing all relevant positive and negative factors pertaining to the habitat. Unfortunately this is seldom done. How many times have you read that a certain orchid grows only on such and such a tree in a stated area? An example is that in Mindanao *Euanthe sanderiana* grows almost exclusively on Dipterocarpaceae. In this area dipterocarps are more abundant than any other tree. No doubt you are familiar with this type of statement made by observers who fail to add contributing data, much of which they cannot measure, but they could at least offer a present-or-absent estimation.

An assessment of habitat must firstly be done in respect of seed germination, for if this does not occur the tree will not host the orchid. Secondly, once the seed germinates, the factors which contribute to growth must be above the minimum needs of the plant, otherwise the seedling will die.

In respect of epiphytes some factors relative to the tree itself are: (1) The type of bark, its relief, its permanency, its water retention; does it produce toxic phenolic-like substances, does it have a high salt content, has it high acidity, does it harbour lichens and mosses? Lichens provide a wide range of acids as described by Rogers (1981) so the degree of lichen content near the orchid should be stated. (2) How much light is transmitted through the canopy and its neighbours? Duration of light, amount and duration of sun-flecks. (3) Where does the orchid grow on the tree? On branches high or low, on the top or underneath, on the trunk or in a fork? (4) Is the canopy so dense as to inhibit throughfall? Is stem flow likely to be sparse or plentiful?

The habitat of the geophyte is the soil and here relevant factors are soil texture, albedo, pH, type and amount of litter and its probable decomposition rate, throughfall, sun flecks and spectral quality of light through the canopy. Is the canopy deciduous or evergreen? How much diffuse light is there from the sky-dome, and what is its duration?

Having assessed all these matters we can move on to consider some environmental factors in more detail.

The Symbionts

Practically all texts dealing with orchid seed dispersal limit the germination of the seed to places where a symbiotic fungus exists, either carried with the seed or present prior to its arrival.

But is this really necessary? Remember the work of Lewis Knudson (1884–1958) who demonstrated that orchid seed can germinate on organic and inorganic mixtures without the presence of a fungus. He added 1% sucrose (to provide the carbon source) to an already existing plant nutrient medium (Pfeffers solution). Subsequent experiments resulted in the Knudson B and C media with sucrose again providing the carbon source and nitrate the nitrogen source (Arditti 1990).

The principal sources of nutrition for epiphytic orchids are throughfall and stem flow containing mineral nutrients leached from the leaves and stem of the phorophyte. Despite the large amounts of inorganic nutrients so leached, carbohydrates account for a substantial, if not the major, quantity of leached materials. Dalbro (1956) as cited by Tukey (1970) calculated the loss of carbohydrates from apple trees to be as great as 800 kg per hectare per year. This leaching does not occur from the cell content but from the tissue involved in the transport of sugars from the leaf, i.e. the phloem tissue, and is greater from mature leaves than from young actively growing ones. Although glucose is the major sugar made from photosynthesis this is converted to sucrose for transport within the plant and it is this sucrose which is leached into throughfall and stem flow.

Sanford (1974) states that he found relatively high sugar content, particularly sucrose, in some barks of trees. It is not clear whether these are bark exudates from underlying living tissue (the phloem) or are due to absorption from stem flow. It does not really matter which, the presence of sucrose is the main point.

It is this sucrose along with other nutrients which could provide a fungal-free substrate in and on the bark of a tree, almost any tree, to permit the germination of an orchid seed. This would overcome the difficulties raised by many authors to dispersal of orchid seed without co-dispersal of symbiotic fungi.

I am not aware of any papers detailing experimental work to prove seed germination occurs under these conditions so it remains speculation, but it is speculation based on some known data and seems plausible. What we have is virtually a seed-germinating medium neither enclosed in a flask nor sterile. Plant hormones are also leached from leaves.

Toxic substances

In the forest it is not uncommon to see one tree laden with epiphytes of all kinds yet adjacent trees are devoid of such epiphytes, even though these have branches penetrating into the space of the laden tree. While this phenomenon does not appear to have been investigated thoroughly some critical observations have been made. The latex juice from *Ficus* and *Euphorbia* spp. is very inhibitory to orchid flora. Frei (1976) reported on the extraction of phenolics from bark. However, germination experiments reported were done quantitatively with the pure forms of the various extracts, so ignoring any synergistic effects of phenolics from the bark. Tannic and gallic acids appear to have disposed fairly rapidly of seed germination but the concentrations used in this laboratory work appear to be higher and more persistent in flasks than would occur in nature. There remains quite a lot of difficult work to be done on the toxic properties of tree barks.

Light

Light is energy in the photosynthetically active radiation band (PAR band) and because this coincides with the visible (to us) spectrum we call this energy 'light' (see Chapter 9). It can vary in intensity (the number of photons per square metre per second), duration (not only in length of daylight, but for short periods from one second to two minutes as sunflecks) and also in spectral composition. Plants growing on the forest floor or low down on heavily shaded trunks or branches under a dense canopy receive light which is much depleted in the wavelengths of the PAR band due to absorption of these by the canopy.

Many tree canopies are sparse at all times of the year, others are sparse in seasons. Lee (1989) used a fish-eye lens fitted to a 35 mm camera to photograph the canopy cover. Pictures were taken at ground level, looking upwards into a tropical dediduous forest in India. After the rainy season the canopy was relatively dense (94 ± 3.1%), whereas some four months later in the dry season leaf fall had reduced the coverage to 40.6 ± 18.8%. Those who explore habitats in the wild could well adopt this method of measuring canopy cover change with seasons so that the habitat can be more fully described.

In this same report the effect of seasonal foliage density showed that the forest floor light intensity was only 10% of that in direct sunlight after the rainy season and 44 ± 17% of this was due to sunflecks. In the dry season the forest floor received 54% of direct sunlight intensity due to the open canopy and sunflecks were no longer relevant.

Sunflecks are produced by the penetration of sunlight through gaps in the canopy and provide a significant amount of light to plants at or near ground level. In sunflecks the critical photosynthetic wavelengths have not been absorbed by the canopy leaves so the whole photosynthetic spectrum is available to plants. Short sunflecks of say 0.5 minutes duration but occurring 20 times per hour contribute only 87% of the photosynthate obtained from sunflecks of two minutes duration occurring five times per hour, although the total exposure to light is the same in both cases (Gross 1982).

This poorer response to short duration sunflecks is thought to be due to enzyme activity not responding immediately to a burst of received energy. The enzyme takes a little time to build up to its maximum activity rate. Even shorter periods of just a few seconds are likely to be even less productive. Although observers will not normally be able to measure photon flux density over the PAR band, the duration and recurrence times of the sunflecks can be measured readily.

Spectral composition will not be discussed in detail here but the effect of the canopy on this is measured by the ratio of 'red' light which is absorbed by the canopy to provide photosynthetic energy, compared to 'far red' light which is not absorbed by the canopy.

That is $$\frac{\text{'red' light at forest floor}}{\text{'far red' light at forest floor}}$$

For a canopy of high but not complete density this ratio is commonly 0.2 but for some tree species this may fall to 0.09 (Lee 1989). So the canopy coverage is important for plants on the forest floor; their photosynthetic efficiency needs to be high. Bjorkman (1971–72) gave similar low ratios for tropical rain forest in Queensland.

Diffuse radiation is also important as on a tropical rain forest floor, under a dense canopy, this may contribute as much as 40% to the light intensity, sunflecks contributing the remainder. In England, with extensive cloud cover, diffuse radiation may contribute 50 to 100% of the total radiation. Diffuse radiation comes from the skydome which reflects this radiation to earth from the atmosphere and clouds. It varies typically from 15% to 30% of full sunlight in the open and is important in the tropics where a substantial part of the day is often obscured by cloud. As it arrives from all angles it can penetrate under the canopy to ground level and so is often not changed in spectral composition, but this, of course, depends largely on the density of sub-canopy vegetation and is difficult to assess.

The foregoing has largely been about plants growing on the forest floor or on low branches or trunks. Epiphytic orchids are usually found in more exposed positions in tree forks or high branches where direct or diffuse light is predominant; sunflecks are not relied upon to deliver the energy needed and there is very little spectral distortion to the PAR band by the canopy. The ratio of 'red' to 'far red' light is usually about 1.2:1 indicating a predominance of 'red'.

Climate

This must be a major factor in continued growth particularly for epiphytes exposed to the rather difficult environment of tree tops. Geophytes are somewhat better off as they have a substrate which is potentially moist. This section will be concerned mainly with the microclimate around epiphytes.

Too often we see in orchid journal articles which purport to state the climatic conditions existing around the orchid site. The climate as reported by the nearest weather station, which may be many kilometres from the site, has only a little bearing on the weather conditions to which the orchids are exposed. True, such information will indicate wet and dry seasons for the area, but hills and valleys around the orchid site will modify these to some extent.

Epiphytic orchids can do quite well without precipitated water; they are adapted to survive on moisture from clouds which frequently occur along valleys in otherwise dry surroundings. So area weather statistics may have little bearing on the microclimate of epiphytes.

Although microclimate also affects nutrition, this is considered later as a separate subject.

Factors which produce varying microclimates at the orchid habitat are:

1. Minimum and maximum temperatures and their duration.
2. Rainfall directly onto the plants or through the canopy (throughfall) or down the stem (stem flow).
3. The condensation of water vapour onto the leaves and roots of the orchid or onto the leaves of the phorophyte.
4. Cloud, mist and fog.
5. Wind.
6. Carbon dioxide concentration.

Chapters 5 to 9 inclusive deal with the physiological responses of orchids to some of the above; this need not be repeated here as it applies in the wild the same as in cultivation.

When assessing the microclimate of the orchid site all these factors should be considered. Some can be measured or estimated if one knows what to look for, as measurement usually involves equipment not available to the casual observer.

1. Temperatures depend on the season, altitude and latitude, and the height at which the temperature is measured. For example in the tropical forest at sea level in the dry season the air temperature 24 m above ground exceeds 30°C but is less than 30°C at 0.7 m above ground, these maxima occurring at 1300 hours. The lowest temperatures occur at 0700 hours, around 25°C. So there is little difference between day/night temperatures near the forest floor, and a difference of about 6+ °C at 24 m above the floor.

In the wet season both maximum temperatures are somewhat lower (about 2°C). The minimum temperatures occur at 0700 hours, the night temperatures being lower in the wet season than in the dry; the day/night difference is about 9°C. This difference in day/night temperature is important for flower initiation. For example many orchids will not flower in Singapore due to equable day/night temperatures.

For temperate forests at low altitudes the day/night variation is likely to be much greater in summer (about 15°C); the maximum summer temperature occurring at 1500 hours, to 35°C. In winter the maximum temperature is about 25°C at 1400 hours and the minimum very variable at 0600 hours. These are just typical figures modified by lakes, sea and rivers and in general temperatures are much more variable than in the tropics.

Temperature measurement should be taken as near as possible to the orchid location.

2. Rainfall is even more variable than temperature and is influenced by localised topography. Within a few degrees on either side of the equator rain falls at all times of the year. Seasonal distribution of rainfall with latitude depends on the cyclic passage of the sun. From 3 to 10 degrees south there are two wet seasons from about February to April and September to November. These are separated by a long dry season May to August and a short dry season December and January.

In the 3 to 10 degrees north latitudes the wet seasons are April and May and later August to October. These two wet seasons are separated by a short dry season in June and July and a long dry season from November to February.

Dry conditions at 30 degrees south and north latitudes are usual, particularly in inland areas. Circulating ocean currents have a major effect on rainfall. A warm current along the coast produces high evaporation and precipitation as rain on the coastal strips. With a cold current sweeping along the coast from Arctic or Antarctic waters the evaporation is small and the coastal strips are dry, e.g. the western coast of South America.

Whether a canopy is open or closed will affect the amount of rain falling directly on the epiphytes. A closed canopy will produce a throughfall of water washing over the tree leaves and dropping to the ground. Part of this is caught by branches of all sizes and becomes stem flow. Both throughfall and stem flow carry nutrients and hence are important factors. Total precipitation, both throughfall and stem flow, is not difficult to measure if one has frequent access to the site, but this seldom occurs, so it must be estimated. When the canopy is dense it stores a large part of the total precipitation and gradually releases this as throughfall (as high as 80 to 90% of the precipitation), while stem flow can be about 7 to 8% of precipitation. Open canopies typical of temperate forests store very little of the rainfall, most of which wets the ground, branches, trunks and epiphytes directly.

3. Humidity is the measure of the amount of water vapour in the air. There are two direct measurements of this, absolute humidity which is the mass of water vapour in a volume of air (kilograms per cubic metre) and specific humidity which is the mass of water vapour in a mass of air (kilograms per kilogram). Indirect measurements are more frequently used. One is vapour pressure deficit (Chapter 9) and the other relative humidity stated as either a fraction or a percentage. This latter measurement is explained in this section.

Water vapour is an invisible gas, so that cloud, fog and mist are forms of liquid water, not water vapour. The amount of water vapour the air can hold (at sea level) and at various temperatures is shown by a psychrometric curve in Fig. 14.1. This curve relates the water vapour pressure (in hectopascals) to the temperature of air (°C). It is not a straight line and the water vapour pressure increases sharply with temperature rise.

Consider point A of Fig. 14.1. This represents an RH of 0.8 (80%) as $0.8 = x/x+y$. Here $x+y = 35.5$ and $x = 28.5$ hence RH = 0.8.

Point B is also at RH = 0.8 as $x+y = 31.7$ and $x = 25.5$. Note at point B there is a lower water vapour pressure (hence less humidity) than at point A although both have an RH of 0.8.

Point P has a lower value of RH although it is the same temperature as point B. Here $x = 19$ and $x+y = 31.7$ as before, so RH = 0.6. Note that RH is purely a ratio of the amount of water vapour in the air to the amount it could hold at saturation at that temperature. RH values without temperature being stated are rather meaningless.

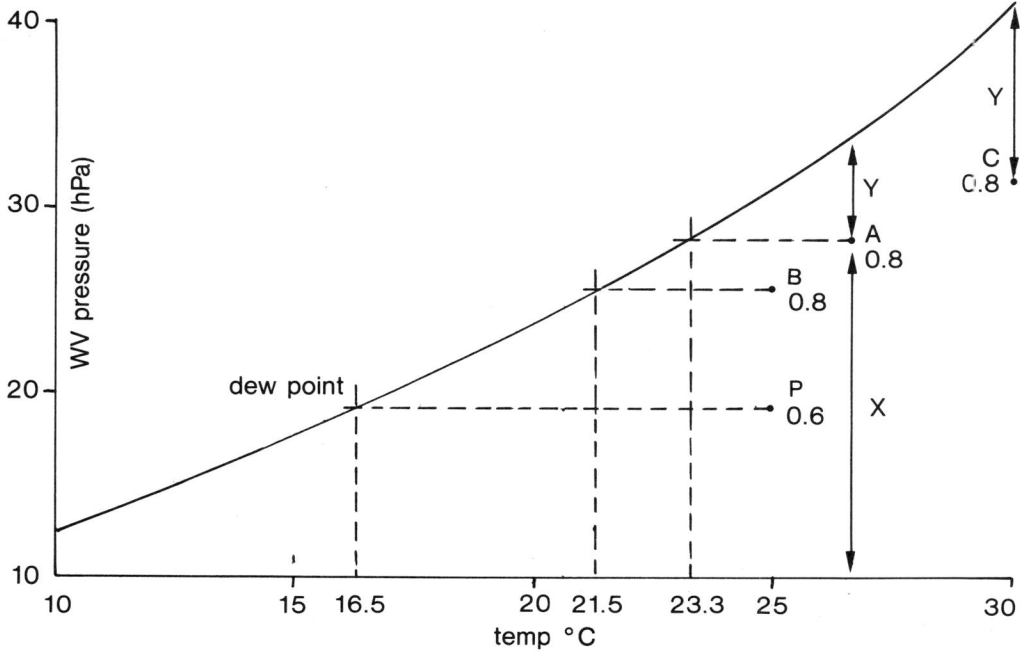

Fig. 14.1

The horizontal lines drawn from points A, B and P show the dew point temperature at which point the water vapour in the air will settle out on surfaces. Point P has a dew point temperature of 16.5°C whereas point B has a dew point temperature of 21.5°C. So the lower the RH the colder the air has to become before dew point is reached. Actually dew point is not always sharply defined. As water settles out from the air at saturation, so the water vapour lost from the air decreases the saturation and the air needs to become colder for dew to occur. Also, each gram of water settling as dew releases about 2400 joules of energy as heat which must be dissipated away for continued cooling to be maintained. This is usually done by convection, forced or free, or radiation from the heated surface. At night leaves and roots are at substantially the same temperature as air so dew deposition can provide water to these parts of the epiphyte or the leaves of the phorophyte. In some observed cases leaves are colder by 0.4 to 1.4°C than the air (Monteith 1957) so deposition of dew occurs before saturation level is reached, say at 0.9 to 0.99 RH.

As shown in Chapter 5 it is the VPD which is the driving force of water loss from the leaf. In Fig. 14.1 this is the value y, that is saturated water vapour pressure minus the actual water vapour pressure in the air. As the temperature increases from 25 to 27 to 30°C, keeping the RH constant at 0.8, the VPD increases from 6.2 to 7.2 to 8.8 hPa (for points B, A and C).

The above values are for still conditions at sea level pressures. As the altitude increases the partial pressures of all atmospheric gases decrease in proportion. However, water vapour partial pressure decreases more rapidly because, as the temperature falls with height, condensation increases. RH tends to increase with altitude as the cold air saturates at lower temperatures. The VPD tends to decrease with lower temperatures as shown in Fig. 14.1.

Measurements taken in Europe show an average summer air temperature (July) as 18°C with water vapour pressure of 14.7 hPa at 600 metres. At 2400 metres altitude these had fallen to 5°C and 6.9 hPa (average figures) (Korner & Mayr 1981).

Plants growing at high altitudes are reported to have stomata on the upper surface of the leaf only, whereas orchids have stomata on the lower surface only. How does this variation interact with the effect of wind, wet and low pressures? There is a very pronounced deficiency of measurements made on orchids at high altitudes, in particular their reaction to low atmosphere partial pressures, so we must remain ignorant on this subject.

4. Cloud, mist and fog. In the tropical highlands cloud cover at tree top level occurs quite regularly in late afternoon and persists throughout the night, disappearing at sun-up. The empty cells of the velamen of the epiphytic orchid roots become filled with liquid water from the cloud and this water passes into the root interior. Cloud appears firstly in the valleys due to the evaporation of water from a river or stream and the water vapour condenses as it rises to form cloud which is moved by the wind. Water vapour has a molecular weight of 18 compared to the equivalent molecular weight of air of 29, hence moist air will generally rise from the ground.

Condensation of water vapour at ground level is defined as fog when the visibility is less than 1 kilometre, and is mist when the visibility is greater than 1 kilometre.

The whole environment in a forest is altered by fog, which changes the length of the light period, the temperature and water availability and, concomitant with these, photosynthesis, respiration and transpiration.

When fog or mist is formed, it often remains at ground level for some time. The fog layer radiates more energy into space from its upper surface than it receives from the ground beneath because its water vapour gives it greater emittance. This cooling of the fog layer causes it to become more dense. The top of the layer has a high albedo and reflects SW radiation from the sun; this results in the fog being persistent even after sunrise. It is finally dissipated by wind which mixes it with the air. Upslope fog occurs when humid air is forced up a steep slope and cools below its dew point.

5. Wind. One of the most obvious features of a tropical forest to the newcomer is the lack of air movement unless a storm is active. Freise (1936) as quoted by Richards (1952) measured the wind speed outside the forest as 28.8 metres per second. At only 100 metres inside the forest this was reduced to 6 metres per second, an attenuation of 4.6. Wind around the plant leaves produces air turbulence and decreases the resistance offered by the boundary air layer to carbon dioxide intake and transpiration (Chapter 6). Wind direction is also of some importance, as when it sweeps rain in from the sea the phosphorus content of the rain is increased, so providing a valuable nutrient to the forest. A Turbo-Meter made by Davis Instruments, San Leandro, CA, USA is very portable and inexpensive and measures wind speed in metres per second.

6. Carbon dioxide might be considered as both a nutrient and a factor of climate. In wet forests where decomposition of litter is rapid, there is a high concentration of carbon dioxide (550 volumes per million) in the early morning. Normal plant respiration in the dark on the forest floor also adds to this concentration. From midday onwards the concentration falls to normal (340 vpm) after wind has caused air mixing.

In temperate or not-so-wet tropical forests the decomposition of leaf litter is much slower and observers have failed to notice a high carbon dioxide concentration in the early morning; no diurnal trend was apparent.

Epiphytic orchids having CAM metabolism, with stomata open at night, do not suffer from carbon dioxide competition from their host trees. Geophytes on the forest floor may profit from the high carbon dioxide concentration during the early morning, but these are mostly C3 plants which do not absorb carbon dioxide during the night.

The measurement of carbon dioxide concentration requires special equipment. It can be assessed by the amount of leaf litter, its type and wetness, and this is usually based on the time taken for half the litter to decompose. For a warm wet forest this ranges from 44 days to 63 days for a drier type forest. The comparable time for a temperate deciduous forest is one year or for schlerophyllous leaves a period of three years. It is only in the warm wet forest that litter would make any significant contribution to diurnal fluctuations of carbon dioxide concentration.

Mineral nutrients

For epiphytes the main source of mineral nutrients is throughfall and stem flow where rainwater, passing over the leaf surfaces, leaches out mineral ions which have been taken up by the phorophyte or its neighbours and not yet incorporated into the leaf. Mature leaves are slower to incorporate these ions, hence leaching from mature leaves is greater than from young leaves which are metabolically active and lose very little as leachate.

The amount of mineral ions in the throughfall is always (as measured) greater than the minerals in the incident precipitation. Over long periods of rain when leaching is extensive, the leachates collected contained more inorganic nutrients than originally in the leaf, indicating that leached substances are replaced by the plant. Leaching ensures that the inorganic nutrients within the soil and the plants are cycled continuously and that this does not occur only at leaf fall and litter decomposition.

Leaching occurs readily and the leaves only need to be wetted to be leached, so dew, fog and light rain are very effective agents. Also leached from tree leaves are sugars, amino acids, gibberellins and vitamins (Tukey 1970) which can greatly assist microorganism growth and litter decomposition on the forest floor, thereby releasing more mineral ions for new growth.

Leaf litter is a poor nutrient compared to throughfall. It is well known that the plant salvages much nutrient from the leaves before they are shed. Calcium is not mobile within the phloem tissue and largely remains in the leaf, but other elements are withdrawn to some extent prior to leaf fall. So, other than calcium, leaf litter is not very rich in minerals or nitrogen. Fresh leaf litter tends to have a high C:N ratio of 100:1 or greater, hence is of no value as a nutrient for epiphytes. If the C:N ratio is 22:1 or more very little nitrogen is released for plant use. As nitrogen is low the decomposition will be slow, particularly in the drier type of forest. In wet forests this nitrogen is supplied as amino acids leached from the leaves, which lowers the C:N ratio to values of 12:1 to 14:1 giving rapid decay.

For those interested in this subject in greater detail refer to Morrison (1988) Topic 1.

References

Arditti Joseph (1990) Lewis Knudson, His Science, His Times and His Legacy. *Lindleyana* 5(1); 1–79.

Bjorkman Olle (1971–72) Photosynthetic adaption to contrasting light climates. *Carnegie Y.B.* Vol. 71.

Frei Sr John Karen (1976) The ecology of epiphytic orchids in relation to their substrates. In *First Symp. of Scientific Aspects of Orchids.* Eds. H. Harry Szmant & James Wemple. Uni. of Detroit.

Gross Louis (1982) Photosynthetic dynamics in varying light environments. *Ecol.* 63(1); 84–93.

Korner C.H. & Myer R. (1981) Stomatal behaviour in alpine plant communities between 600 and 2400 m above sea level. In *Plants and Their Environment.* Eds. J. Grace *et al.* Blackwell Scientific Pubs.

Lee David W. (1989) Canopy dynamics and light climates in tropical moist deciduous forest in India. *J. Trop. Ecology* 5; 65–79.

Monteith, J.L. (1957) Dew. *Q. J. Roy. Meterol. Soc.* 83; 322–341.

Morrison Gordon C. (1988) *The Orchid Grower's Manual.* Kangaroo Press.

Richards P.W. (1952) *The Tropical Rain Forest.* Cambridge Univ. Press.

Rogers Roderick W. (1981) *The Genera of Australian Lichens.* Uni. of Queensland Press.

Tukey H.B. (1970) The leaching of substances from plants. *Ann. Rev. Plant Physiol.* 21; 305–324.

Glossary

Note: Many words are formed by adding 'a' in front to indicate 'not', e.g. asexual meaning not sexual, achlorophyllous meaning no chlorophyll. Such words have not been included in this glossary.

Abaxial   Away from the axis, underside of leaf.

Abscission   Disconnection of leaves and organs from the plant at abscission layer.

Acid   A substance which donates H^+ ions, usually in an aqueous solution.

Adaxial   Towards the axis, upper side of leaf.

Adnate   Fusion of one organ to another.

ADP/ATP   Adenosine diphosphate and adenosine triphosphate, energy storing compounds.

Adventitious   Neither primary nor secondary, roots from cuttings.

Adventive   Dispersed exotic plant growing as a native.

Agar   A gel-forming polymer of galactose derived from seaweed.

Albedo   The amount of SW radiation reflected from ground surfaces.

Alga   A eukaryotic green plant rarely differentiated into specialised organs.

Alkali   A basic substance, forms OH^- ions in water.

Alleles   One of two or more genes of a heterozygote occupying identical positions on homologous chromosomes.

Allopatric   Originating from, or occupying, different geographic regions. Cf. sympatric.

Amphipathic   Having two parts, one part 'water loving' and the other 'water hating'. Refers to many compounds active in organisms.

Anaerobic   Avoiding free oxygen or tolerating its absence.

Analagous   Related in function or usage but not of same origin.

Anatomy   The structure of an organism as distinct from its functioning.

Androecium   Male or stamen part of a flower.

Aneuploidy   Loss or gain of a chromosome from normal number.

Angiosperm   A subdivision of plants where the seed is encased in an ovary; in modern terms called Magnoliophytina.

Anther   Pollen-producing part of stamen.

Anthesis   Expansion and opening of flower from bud opening to fruit set.

Antrorse   Projecting forward. Cf. retrorse.

Apiculate   An apex terminating in a short flexible tip.

Apomixis   Reproduced by other than sexual means, vegetative.

Apoplast   The path through tissue formed by cell walls and air spaces through which water and nutrients can flow without entering the cell proper. Cf. symplast.

Autogamy   Self pollination.

Autotrophic   Grows by inorganic substances and sunlight, not dependent on organic substances.

Auricle   A lobe.

Axenic   A population of only one species derived from a single organism.

Axile   Central placentation in ovary.

Back bulb   In sympodial orchids older pseudobulbs which have lost their leaves.

Back cross   A mating between a heterozygote and homozygote, usually one of the parents.

Basipetal   Developing down from the tip as in a raceme where the first flower is at the tip and later flowers lower down.

Bifid   Two lobes or segments, forked.

Bifoliate   Having two leaves at the top of one pseudobulb.

Bigeneric   A hybrid having two distinct genera as parents.

Binomial   A two word name consisting of the generic name plus a specific epithet.

Biometry   Statistical analysis of living organisms.

Biotope   A small habitat in a large community, e.g. epiphytic biotope in a tropical forest.

Bract   Small leaflike organ around base of flower pedicel or peduncle.

Bracteole   A small bract usually of a pedicel.

Buffer   A salt of a weak acid resisting change in pH.

Bulb   Short vertical subterranean stem with fleshy leaves as in a lily.

C3, C4   Names given to two different methods of carbon fixation, type C3 being common in orchids.

Callus A hardened and thickened region, a fleshy growth on the lip.

CAM Crassulacean acid metabolism, a method of photosynthesis common in orchids particularly epiphytes.

C/N ratio The carbon/nitrogen ratio; substances with a high ratio are resistant to decay, substances for composting should have a low C/N ratio of 22:1 or less.

Capsule A fruit, dehiscent when dry with two or more locules.

Carbohydrate A substance having the general formula $C_n(H_2O)_n$, a typical one being glucose $C_6H_{12}O_6$.

Carbon An element with an atomic weight of 12 which forms the skeleton of all living organisms from a cellular viewpoint.

Carotene A yellow-red pigment insoluble in water, present in leaves.

Casparian strip A non-water-conducting band of cells in the endo- and exodermis.

Cation A positively charged ion, e.g. H^+ K^+ Ca^{++}.

Caudicle A stalk-like part of the pollinarium.

Cell The self-regulating and reproducing unit of an organism, its function determined by its position.

Cell cycle The process which a cell undergoes to assemble the components to grow and reproduce itself.

Chlorophyll The principal light-absorbing pigment of plants. It has several variants but the principal one is chlorophyll 'a'.

Chloroplast An organelle containing chlorophyll and many other substances which is located in the cytoplasm. It is the site of the energy reaction of photosynthesis.

Chlorosis Loss of chlorophyll, yellowing of tissue.

Chromosomes The assembly of chromatin into short thick bodies when the cell is ready for division.

Chromotids The two parts, still joined, of a chromosome which has split into two parts.

Chromotin DNA which is very thin and distributed throughout the nucleus and is microscopically invisible. It forms into chromosomes when the cell is ready for division to occur.

Ciliate Fringed with fine soft hairs.

Clone A single plant raised from seed plus all of its subsequent progeny derived from vegetative propagation.

Column An organ in an orchid flower formed by the union of stamens and pistils with their supporting tissue.

Column foot This is an extension of the base of the column, not always occurring, to which the lip is attached.

Conduplicate Folded together lengthwise.

Congeneric Of the same genus.

Convection In orchid culture it is the movement of air by temperature difference (free convection) or wind (forced convection).

Cortex Primary tissue of a root-shoot system.

Cultivar A plant of cultivated origin and those plants derived vegetatively from it. Applicable to hybrids and not to be confused with variety.

Cytology Study of cell structure.

Cytoplasm That part of a cell other than a nucleus and vacuole; it contains the organelles.

Cytorrhysis Collapse of cell walls in wilting leaves when cells are losing water faster than it can be replaced.

Decurrent Extending downwards.

Dehiscent Splitting open (of ripe fruit).

Denticulate Having small teeth at the margin.

Diagnosis A plant description used to differentiate one taxon from another.

Diffusion The migration of ions or molecules in a fluid, usually under the influence of a concentration difference.

Disc The upper part of the middle section of the lip.

DNA De-oxyribonucleic acid. Provides the supporting structure for the genes in the nucleus of the cell.

Dominant Refers to an allele producing a trait which is developed in both homozygous and heterozygous plants.

Dorsal The back or outer surface of an organ. Also used to indicate the upper sepal of a flower.

Ecology Relationship of organisms to their environment.

Ecotype An individual or group of a species which maintains distinct variation due to environment and isolation.

Electrolytes Solutions which contain ions and conduct an electric current.

Electrons Negative charges contained within the atom.

Element A substance having such a simple form it cannot be further simplified chemically.

Endemic Not found outside a country or region.

Endoclimate The climate within a leaf tissue.

Enzyme   A protein which performs a specific reaction, say by joining two compounds together. The enzyme is then released for further action. Enzymes catalyse reactions at low energy levels suitable for the interior of organisms.

Epiclimate   The climate at the leaf surface.

Epidermis   The outermost tissue.

Epiphyte   A plant growing on a tree but not parasitic on it.

Epistasis   Where more than one pair of alleles influence a trait.

Epithet   An adjective. The specific epithet qualifies the generic name.

Exodermis   The outer waterproofing layer of cells just inside the velamen in the orchid root.

Exotic   Not native, coming from another country.

Extrorse   Facing outward from the axis.

F1   The first filial generation from a given cross.

F2   The second filial generation obtained by interbreeding the F1 generation.

Facultative   Not obligate, able to adapt from one mode to another.

Family   A major taxon in the plant hierarchy.

Fasciation   Abnormal growth, usually stems flattened and fused into one.

Fertilisation   The union of male and female gametes. Also refers to artificial feeding of plants.

Fimbriate   Bordered by fine hairs or fringed.

Foliar feeding   The application of nutrient solutions to leaves.

Fruit   That part which bears the seeds.

Funicle   Supporting attachment for ovule or seed.

Gamete   Reproductive cells of either sex.

Gene   Hereditary unit controlling production of traits or characteristics.

Generic name   A noun, the first word of a binomial.

Genotype   An organism's genetic composition. Cf. phenotype.

Geophyte   A plant which grows in the ground.

Glucose   A simple sugar, $C_6H_{12}O_6$.

Grex name   A new generic name given to a hybrid.

Guard cells   Two crescent-shaped cells surrounding a stoma.

Gynaecium   Ovule-bearing structure.

Gynostemium   The column, fusion of stamens and style.

Habitat   The environment in which an organism grows.

Hamulus   Small hook or barb, pl. hamuli.

Haploid   Cells with only one of each type of chromosome (n) or an organism composed of these cells.

Hectopascals   One hundred pascals, symbol hPa.

Heterozygote   An individual in which given pairs of alleles are dissimilar.

Hirsute   Covered with stiff coarse hairs.

Hispid   A surface with bristle-like hairs.

Homonym   A name applied to a taxon which has had prior application to another taxon, hence is not legitimate.

Homozygote   An individual in which given pairs of genes are similar.

Hydathode   A water gland on a leaf where water under pressure is passed out.

Hydrogen bonding   A weak bond; an electrostatic interaction between a hydrogen proton and electrons in a neighbouring atom, usually oxygen or nitrogen in organisms.

Hydrophilic   Having an affinity for water.

Hydrophobic   Lacking affinity for water.

Inflorescence   That part of the floral shoot bearing and including flowers.

Insolation   Exposure to sun's radiation.

Ion   An atom or molecule with an electric charge due to loss or gain of one or more electrons.

Irradiance   The rate at which radiation is received at the earth's surface.

Isotopes   Atoms having a different number of neutrons in the nucleus from that present in the normally occurring atom.

Joule   The unit of energy. One joule per second equals one watt.

Keel   A central ridge on a surface.

Keiki   An offshoot arising from the stem of a plant.

Kinesis   A process of division; karyokinesis is division of nucleus, cytokinesis is division of cytoplasm.

Kingdom   The highest taxon in plant hierarchy.

Labellum   Lip or modified petal of orchid.

Latent heat   Heat energy used to change the phase of a liquid and which does not produce an increase in temperature.

Leaf trace   A strand of vascular tissue forming an extension of a primary vascular bundle from stem to leaf.

Liliopsida The modern name for the taxon 'monocotyledon'.

Linkage A tendency of some genes carried on the same chromosome to stay together.

Locule A cavity formed by partitioning, especially in an ovary or fruit.

Locus The position occupied by a gene on a chromosome.

Magnoliopsida The modern name for the taxon 'dicotyledon'.

Meiosis Two divisions of the nucleus to halve the number of chromosomes in daughter cells, produces gametes.

Membrane A very thin permeable tissue which surrounds the cytoplasm and other cell enclosures and consists of lipid-protein.

Mentum A chin-like structure formed by sepals at the foot of the column.

Mesophyll A spongy cell arrangement inside the leaf adjacent to the abaxial surface and below the palisade tissue.

Mesophyte A plant having maximum growth within modest temperature and moisture conditions.

Mitochondria Organelles in the cytoplasm which degrade sugars and release energy to the plant cell.

Mitosis The process by which the nuclei normally divide without reduction in the number of chromosomes. Cf. meiosis.

Molecule An assembly of two or more atoms.

Monandrous With one stamen.

Monoecious Having stamens and pistils on separate flowers on the same plant.

Morphology The external structure of a plant and its parts.

Mucro A short hard flexible point terminating a structure, typically a leaf.

Mutation A change in the genetic system of a cell which produces a variant (mutant).

Mycelium The vegetative part of a fungus composed of thread-like tissue.

Mycorrhiza The infection of a root by a fungal mycelium, usually considered to be of mutual benefit to both plant and fungus by interchange of different nutrients.

Necrotic Dead, refers to dead tissue.

Nectary A nectar-secreting organ either on the flower or on the stem or axils.

Niche An organism's niche depends not only on where it lives but also on what it does and how it responds to its environment. Do not confuse with habitat.

Nototribic When pollinia are stuck to the dorsal surface of the insect. Cf. sternotribic.

Nucleic acids These form the structure upon which genes are mounted or genetic code is transmitted from the nucleus.

Nucleus An organelle embedded in the cytoplasm and responsible for housing the genetic material. It is bounded by a membrane.

Obligate Limited to a particular condition, nutrient or mode. Cf. facultative.

Ontogeny The development cycle of an organism.

Order The level of a taxon above family but below class.

Organelle An inclusion in a cell which operates more or less autonomously, e.g. chloroplast, mitochondrion.

Organic acid An organic compound containing a carboxyl group ($COOH$) and which ionises to lose the H^+.

Ovary The structure connected to the pistil and in which ovules are formed.

Ovule The 'egg' cell of the plant which when fertilised develops into a zygote within a seed.

Oxidation-reduction Sometimes called redox; the interchange of electrons between atoms or molecules, the one gaining electrons is reduced and the one losing electrons is oxidised. A very common and frequently occurring reaction in metabolism.

Palisade Elongated cells forming the upper tissue within a leaf. The major site of photosynthesis.

Panicle A branched inflorescence, often in loose clusters of flowers; a branched raceme

PAR band Photosynthetic active radiation band, from 0.4 to 0.7 μm.

Parasexual The fusion of two vegetative cells from different parents; protoplast fusion.

Parenchyma Tissue forming the fundamental structure of the plant; ground tissue, usually thin-walled and actively functioning.

Parietal Refers to wall, e.g. location of ovules on wall of ovary.

Passage cell A cell in the exo- or endo-dermis of a root, usually opposite the xylem, and which allows water and nutrient to flow.

Patulous Spreading outward or divergent.

Pedicel The stalk of an individual flower.

Peduncle The unbranched flower stalk below the flowers; or the main axis of a compoundly branched inflorescence.

Peloria An abnormal condition where flowers depart from the normal structure

PEP Phosphoenolpyruvate.

Perianth The whole flower, sepals and petals.

Pericarp The matured wall of an ovary which encloses the seed.

Petiole The leaf stalk.

PFD Photon flux density, being the number of photons, expressed as moles of photons per square metre per second.

pH A logarithmic measure of the concentration of hydrogen cations in a litre of water.

Phenology The correlation of climatic factors with vegetative and reproductive development.

Phenotypes Plants having observable characteristics all similar. Cf. genotype.

Phloem Vascular tissue continuous throughout the plant and used for the translocation of synthesised nutrients.

Phorophyte The host tree to epiphytes.

Photon A quantum of visible light.

Photosynthesis A process whereby energy from the sun is utilised to carry out the combination of CO_2 and ribulose 1.5 biphosphate to form sugars.

Phyllody The abnormal conversion of flowers to vegetative shoots.

Pith A centrally located cylinder of parenchyma tissue within root or shoot.

Plasmalemma The membrane enclosing the cytoplasm of a cell. It abuts the inner surface of the cell wall.

Plasmodesma A strand of cytoplasm traversing holes in the cell wall and which interconnects adjacent cells. All living cells in the plant are connected by plasmodesmata.

Plicate Folded lengthwise like a closed fan.

Pollinarium The pollinia plus stalks, sticky discs and other attachments.

Pollinia Pollen masses in the orchid flower, sing. pollinium.

Polyphyletic A taxonomic group of mixed origin without a common phylogeny.

Polyploid Higher than diploid, that is 3n, 4n, 5n etc.

Porrect Extending outwardly.

Procumbent Trailing or lying flat.

Protoplasts Single cells from which the cell wall has been removed.

Quantum General term for the indivisible unit of any form of physical energy; an excitation in electromagnetic fields giving a particle-like interpretation to the field.

Raceme An inflorescence with flowers attached by pedicels.

Rachis The axis of inflorescence bearing flowers singly or in groups. Cf. peduncle.

Raphide Needle-like crystals of calcium oxalate occurring in cells, common in orchids.

Recessive A trait which is only expressed when all alleles are homozygous.

Reflexed Abruptly curved or bending backwards.

Respiration A cellular function, being the breakdown of sugars or fats to provide energy. This occurs in the mitochondria at all times.

Resupinate Turned through 180° to appear upside down.

Retrorse Directed backwards.

Retuse A leaf apex with a central notch.

Rhizome A main stem usually horizontal; may be subterranean or prostrate, developing adventitious roots and stems.

RNA A form of nucleic acid derived from genetic information and used to carry this information out from the nucleus into the cytoplasm and for tasks associated with the construction of proteins.

Rostellum A slender part of the upper edge of the stigma.

Rugose Having a wrinkled surface.

Rupicolous Growing on or among rocks.

Saccate Forming a sac, said of a sepal or petal forming depressions.

Salts A name commonly given to the substance resulting when an acid reacts with a metal, e.g. potassium sulphate, magnesium chloride.

Saprophyte An organism depending for nutrition on dead organic matter.

Scabrous A surface roughened by minute protuberances, rough feel.

Scape A peduncle arising from the ground on a stemless plant and bearing one or more flowers.

Sciophyte A plant adapted to constant shade.

Sectile Cut into parts.

Sepal One of the three outer parts of an orchid flower.

Septate Divided by a partition.

Sessile Having no stalk; in flowers, having no pedicel and attached directly to rachis.

Setose Covered with bristle-like hairs; *seta* = bristle.

Sinus A cavity or cleft, e.g. between the lobes of a flower.

Solar constant The solar flux density above the atmosphere = 1360 watts per square metre.

Solutions Consist of a solute (the solid) dissolved in a solvent (the liquid).

Somatic The body cell as distinct from reproductive cell.

Stamen Part of androecium comprising anther and supporting filament.

Staminode A sterile stamen or structure without anther.

Stele The central vascular cylinder of a root system.

Sternotribic When pollinia stick on to the ventral surface of insects when the reward is behind the column as in resupinate Disinae. Cf. nototribic.

Stigma Part of a flower which is pollen receptive.

Stipe Supporting structure or stalk.

Stomata Pores on the underside of the orchid leaf.

Stochastic Random, having an element of chance.

Striate A surface having longitudinal lines, grooves or ridges.

Style Part connecting stigma to the ovary and through which the pollen tube travels.

Superior An ovary above the calyx, not found in orchids.

Surfactant A wetting agent, able to reduce surface tension of water.

Sympatric A distribution of plants duplicated in same or overlapping regions. Cf. allopatric.

Symplast The passageway of water and nutrients through the plant via the cell cytoplasm. Cf. apoplast.

Synonym A name rejected for a species in favour of a name having precedence.

Tactile Sensitive to touch.

Taxon A taxonomic unit covering any one of the categories in classification.

Terete Circular in cross section, used to describe 'round' leaves.

Tessellated Checkered; marked in pattern of squares.

Test cross A pollination from one individual to a double recessive individual for the trait under examination. Cf. back cross.

Thigmotrophic Responsive to the stimulus of contact.

Tissue A collection of cells from the same origin.

Tonoplast The membrane surrounding the vacuole.

Torose Knobbly, swelling of tissue.

Trace elements Minerals required in very small amounts for nutrition.

Transcription The production of messenger RNA in accordance with the genetic code in the DNA.

Translation The conversion of the genetic code in mRNA into proteins.

Transpiration The passage of water vapour from plant to atmosphere.

Trichome A hair (on leaf), uni- or multi-cellular.

Tropism The tendency of an organism to respond to environmental influences as in phototropic and geotropic.

Turbulence The break up of layered air by forced convection.

Type specimens A sample plant lodged in a recognised herbarium by the person who proposes its name or its family or genus.

Umbel An inflorescence where pedicels join the peduncle at one point, the apex.

Vacuole A membrane-surrounded enclosure within a cell containing dissolved salts, pigments and other water soluble substances.

Valence Of an atom, its capacity to unite with other atoms.

Variety A minor classification below a species, does not apply to hybrids. Cf. cultivar.

Velamen One or more layers of spongy cells surrounding the root.

Ventral The opposite to dorsal which is the back; so ventral becomes the front. Very confused with leaves, sometimes upper surface sometimes lower surface.

Viscidium Part of the rostellum and attached to pollinia, usually sticky.

VPD Vapour pressure deficit, the difference between water vapour pressure in the leaf and in the surrounding air.

Watt The SI unit of power, one volt × one ampere = one watt; one joule per second = one watt.

Wetting agent See surfactant; an agent which allows water to wet a surface.

Whorl Leaves or floral parts attached at a common point on the stem and forming a 'circle' of leaves or petals.

Note X is pronounced as Z.

Xeric Dry, referring to environment.

Xerophyte A plant which withstands dry conditions.

Xylem The water and nutrient conducting tissue in stems and leaves.

Zygomorphic Bilaterally symmetrical; divisible into two similar halves in one plane.

Zygonema The stage where homologous chromosomes pair.

Zygote A product of the fusion of gametes.

Index of coloured plates

Index